Iowa Legal Research

CAROLINA ACADEMIC PRESS
LEGAL RESEARCH SERIES

Suzanne E. Rowe, Series Editor

❧

Arizona—Tamara S. Herrera
Arkansas—Coleen M. Barger
California—Hether C. Macfarlane & Suzanne E. Rowe
Colorado—Robert Michael Linz
Connecticut—Jessica G. Hynes
Florida, Third Edition—Barbara J. Busharis & Suzanne E. Rowe
Georgia—Nancy P. Johnson, Elizabeth G. Adelman & Nancy J. Adams
Idaho—Tenielle Fordyce-Ruff & Suzanne E. Rowe
Illinois, Second Edition—Mark E. Wojcik
Iowa—John D. Edwards, M. Sara Lowe, Karen L. Wallace, & Melissa H. Weresh
Kansas—Joseph A. Custer & Christopher L. Steadham
Louisiana—Mary Garvey Algero
Massachusetts—E. Joan Blum
Michigan, Second Edition—Pamela Lysaght & Cristina D. Lockwood
Minnesota—Suzanne Thorpe
Missouri, Second Edition—Wanda M. Temm & Julie M. Cheslik
New York—Elizabeth G. Adelman & Suzanne E. Rowe
North Carolina—Scott Childs
Ohio—Katherine L. Hall & Sara Sampson
Oregon, Second Edition—Suzanne E. Rowe
Pennsylvania—Barbara J. Busharis & Bonny L. Tavares
Tennessee—Sibyl Marshall & Carol McCrehan Parker
Texas—Spencer L. Simons
Washington, Second Edition—Julie Heintz-Cho, Tom Cobb & Mary A. Hotchkiss

❧

Iowa Legal Research

John D. Edwards
M. Sara Lowe
Karen L. Wallace
Melissa H. Weresh

Suzanne E. Rowe, Series Editor

CAROLINA ACADEMIC PRESS
Durham, North Carolina

Copyright © 2011
Carolina Academic Press
All Rights Reserved.

Library of Congress Cataloging-in-Publication Data

Iowa legal research / John D. Edwards ... [et al.].
    p. cm. -- (Carolina Academic Press legal research series)
Includes bibliographical references and index.
ISBN 978-1-59460-872-8 (alk. paper)
1. Legal research--Iowa. I. Edwards, John (John Duncan), 1953-
KFI4275.I587 2011
340.072'0777--dc22

                        2010048014

Carolina Academic Press
700 Kent Street
Durham, North Carolina 27701
Telephone (919) 489-7486
Fax (919) 493-5668
www.cap-press.com

Printed in the United States of America.

Summary of Contents

Contents		vii
List of Tables and Figures		xvii
Series Note		xxiii
Foreword		xxv
Acknowledgments		xxvii
Chapter 1	The Research Process and Legal Analysis	3
Chapter 2	Legal Research Sources and Techniques	21
Chapter 3	Secondary Sources	51
Chapter 4	The Constitution	87
Chapter 5	Judicial Opinions, Reporters, and Digests	103
Chapter 6	Statutes, Court Rules, and Ordinances	139
Chapter 7	Legislative History	163
Chapter 8	Administrative Law	191
Chapter 9	Updating with Citators	215
Chapter 10	Practice Aids	237
Chapter 11	Legal Ethics	251
Chapter 12	Research Strategies	267
Appendix	Legal Citations	281
About the Authors		291
Index		293

Contents

List of Tables and Figures	xvii
Series Note	xxiii
Foreword	xxv
Acknowledgments	xxvii
Chapter 1 · The Research Process and Legal Analysis	3
I. Introduction to Iowa Legal Research	3
II. The Intersection of Legal Research and Legal Analysis	4
III. Types and Sources of Legal Authority	5
IV. Court Systems	8
V. Overview of the Research Process	10
A. Ethical and Professional Considerations	10
B. Getting Started on a Research Project	12
1. Identify the Issues, Jurisdiction, and Scope of the Project	12
2. Gather Facts and Identify Preliminary Search Terms	13
3. Consult Secondary Sources and Practice Aids	14
4. Retrieve, Read, and Evaluate Primary Sources	15
5. Update Authorities with a Citator	16
6. Determine When to Stop	16
C. Keeping an Efficient Research Trail	16
D. The Most Overlooked Research Resource in the Law Library	17
VI. Researching the Law—Organization of This Text	17
VII. Legal Research in Context	18

Chapter 2 • Legal Research Sources and Techniques			21
I.	Introduction		21
II.	Key Resources		21
	A. Librarians and Library Catalogs		21
	B. Government, Organization, and Educational Websites		24
	C. Commercial Databases		28
III.	West Key Number System		29
IV.	Updating		30
V.	Print Search Techniques		31
	A. Why Use Print?		31
	B. Indexes		31
	C. Tables of Contents		33
	D. Understanding and Using Legal Citations		35
VI.	Electronic Search Techniques		37
	A. Introduction		37
	B. Developing a Search Strategy		38
		1. Choosing Databases	38
		2. Searching with Terms and Connectors (Boolean)	40
		3. Searching with Natural Language	41
		4. Working with Search Results	42
		5. Using Special Features and Techniques	43
	C. Starting with a Citation		46
	D. Topic Limits		46
VII.	Recording Legal Citations		47
	A. Introduction		47
	B. Citation Examples		48
		1. Cases	48
		2. Statutes	49
		3. Constitutions	49
Chapter 3 • Secondary Sources			51
I.	Introduction		51
II.	Types of Secondary Sources		54
	A. Treatises and Other Books		54

			1. Updating Treatises	54
			2. Finding Relevant Treatises	55
	B.		Restatements of the Law	56
	C.		Uniform Laws and Model Codes	59
	D.		Legal Periodicals	62
		1.	Introduction	62
		2.	Types of Legal Periodicals and Their Use	62
		3.	Finding Articles by Topic: Indexes and Full-Text Databases	63
		4.	Finding an Article When You Already Have a Citation	67
		5.	Locating Recent and Forthcoming Articles	68
	E.		Looseleaf Services and Portfolios	70
		1.	Using a Print Looseleaf Service	70
		2.	Using a Print Portfolio	71
		3.	Electronic Options	72
	F.		*American Law Reports*	72
	G.		Legal Dictionaries	75
	H.		Legal Encyclopedias	76
		1.	Using the Index to Find Encyclopedia Articles	79
		2.	Using the Topic Outline to Find Encyclopedia Articles	81
		3.	Conducting a Keyword Search to Find Encyclopedia Articles	82
	I.		Research Guides	82
		1.	Finding Guides Using Web Search Engines	84
		2.	Finding Guides Using Law Library Catalogs	84
		3.	Finding Guides Using Law Journal Article Indexes	85

Chapter 4 · The Constitution — 87

I. Introduction — 87
II. Historical Context and Constitution of 1857 — 89
III. Constitutional Amendments — 90
IV. Interpreting the Iowa Constitution — 91
V. Researching the Iowa Constitution — 93

	A.	Print Sources for the Iowa Constitution	95
		1. *Iowa Code Annotated*	95
		2. *Code of Iowa*	96
	B.	Free Online Sources of the Iowa Constitution	98
	C.	The Iowa Constitution in LexisNexis and Westlaw	98
		1. Finding Relevant Provisions	98
		2. Using a Citator	99
VI.	United States Constitution	100

Chapter 5 • Judicial Opinions, Reporters, and Digests 103

I.	Introduction	103
II.	Court Systems	104
	A.	Iowa Courts	104
		1. Iowa District Courts	105
		2. Iowa Court of Appeals	105
		3. Iowa Supreme Court	106
	B.	Federal Courts	106
	C.	Courts of Other States	107
III.	Published Case Law	108
	A.	Slip Opinions	109
	B.	Advance Sheets	110
	C.	Reporters	110
		1. Features of a Reported Case	111
		2. Other Features of a West Reporter	116
	D.	Reporters for Iowa Cases	117
	E.	Other Sources for Finding Iowa Cases	117
	F.	Reporters for Federal Cases	118
		1. United States District Courts Cases	119
		2. United States Court of Appeals Cases	119
		3. United States Supreme Court Cases	120
IV.	Digests	122
	A.	Digest Features	124
		1. Topic and Key Numbers	126
		2. Headnotes	127
		3. Words and Phrases	127
		4. Table of Cases	128
	B.	Digest Research	128

	1.	Beginning with a Relevant Case	129
	2.	Beginning with the Descriptive-Word Index	129
	3.	Beginning with the Topic Analysis	133
V.	Online Topic Searching	133
	A.	LexisNexis and Westlaw	133
		1. Known Keywords	133
		2. Known Topic	134
		3. Known Case	134
	B.	Internet Research	135
VI.	Updating Your Research	136
VII.	Reading and Analyzing Cases	137

Chapter 6 · Statutes, Court Rules, and Ordinances — 139

I.	Introduction	139
II.	Session Laws and Codification	139
III.	Iowa Statutory Publications	141
	A. Iowa Slip Laws	141
	B. Iowa Session Laws	141
	C. Iowa Statutes	142
IV.	Iowa Statutory Research	144
	A. In Print	144
	B. Online	148
	C. Updating Your Research	149
V.	Interpreting Statutes	150
VI.	Statutes of Other States	151
VII.	Federal Statutes	152
	A. Slip Laws	152
	B. Session Laws	153
	C. Codified Statutes	154
VIII.	Court Rules	157
	A. Iowa Court Rules	157
	B. Federal Court Rules	158
IX.	Local Ordinances	159
	A. Finding Local Ordinances	159
	B. Updating Ordinances	161

xii Contents

Chapter 7 · Legislative History   163
- I. Introduction   163
- II. Iowa Legislative Process   163
- III. Iowa Legislative History Research   166
    - A. Introduction to Iowa Legislative History Research   166
    - B. Sources of Iowa Legislative History   168
        1. Overview   168
        2. Compiled Legislative History: Annotated Codes and Index to Legal Periodicals   168
        3. Code Section History   170
        4. Session Laws   170
        5. Bill Books   171
            - a. Bill Versions   171
            - b. Bill Explanations   172
            - c. Fiscal Notes   172
            - d. Sources of Bill Books and Older Bill Text   173
            - e. Navigating Bill Books   174
        6. General Assembly Actions: House and Senate Journals   175
        7. Committee Minutes   176
        8. Reports   177
        9. Bill Drafting Files   178
        10. Newspaper Articles   178
- IV. Iowa Bill Tracking   179
    - A. Alert Services   180
    - B. Search Options   180
    - C. Post-Session Publications   181
- V. Federal Legislative Research   181
    - A. Federal Legislative Process   181
    - B. Federal Legislative History   182
        1. Federal Legislative Documents and Their Uses   182
        2. Compiled Legislative History   183
        3. Finding Legislative Documents   184
    - C. Federal Bill Tracking   186
- Appendix: Iowa Legislative History Excerpts   188

Contents xiii

Chapter 8 · Administrative Law — 191
I. Introduction — 191
II. Administrative Agencies — 192
III. Administrative Rules — 192
IV. Iowa Administrative Rules — 193
    A. Finding Iowa Rules — 194
        1. *Iowa Administrative Bulletin* — 194
        2. *Iowa Administrative Code* — 194
    B. Researching Iowa Rules — 197
    C. Currentness of Iowa Rules — 200
V. Federal Regulations — 201
    A. Finding Federal Regulations — 202
        1. *Federal Register* — 202
        2. *Code of Federal Regulations* — 204
    B. Researching Federal Regulations — 206
    C. Updating Federal Regulations — 209
        1. Online — 210
        2. In Print — 211
VI. Other Documents from the Executive Branch — 212
    A. Decisions of Agencies — 212
        1. Iowa — 212
        2. Federal — 212
    B. Executive Orders and Proclamations — 213
        1. Iowa — 213
        2. Federal — 214

Chapter 9 · Updating with Citators — 215
I. Introduction — 215
II. Purposes of Updating — 215
    A. Ethical and Professional Considerations — 216
    B. Practical Considerations — 217
III. Updating: An Overview — 217
    A. Using Shepard's on LexisNexis — 218
        1. Accessing the Citator — 218
        2. Selecting the Type of Citing List — 219

			3.	Analyzing the Citing Symbols and Limiting the Search Results	219
			4.	Reading and Analyzing the Citing References	224
		B.	Using KeyCite on Westlaw		226
			1.	Accessing the Citator	226
			2.	Selecting the Type of Citing List	226
			3.	Analyzing the Citing Symbols and Limiting the Search Results	228
			4.	Reading and Analyzing the Citing References	232
		C.	Caution: Additional Limitations on the Use of Citators to Update		233
	Appendix: Shepardizing in Print				233

Chapter 10 • Practice Aids   237

I.	Practice Aids: Types and Use		237
II.	Finding Practice Aids		237
III.	Bar Manuals and Practice Guides		238
	A.	Introduction to Bar Manuals and Practice Guides	238
	B.	Iowa Manuals and Practice Guides	238
	C.	Federal and General Practice Guides	241
IV.	Legal Forms and Sample Documents		241
	A.	Introduction to Form Books	241
	B.	Iowa-Specific Form Books and Electronic Resources	244
	C.	Other Form Books and Electronic Resources	245
	D.	Other Sample Materials	247
V.	Continuing Legal Education (CLE) Publications		248
	A.	Introduction to CLE Materials	248
	B.	Iowa-Specific CLE Resources	248
	C.	Other CLE Resources	249
VI.	Jury Instructions		249
	A.	Introduction to Jury Instructions	249
	B.	Iowa-Specific Instructions	250
	C.	Other Instructions	250

Chapter 11 • Legal Ethics   251

I.	Introduction to Legal Ethics Research	251

II.	Regulating the Conduct of Attorneys — An Overview	252
	A. Sources of Regulation	252
	1. ABA Model Code and Model Rules	252
	2. Legal Ethics Opinions	253
	3. Other Sources of Law Relating to Attorney Ethics	254
	B. State Regulation of Attorney Conduct	255
	C. Regulation of Judicial Conduct	255
III.	The Process of Legal Ethics Research	256
	A. Overview	256
	B. Iowa Rules of Professional Conduct	256
	C. Iowa Ethics Opinions	258
	1. Iowa Ethics Opinions	258
	2. Disciplinary Actions	260
	D. American Bar Association Materials	261
	1. Model Rules of Professional Conduct	261
	2. Model Code of Professional Responsibility	262
	3. ABA Ethics Opinions	262
	E. Materials from Other States	263
	F. Secondary Sources for Legal Ethics Research	264

Chapter 12 · Research Strategies — 267

I.	Introduction	267
II.	Developing a Research Strategy	268
III.	Organizing the Research	269
	A. Getting Started	269
	B. Structuring a Plan	269
	C. Implementing Your Plan	270
	D. Secondary Authorities	273
	E. Primary Authorities	273
	1. Taking Notes on Statutes	275
	2. Taking Notes on Cases	275
	F. Updating	276
IV.	Outlining Your Analysis	277
V.	When to Stop Researching	279

Appendix · Legal Citations   281
   I. Introduction   281
   II. The *Bluebook*   283
   III. *ALWD Manual*   284
   IV. Legal Citation in Iowa   284
      A. Introduction   284
      B. Cases   286
      C. Statutes   287
      D. Constitutions   288
      E. Administrative Regulations   288
      F. Books and Periodicals   288

About the Authors   291

Index   293

List of Tables and Figures

Tables

Chapter 1 · The Research Process and Legal Analysis
Table 1-1.	Examples of Authority in Iowa Research	8
Table 1-2.	Basic Research Process	12
Table 1-3.	Generating Research Terms	15

Chapter 2 · Legal Research Sources and Techniques
Table 2-1.	Iowa Law Library Catalogs	22

Chapter 3 · Secondary Sources
Table 3-1.	Secondary Source Overview	53
Table 3-2.	Current Adopted Restatements	58
Table 3-3.	Additional Sources for Uniform/Model Law Information	62
Table 3-4.	Finding Law Articles on the Web	68
Table 3-5.	Resources for Locating Recent and Forthcoming Articles	69
Table 3-6.	Selected Legal Dictionaries	76
Table 3-7.	Selected Internet Sources for Legal Research Guides	85

Chapter 4 · The Constitution
Table 4-1.	Articles of the Iowa Constitution	88
Table 4-2.	Iowa Bill of Rights and Corresponding U.S. Constitutional Provisions	94
Table 4-3.	Selected Websites Providing Access to the U.S. Constitution	101

Chapter 5 • Judicial Opinions, Reporters, and Digests

Table 5-1.	West's National Reporter System	112
Table 5-2.	Reporters for Federal Court Cases	118
Table 5-3.	Selected List of Free Internet Sources Containing Court of Appeal and District Court Decisions	120
Table 5-4.	Selected List of Free Internet Sources of Supreme Court Opinions	121
Table 5-5.	West Digest System	123
Table 5-6.	Outline for Digest Research with the Descriptive-Word Index	130

Chapter 6 • Statutes, Court Rules, and Ordinances

Table 6-1.	Research Strategy for Statutory Research	140
Table 6-2.	Titles in the *Code of Iowa*	142
Table 6-3.	Iowa Legislature General Assembly Online Resources for Iowa Statutes	146
Table 6-4.	Free Online Resources for Federal Statutes	157
Table 6-5.	Free Online Resources for Iowa Court Rules and Iowa-Related Federal Courts	160

Chapter 7 • Legislative History

Table 7-1.	General Process for Researching Iowa Legislative History	169
Table 7-2.	Iowa Bill Book Color Coding	171
Table 7-3.	Selected Sources for Key Legislative History Materials	187

Chapter 8 • Administrative Law

Table 8-1.	Example from the Table of Contents of the *Iowa Administrative Code*	196
Table 8-2.	Researching Federal Regulations	208
Table 8-3.	Updating a CFR Citation Using GPO Access	210
Table 8-4.	Partial List of Iowa Agency Decisions Available on the Web	212

Tables and Figures   xix

Chapter 9 • Updating with Citators
    Table 9-1. Shepard's Signal Indicators   223

Chapter 10 • Practice Aids
    Table 10-1. Iowa State Bar Association Manuals   239
    Table 10-2. Topics in West's Iowa Practice Series   240
    Table 10-3. Selected Internet Sources for Iowa Forms   245
    Table 10-4. Online Sources for Free or Low Cost Legal Forms (General)   247

Chapter 11 • Legal Ethics
    Table 11-1. Basic Process for Legal Ethics Research   256

Chapter 12 • Research Strategies
    Table 12-1. Sample Analysis Chart   277

Appendix • Legal Citations
    Table A-1. Purposes of Legal Citations   281

Figures

Chapter 2 • Legal Research Sources and Techniques
    Figure 2-1. Screenshot of Drake Law Library Catalog Record: Catalog Record View   25
    Figure 2-2. Screenshot of Drake Law Library Catalog Record: Item Information View   26
    Figure 2-3. Excerpt from *Iowa Practice General Index*   33
    Figure 2-4. Excerpt from *Iowa Practice: Criminal Law*   34
    Figure 2-5. Excerpt from *Iowa Practice: Criminal Law* Index   35
    Figure 2-6. Westlaw Screenshot Showing Star Pagination   44

Chapter 3 • Secondary Sources
    Figure 3-1. Screenshot of Westlaw JLR Search Results   67
    Figure 3-2. ALR Outline Excerpt   74
    Figure 3-3. Excerpt from AmJur   78

Figure 3-4.	Excerpts from AmJur General Index	79
Figure 3-5.	Excerpt from AmJur Table of Abbreviations	80

Chapter 4 • The Constitution

Figure 4-1.	Excerpt of Iowa Constitution from *Iowa Code Annotated* v. 1, 2	97
Figure 4-2.	Sample Case Annotation from ICA	98

Chapter 5 • Judicial Opinions, Reporters, and Digests

Figure 5-1.	Case Excerpt from *North Western Reporter 2d*	113
Figure 5-2.	Case Excerpt from Westlaw	115
Figure 5-3.	Example of the Analysis Outline from the *North Western Digest*	124
Figure 5-4.	Example from the *North Western Digest 2d*	125
Figure 5-5.	Example from Words and Phrases	128
Figure 5-6.	*Descriptive-Word Index* Excerpt from *North Western Digest 2d*	131

Chapter 6 • Statutes, Court Rules, and Ordinances

Figure 6-1.	*Code of Iowa* Example	144
Figure 6-2.	*Iowa Code Annotated* Example	145
Figure 6-3.	Sample from *Code of Iowa* Index	146
Figure 6-4.	Sample of *United States Code* Index	155
Figure 6-5.	Sample Entry in *United States Code*	156

Chapter 7 • Legislative History

Figure 7-1.	Iowa Legislative Process Flowchart	165
Figure 7-2.	Iowa Code § 4.6	167
Figure 7-A.	Screenshot of Westlaw's 2002 Version of Iowa Code § 598.35	188
Figure 7-B.	Sample *Acts and Joint Resolutions of the General Assembly*	189
Figure 7-C.	Screenshot of Iowa Heritage Digital Collection Bill Book Search	189
Figure 7-D.	Screenshots from the Iowa Heritage Digital Collection	190

Tables and Figures

Chapter 8 • Administrative Law

Figure 8-1.	Example from the Index of the *Iowa Administrative Code*	198
Figure 8-2.	*Iowa Administrative Code*	199
Figure 8-3.	Example from the *Iowa Administrative Code*	200
Figure 8-4.	Example from the *Federal Register*	203
Figure 8-5.	Example of the *Code of Federal Regulations* Index and Finding Aids	205
Figure 8-6.	Example from the *Code of Federal Regulations*	207

Chapter 9 • Updating with Citators

Figure 9-1.	Shepard's for Validation: *Santi v. Santi*, 633 N.W.2d 312 (Iowa 2001)	220
Figure 9-2.	Shepard's for Research: *Santi v. Santi*, 633 N.W.2d 312 (Iowa 2001)	221
Figure 9-3.	Shepard's for Validation: Iowa Code § 598.35(7) (1999)	222
Figure 9-4.	Focus Feature on Shepard's	225
Figure 9-5.	KeyCite Full History: *Santi v. Santi*, 633 N.W.2d 312 (Iowa 2001)	227
Figure 9-6.	KeyCite Citing References: *Santi v. Santi*, 633 N.W.2d 312 (Iowa 2001)	229
Figure 9-7.	KeyCite Citing References: Iowa Code § 598.35(7) (1999)	230
Figure 9-8.	KeyCite Signal Indicators	231
Figure 9-9.	Limit KeyCite Display Options: *Santi v. Santi*, 633 N.W.2d 312 (Iowa 2001)	232
Figure 9-10.	"Locate" Feature within "Limit KeyCite Display"	232
Figure 9-A.	Shepard's Results in Print	235

Chapter 10 • Practice Aids

Figure 10-1.	Sample Forms	242

Series Note

The Legal Research Series published by Carolina Academic Press includes titles from many states around the country. The goal of each book is to provide law students, practitioners, paralegals, college students, laypeople, and librarians with the essential elements of legal research in each state. Unlike more bibliographic texts, the Legal Research Series books seek to explain concisely both the sources of state law research and the process for conducting legal research effectively.

Foreword

Chief Justice Mark S. Cady
Iowa Supreme Court

Lawyers and law students endure years of formal education in a wide variety of subjects and are institutionally trained in the art of critical analysis and precise communication. These tools are refined for years following graduation, and they are tested outside the classroom with issues affecting citizens of our state every day. Of course, these trials in research can be motivated to excellence by the desire to more efficiently serve clients in order to make a living, and every lawyer in Iowa has an obligation to the client, the courts, and the profession to uphold the established standards of service to society. But Iowa lawyers have long been committed to providing legal service above and beyond the call of duty. When the rule of law is critically examined in each new factual circumstance, well-trained servants of the law can also be agents of change in our laws because they have a new understanding of the world in which we live. This ability to provide legal counsel that constantly challenges established principles is our strength as a community. It is only through a spirited commitment to resolving the legal issues presented in each case that our law develops over time. As advocates for this standard of practicing law, it is essential that the most effective method of performing legal research be the cornerstone of our practice.

Because effective legal research is so fundamental, a lawyer's education is not complete without it. For over one hundred years, the Iowa legal community has had the benefit of the Drake University Law School's legal research program, which has been at the forefront of both technological and methodological innovations. True to their reputations as dedicated legal research educators, Dean John Edwards and Professors Sara Lowe, Karen Wallace, and Melissa Weresh have tirelessly worked to produce this invaluable guide for law students and Iowa lawyers. *Iowa Legal Research* is the first comprehensive research book that synthesizes various sources of Iowa law with the process necessary to isolate a research path among those sources and follow it confidently to its conclusion. I am honored to have the opportunity to introduce such an exemplary piece of the work done to advance Iowa legal research.

The book begins where all legal practice should: by keeping the client's problem central to the research process. As a result, the researcher's understanding of the issue will sharpen as the research evolves. Effective research does not always unveil a definitive answer to the problem that is presented like a treasure at the end of a rainbow; instead, effective research typically creates more need for research. This book identifies that the sustainable practice of legal research starts with the recognition that research and analysis are intertwined and their development is codependent. As the authors point out, "[l]egal research cannot be divorced from legal analysis." Yet, under the direction of this Iowa-specific guide, researchers in Iowa can begin the intricate process of research and analysis without first having to spend countless hours acquainting or reacquainting themselves with methods for finding the applicable sources of law.

The authors have left no practical stone unturned. Consistent with the practice in most other industries today, much of Iowans' legal work is done electronically. Researchers unfamiliar with local web hosts need not spend time attempting to assess the credibility of these sources on their own; this book includes reputable Iowa-specific online databases and websites for lawyers and law students looking for Iowa-specific practice aides at little or no charge. Additionally, this book presents information about researching legal ethics opinions and disciplinary actions in Iowa. Sources of law related to professional regulation can be particularly difficult to locate as a new attorney, but this thorough guide lightens the burden of the search considerably.

The legal community is enriched by the publication of this book, which gives law students, practitioners, and anyone seeking the sources of Iowa law a firm foundational tool for any research task that lies before them.

Acknowledgments

Thanks to Amy Cutler, administrative assistant, for her work securing permissions, submitting the manuscript, and attending to myriad other details of this project. Thanks also to Ann Naffier, law student (class of 2011), for her comments on the draft manuscript. We also wish to thank series editor Suzanne Rowe, who has been extraordinarily helpful throughout the entire process.

Iowa Legal Research

Chapter 1

The Research Process and Legal Analysis[1]

I. Introduction to Iowa Legal Research

The process of legal research — finding the law — is essentially the same in every American jurisdiction. Locating applicable law requires that the researcher understand certain basic components, including the legal issue, potential sources of law that may be applicable to the resolution of that issue, the resources that may contain that law, and an understanding of how those resources are organized. Beyond these basic issues, there may be variations between jurisdictions in terms of the substantive law; the law-making processes; and the type, variety, and organization of the sources. While some of these variations are minor, others require specialized knowledge of the resources available and the analytical framework in which those resources are used. This book focuses on sources of Iowa law and the techniques for locating relevant Iowa authority. It supplements this focus with brief explanations of federal research and research into the law of other states, both to introduce and to highlight some of the variations.

---

1. Portions of this chapter are based on Suzanne E. Rowe, *Oregon Legal Research* (2d ed., Carolina Academic Press 2007).

II. The Intersection of Legal Research and Legal Analysis

While all researchers understand that legal analysis is difficult, some falsely assume that legal research is a distinct, mechanical task. Researchers may form this impression because many of the basic *techniques* of legal research are relatively simple. For most print resources, you will begin with an index, find entries that appear relevant, and read those sections of the text. You will then locate additional sources identified within the text, and update your research to determine whether more recent material is available. For online research, you will search particular databases or websites using words likely to appear in the text of relevant documents, or you will construct searches that seek to find information on a particular topic. Chapter 2 describes basic print and online search techniques in detail.

The simplicity of those techniques, however, can be misleading. Legal analysis is implicated in all steps of the research process, raising challenging questions. In print research, which words will you look up in the index? How will you decide whether an entry looks promising? With regard to online research, how will you choose relevant words and construct a search most likely to produce the documents you need? When you read the text of a document, how will you determine whether it is relevant to your client's situation? How will you learn whether more recent material changed the law or merely applied it in a new situation? In order to answer these questions, a researcher must engage in legal analysis. This interdependency of research and analysis can make legal research complex, especially for the novice.

As someone just starting out—either in law school or as a new lawyer in Iowa—take this opportunity to carefully consider what the process of legal research entails. Legal research cannot be divorced from legal analysis and entails far more than simply understanding the available resources. To be useful and effective, the legal researcher must consistently and recursively analyze the client's problem and the resources discovered during the research process. This takes time, creativity, and patience. As Peter Friedman observed:

The answers to difficult legal questions don't lie around waiting to be found as if they are treasure chests left lying on forest floors. They are constructed and created by elements buried within our universe of databases. Thus, research that is genuine research not only requires Sisyphean patience in combing through the sources, it requires also consideration, observation, and study of what one finds within those sources so that one can, first, *identify the elements that matter*, and, second, *put those important, buried, and isolated elements together in some useful and novel way.*

* * *

In short, research, analysis, and theorizing are all a single activity—finding things, making sure they are the right things, and putting them together in the right ways.[2]

This book is not designed to be a blueprint for every resource in the law library or search engine on the Internet; many resources contain their own detailed explanations in a preface or a "help" section. This book is more like a manual or field guide, introducing the various resources available and explaining when and how to use them.

III. Types and Sources of Legal Authority

In finding the law that is applicable to your client's problem, you need to distinguish between resources that control the client's situation—primary, mandatory authority—and those that may be merely applicable to the situation—persuasive authority. *Primary authority* is law produced by governmental bodies with law-making power. Sources of primary authority include constitutional provisions, statutes, and administrative regulations. These sources are known as *enacted law*. The other source of primary authority comes from the judiciary. Judicial opinions are primary authority whether they in-

---

2. Peter Friedman, *Research Only Begins with Information: Patience, Insight, and Imagination Are the Most Important Parts of It*, http://blogs.geniocity.com/friedman/2010/03/research-only-begins-with-information-patience-insight-and-imagination-are-the-most-important-parts-of-it (posted March 26, 2010).

terpret statutes or develop the *common law*, the legal principles established through court decisions. Primary authority is distinguished from *secondary* authority, which includes all other legal sources such as treatises, law review articles, and legal encyclopedias. Secondary authority is typically written by individuals who do not have law-making authority, or who are not writing in their law-making authority capacity.[3] These secondary sources summarize, clarify, and comment on primary authorities and are therefore designed to aid in understanding the law and locating primary authority. Secondary sources often cite extensively to primary authority, making these sources valuable research tools.

In terms of beginning a research project, your principal objective is typically to locate primary authority, which is the law that controls the client problem. For any legal problem, you need to determine the applicable sources of law. Thus, in every situation, you will need to ascertain whether the client matter is controlled by a constitutional provision, a statute, or an administrative regulation. In any of these instances, there are also likely to be relevant judicial opinions that interpret the enacted law and are therefore applicable to the client problem. For some client problems, the only source of authority is judicial opinions that develop the common law. In short, you are searching for the controlling authority—primary, mandatory authority, as opposed to authority that is merely persuasive.

Mandatory authority is binding on the court that would decide a conflict if the situation were litigated. In a question of Iowa law, mandatory or binding authority includes the Iowa Constitution, statutes enacted by the Iowa legislature, Iowa administrative regulations, and opinions of the Supreme Court of Iowa.[4] *Persuasive au-*

---

3. Note that judges and legislators may author law review articles and other secondary authority. Notwithstanding, judges only have law-making authority when they author primary authority in the form of a judicial opinion and legislators only have law-making authority when they author primary authority in form of enacted law (statutes and regulations).

4. An opinion from the Court of Appeals is binding on the trial courts if the Supreme Court of Iowa has not addressed a particular topic.

thority is not binding, but may be followed if relevant and well reasoned. Authority is merely persuasive if it is from a different jurisdiction or if it is a resource that has not been produced by a law-making body. In a question of Iowa law, examples of persuasive authority include primary authorities from outside Iowa, such as a similar Nebraska statute or an analogous opinion of an Illinois state court.

Secondary materials, such as a law review article or a treatise written by a legal scholar, are also considered persuasive authority.[5] The impact or influence of different sources of persuasive authority varies by source. For example, the Restatements of Law, a secondary resource produced by the American Law Institute and discussed in Chapter 3, may have more persuasive weight in a particular jurisdiction than the primary authority from a different jurisdiction.[6] See Chapter 3 for a further discussion of secondary sources.

Table 1-1 provides a list of the most frequently encountered sources of law. Each source is explained later in this book. Notice in Table 1-1 that persuasive authority may be either primary or secondary authority, while mandatory authority is always primary.

For sources of mandatory authority, there is a hierarchy of law involving constitutions, statutes, administrative rules, and judicial opinions. The constitution of each state is the supreme law of the state. If a statute is on point, that statute comes next in the hierarchy, followed by administrative rules. Judicial opinions may interpret the statute or rule, but they cannot disregard them. A judicial opinion may, however, decide that a statute violates the constitution or that an administrative regulation is overbroad. In that instance, the judicial opinion that invalidates the statute controls. Finally, if there is no constitutional provision, statute, or administrative regulation applicable to the client matter, the issue will be controlled by the common law (judicial opinions).

---

5. This should make sense because secondary authority is generally written by individuals who do not have law-making authority.

6. Indeed, courts routinely adopt restatement rules, although they are not obligated to do so. According to the 2004 Annual Report of ALI, as of March 1, 2004, there were approximately 160,000 case citations to the restatements.

Table 1-1. Examples of Authority in Iowa Research

	Mandatory Authority	Persuasive Authority
Primary Authority	The Iowa Constitution Iowa statutes Iowa regulations Iowa Supreme Court cases	The Nebraska Constitution Illinois statutes Missouri regulations South Dakota cases
Secondary Resources		Treatises and other books Restatements Uniform Law and Model Code Commentary Law journal articles Looseleafs and portfolios Legal dictionaries

IV. Court Systems

Legal research often includes reading judicial opinions, so researchers need to understand the court system. The basic court structure includes a trial court, an intermediate court of appeals, and an ultimate appellate court, often called the "supreme" court. These courts exist at both the state and federal levels. In Iowa, trial courts are known as district courts. Iowa has two appellate courts: the Court of Appeals and the Supreme Court. All appeals from Iowa trial courts proceed directly to the Supreme Court. The Supreme Court then transfers a majority of those appeals to the Court of Appeals. For a more detailed discussion of the Iowa court system, see Chapter 5.

In the federal judicial system, the trial courts are called United States District Courts. There are ninety-four district courts in the federal system, with each district drawn from a particular state.[7] The

---

7. An illustrative map of the federal districts can be accessed at the website for the federal courts: http://www.uscourts.gov/uscourts/images/CircuitMap.pdf.

state of Iowa has been divided into two geographic regions for federal district court jurisdiction. The United States District Court for the Northern District of Iowa is headquartered in Cedar Rapids, and the United States District Court for the Southern District of Iowa is headquartered in Des Moines.

Intermediate appellate courts in the federal system are called United States Courts of Appeals. There are courts of appeals for each of the thirteen federal circuits. Twelve of these circuits are based on geographic jurisdiction. In addition to eleven numbered circuits covering all the states, there is the District of Columbia Circuit. The thirteenth federal circuit, called the Federal Circuit, hears appeals from certain specialized courts and agencies as well as appeals on issues related to patent law from district courts in all circuits. Iowa is in the Eighth Circuit. This means that cases from the United States District Court for both the Northern and Southern Districts of Iowa are appealed to the United States Court of Appeals for the Eighth Circuit. This circuit encompasses Arkansas, Iowa, Minnesota, Missouri, Nebraska, North Dakota, and South Dakota.

The highest court in the federal system is the United States Supreme Court. It decides cases concerning the United States Constitution and federal statutes. This court does not have the final say on matters of purely state law; that authority rests with the highest court of each state. Parties who wish to have the U.S. Supreme Court hear their case must file a petition for *certiorari*, as the court has discretion over which cases it hears.

Not all states have the three-tier court system of Iowa and the federal judiciary. A number of states do not have an intermediate appellate court, just as Iowa did not until 1977. Another difference in some court systems is that the "supreme" court is not the highest court. In New York, the trial courts are called supreme courts and the highest court is the Court of Appeals. Two states, Massachusetts and Maine, call their highest court the Supreme Judicial Court.

Citation manuals are good references for learning the names and hierarchy of the courts, as well as for learning proper citation to legal authorities. The two most popular are the *ALWD Citation Manual: A Professional System of Citation,* written by Dean Darby Dickerson and the Association of Legal Writing Directors,[8] and *The Bluebook: A Uniform System of Citation*, written by students from several law schools.[9] Both manuals provide information on federal and state courts.

V. Overview of the Research Process

A. Ethical and Professional Considerations

Conducting effective research is more than an important part of an attorney's role in assisting clients; it is an ethical obligation of the attorney. The Iowa Rules of Professional Conduct[10] govern the conduct of lawyers who are admitted to practice in Iowa. The Rules require that an attorney be competent in all aspects of legal practice, including the research and analysis of client issues. Section 2 of the Preamble notes that lawyers engage in a variety of functions:

> As advisor, a lawyer provides a client with an informed understanding of the client's legal rights and obligations and explains their practical implications. As advocate, a lawyer zealously asserts the client's position under the rules of the adversary system. As negotiator, a lawyer seeks a result advantageous to the client but consistent with requirements of honest dealings with others. As an evaluator, a lawyer acts by

---

8. ALWD & Darby Dickerson, ALWD *Citation Manual* (4th ed., Aspen Publishers 2010)("*ALWD Manual*"). Most citations in this book conform to the *ALWD Manual* unless there is a clear preference in Iowa for a different form.

9. *The Bluebook: A Uniform System of Citation* (The Columbia Law Review et al. eds., 19th ed., The Harvard Law Review Assn. 2010).

10. The Iowa Rules of Professional Conduct are codified in Chapter 32 of the Iowa Court Rules and can be accessed electronically through the Iowa Courts website at http://www.legis.iowa.gov/IowaLaw/courtRules.apsx. The rules are modeled after the Model Rules of Professional Conduct. As such, they mimic the numbering system of the Model Rules, but are prefaced with their designation in Chapter 32 of the Iowa Court Rules. So, for example, the Model Rule on competence is Rule 1 in the Model Rules, and is referenced in the Iowa Court Rules as Iowa R. Prof. Conduct 32:1.1.

examining a client's legal affairs and reporting about them to the client or to others.[11]

In terms of research and analysis, the rules require that lawyers provide competent representation and, in Rule One, note that "[c]ompetent representation requires the legal knowledge, skill, thoroughness, and preparation reasonably necessary for the representation."[12]

Comments to the rule on competence clarify that "[c]ompetent handling of a particular matter includes inquiry into and analysis of the factual and legal elements of the problem, and use of methods and procedures meeting the standards of competent practitioners."[13] The obligation of competence is continuing, requiring that lawyers "keep abreast of changes in the law and its practice."[14]

In terms of a lawyer's ethical obligation as an officer of the court, there is a prohibition against asserting claims that are not supported by law.[15] Further, lawyers must provide the court with all relevant authority, including authority that may be adverse to the client's position.[16] These prohibitions and responsibilities require that the competent, ethical lawyer be capable of locating and analyzing applicable authority.

---

11. Iowa R. Prof. Conduct Preamble 2.
12. Iowa R. Prof. Conduct 32:1.1.
13. *Id.* at cmt. 5.
14. Iowa R. Prof. Conduct 32:1.1, cmt. 6.
15. Iowa R. Prof. Conduct 32:3.1 provides, "A lawyer shall not bring or defend a proceeding, or assert or controvert an issue therein, unless there is a basis in law and fact for doing so that is not frivolous, which includes a good faith argument for an extension, modification, or reversal of existing law."
16. Iowa R. Prof. Conduct 32:3.3 notes that a "lawyer shall not knowingly ... fail to disclose to the tribunal legal authority in the controlling jurisdiction known to the lawyer to be directly adverse to the position of the client and not disclosed by opposing counsel." Comment 4 further explains that "[t]he underlying concept is that legal argument is a discussion seeking to determine the legal premises properly applicable to the case."

Table 1-2. Basic Research Process

1.	Identify the issues, jurisdiction, and scope of the project.
2.	Gather facts and identify preliminary search terms.
3.	Consult secondary sources and practice aids.
4.	Retrieve, read, and evaluate primary sources.
5.	Update authorities with a citator.
6.	Determine when to stop.

B. Getting Started on a Research Project

Conducting efficient, effective, ethical legal research means following a process. This process leads to the authority that controls a legal issue as well as to commentary that may help you analyze new and complex matters. All too often the novice researcher embarks on a research project without an appropriate plan, which can result in lost opportunities and wasted time. The following brief description of the research process is outlined in Table 1-2 and further explored in Chapter 12.

1. Identify the Issues, Jurisdiction, and Scope of the Project

The first step in developing a research plan is to have a firm understanding of the project. This will require that you evaluate the client's problem to determine, at least initially, what legal issues arise. A good preliminary step is to determine the relevant area of law. Is this a criminal or civil matter? Is this an issue of property, or does the client problem involve personal injury? Note that you will further develop the issue(s) as you conduct research.

You should also determine the jurisdiction. If you practice in Davenport, Iowa, which sits on the Iowa-Illinois border, for example, you should carefully consider whether the client's issue will be governed by the law of Iowa or if the facts indicate the law of Illinois could apply. If you have a client who has received correspondence regarding, for example, an environmental matter, you must determine whether the issue is likely to be governed by state or federal law.

Finally, you need to determine the scope of the project. You should ascertain what the form of the final work product should be and approximately how much time the client expects you to spend on the matter. To that end, you should inquire as to whether there are any limitations on research including how much expensive electronic research is appropriate. In terms of evaluating the scope of the project, you should also consider whether there are resources available to you, such as reference librarians or other associates in a law firm, whose assistance might be beneficial to the project.[17]

2. Gather Facts and Identify Preliminary Search Terms

Getting started on a research project will require you to familiarize yourself with the facts and, in many cases, to learn additional facts. The facts should suggest preliminary search terms so you can begin your research.

Many legal resources in print use lengthy indexes as the starting point for finding legal authority. Electronic sources often require the researcher to enter words that are likely to appear in a synopsis or in the full text of relevant documents. Alternatively, the researcher might begin research by focusing on a particular topic. The terms used to search topically might appear in the topic heading, but not the resulting documents (or vice versa), even though the resulting documents are on point. To ensure you are thorough in beginning a research project, you will need a comprehensive list of words, terms, and phrases that may lead to law on point. These may be legal terms or common words that describe the client's situation. The items on this list are *search terms*.

---

17. By the same token, you should consider whether there are limitations on using such outside resources, as is likely to be the case in a law school project.

Organized brainstorming is the best way to compile a comprehensive list of search terms. Some researchers ask the journalistic questions Who? What? When? Where? Why? How? Others use a mnemonic device like TARPP, which stands for Things, Actions, Remedies, People, and Places.[18] Whether you use one of these suggestions or develop your own method, you should attempt to generate a broad range of terms describing your client's situation. Include in the list both specific and general words. Try to think of synonyms and antonyms for each term since at this point you are uncertain which terms an index may include. Using a legal dictionary or thesaurus may generate additional terms.

As an example, assume you are working for a defense attorney who was recently assigned to a burglary case. Around midnight, your client used a credit card to spring the lock to a stereo store, where she stole $2,000 worth of equipment. She was charged with first-degree burglary and possession of burglary tools. You have been asked to determine whether there is a good argument for challenging the charge of possession of burglary tools based on the fact that she used a credit card and not professional burglary tools. Moreover, you have been asked to consider whether a successful defense of the possession of burglary tools charge will impact the first-degree burglary charge. Table 1-3 provides examples of research terms you might use to begin work on this project.

As your research progresses, you will learn new research terms to include in the list and decide to take others off. For example, you may read cases that give you insights into the key words judges tend to use in discussing the topic. Or you may learn a *term of art*, a word or phrase that has special meaning in a particular area of law. Add these to your list.

3. Consult Secondary Sources and Practice Aids

Secondary sources and practice aids, discussed more fully in Chapters 3 and 10, respectively, are excellent starting points for legal re-

---

18. *See* Roy M. Mersky & Donald J. Dunn, *Fundamentals of Legal Research* 15 (8th ed., Found. Press 2002) (explaining "TARP," a similar mnemonic device).

Table 1-3. Generating Research Terms

	Journalistic Approach
Who:	Thief, robber, burglar, business owner, property owner
What:	Burglary, first degree, second degree, crime
How:	Breaking and entering, burglary tools, trespassing
Why:	Theft, stealing, stolen goods
When:	Midnight
Where:	Store, building, commercial establishment, business, shop

	TARPP Approach
Things:	Burglary tools, stolen goods
Actions:	Burglary, breaking and entering, trespassing, damages, crime
Remedies:	First degree, second degree, incarceration
People:	Thief, robber, burglar, business owner, property owner
Places:	Store, building, commercial establishment, business, shop

search. These sources contain useful commentary and analysis, and can help you broaden both the legal theories and search terms relevant to the client. For most secondary sources, you should be able to use the search terms you created to examine the index for entries in the secondary source that are relevant to the client's issue. You can then use the narrative, analytical material in the secondary sources to find primary legal authorities.

4. Retrieve, Read, and Evaluate Primary Sources

Once you begin to locate primary sources, you will need to read and evaluate their applicability to your client's problem. Resist the urge to skim; print or download and carefully review the source to determine whether it is relevant and helpful. Be aware that this step is likely to be the most time-consuming. Secondary authority may lead you to some primary authority, but be prepared to invest considerable time and energy searching for primary authority. Chapters 4 through 8 discuss how to locate authority in print and online resources. Moreover, consider whether the primary authority itself can lead to additional relevant materials. The information on updating in Chapter 9 should be helpful in this regard.

5. Update Authorities with a Citator

You cannot rely on a legal authority until you determine that it is still good law, or that it has not been overruled or modified by a subsequent authority. Chapter 9 addresses the sources for, and process of, updating.

6. Determine When to Stop

Novice legal researchers tend to stay on the research wheel longer than necessary. For most legal problems, there is no "smoking gun." In instances when there is a *dispositive* authority, one that definitively conveys the rule of law, you should be able to find it efficiently if you have employed appropriate search terms and looked in the relevant resources. However, for some research projects there will not be a dispositive authority. Instead you may have to gather information from a variety of legal sources to synthesize the law and predict a result. A good rule of thumb is to stop researching when the same authorities keep coming up.

This basic process should be customized for each research project. Consider whether you need to follow all six steps, and if so, in what order. If you are unfamiliar with an area of law, beginning your research in a secondary resource may be quite helpful. In contrast, if you know that a situation is controlled by a statute, you may choose to begin with the statute rather than reviewing a secondary resource.

C. Keeping an Efficient Research Trail

One of the most important components of a good research plan is an effective strategy for tracking research. In most cases, a failure to keep track of research will result in lost sources and the frustrating feeling that you have read an applicable source, but no longer know where to locate it. Keeping track of where you have searched, and brief notes about the sources you have reviewed, will save considerable time and make your research more efficient. Some lawyers choose to keep index cards with brief notes about the source including, at a minimum, the citation and the relevant information contained in the source. Other lawyers keep research charts, in either handwritten or electronic format. Different strategies are further explored in Chapter 12, but the importance of a system for tracking research cannot be overstated.

D. The Most Overlooked Research Resource in the Law Library

One of the most effective and overlooked resources in the law library is the librarian. Reference librarians have specialized training and education in legal resources. The efficient lawyer knows this and benefits from the expertise offered by these individuals. Librarians can direct you to relevant resources and help you navigate them. When asking for assistance outside your organization, be careful that you not divulge confidential or privileged information.

VI. Researching the Law — Organization of This Text

The remainder of this book explains how to use your research terms to conduct legal research in a variety of sources. Chapter 2 provides an overview of types of legal research sources and describes basic techniques for their use. Subsequent chapters expand on this introduction in discussing specific sources, both print and electronic, and explaining unique caveats in their use. Because the research process often begins with secondary sources, the book begins its examination of legal sources in Chapter 3 with secondary sources. We then turn to primary legal authority. Chapter 4 addresses the Iowa Constitution, which is the highest legal authority in the state. Chapter 5 contains an overview of the Iowa and federal court systems and explains how to use reporters and digests to research judicial decisions. Chapter 6 addresses statutes and local ordinances, and Chapter 7 explores legislative history. Chapter 8 covers Iowa administrative law resources. After this focus on primary authority, Chapter 9 explains how to update legal authority using citators (e.g., *Shepard's Citations* or Westlaw's *KeyCite*). Chapter 10 introduces the reader to practice aids, and Chapter 11 illustrates Iowa legal ethics research. Finally, Chapter 12 delves into a more detailed explanation of legal research strategy. You may prefer to skim that chapter now and refer to it frequently, even though a number of references in it may not become clear until you have read the intervening chapters. The Appendix provides an overview of the conventions lawyers follow in citing legal authority in their documents.

VII. Legal Research in Context

In order to understand the relationship between legal analysis and legal research, you must examine legal sources in context. To that end, consider the following client problem, the Welch matter, shown in the sidebar. Later chapters will explore this hypothetical situation further, suggesting ways you can use certain legal research sources to analyze this problem.

The Welch Matter

Your client, Mary Welch, has come to see you regarding a family matter. Welch would like your advice concerning her granddaughter, Claire Lewis.

Welch's daughter, Jessica Lewis, had one daughter, Claire, from her marriage to James Lewis. James died when Claire was two years old. He was a chronic drug user and died of an overdose. Jessica has sole, full custody of Claire.

Jessica has also struggled with substance abuse and has attended inpatient substance abuse treatment on three occasions. Welch paid the medical fees associated with those treatment programs and cared for Claire while Jessica underwent treatment. Jessica relapsed after the first two treatments, but has been substance-free for eight months.

Unfortunately, Jessica and Welch have argued recently, and Jessica told Welch that she no longer wants to have a relationship with her. Moreover, Jessica has said that Welch may no longer see Claire. Welch would like to investigate her rights to have visitation with Claire.

Chapter 2

Legal Research Sources and Techniques

I. Introduction

An effective legal researcher knows the available research sources, when to select them, and how to use them. This chapter introduces a few essential research tools and fundamental techniques that will help you proficiently use a wide variety of research sources. Some of these sources and research methods may be familiar from your prior experience, while others are unique to legal research. Later chapters will build on this foundation, introducing more specific research tools and sophisticated search techniques.

II. Key Resources

A. Librarians and Library Catalogs

One of the first places to start researching is the law library. The law library has a wealth of resources and trained personnel to help you find materials to address your research needs. Librarians can be particularly helpful at the initial stages of your research and when you hit an obstacle. Researchers sometimes search fruitlessly for an item that a librarian could have helped them find in a matter of minutes. The type of assistance a law librarian can provide includes: (1) identifying authoritative secondary sources for your project, (2) suggesting databases likely to contain relevant materials, (3) explaining search techniques particular to each research question, (4) guidance

Table 2-1. Iowa Law Library Catalogs

Drake University Law School	http://www.law.drake.edu/library/catalog.html
University of Iowa College of Law	http://infohawk.uiowa.edu
State Library of Iowa	http://iowa.ipac.dynixasp.com/#focus
WorldCat OCLC	http://www.worldcat.org

in navigating the online catalog or a specialized database, and (5) obtaining materials from other libraries through interlibrary loan. Consulting a law librarian provides personalized, expert advice. If you are unable to visit a law library in person, some assistance may be available online or via the phone; check the library's website for headings like public services or reference. (Note: Law librarians will typically only conduct research on behalf of colleagues at the same institution, as indicated in that library's policy.)

Librarians and other informed researchers often consult the online *catalog* to find library materials. It includes *records* for the books, e-books, print periodicals, and non-book materials, e.g., CDs, held at the library. Catalog records briefly describe each item in the collection and indicate where the item can be found in the library.

Many library catalogs can be freely accessed on the web, and Table 2-1 provides addresses for the main Iowa law library catalogs. Iowa's two law schools—Drake University Law School and the University of Iowa College of Law—both offer no-charge catalog access to the vast holdings of all libraries at their institutions. The State Library of Iowa's catalog includes the materials at the State Law Library located in Des Moines. Although smaller than an academic law library collection, the State Law Library's collection includes some unique materials. One of the primary clients of the State Law Library is the state government, including the courts, the legislature, and other agencies. The collection reflects this focus: it includes all Iowa court briefs, materials from legislative sessions, books on statutory construction, and an extensive section on workers' compensation and other administrative matters.

Another catalog of note, WorldCat, offers access to materials from thousands of libraries around the world. After finding books of interest in WorldCat, you can determine which libraries contain these resources. If the library is conveniently located, you can obtain the materials there. Otherwise, you can request that the materials be sent to you through your home library's *interlibrary loan* service.

After accessing a library catalog, you can search it by keyword, subject, author, title, and other options.[1] The search results will provide information to help you start determining which books or other resources will be the most useful. When you access the full record for one of your search results, you will find basic information about the book, such as the author, title, publisher, number of pages, and publication date. Some catalogs also offer additional information, such as synopses, tables of contents, and reviews, to help you winnow your results.

Library catalogs offer helpful cross-references, making your research more efficient. One useful result in the catalog may lead to others if you view the full catalog record and review the subject headings that describe the book's contents. In most catalogs, you can click directly on a subject heading to search for all other materials in the catalog that have that subject.

For instance, Figure 2-1 shows one of the results of a search of the Drake Law Library catalog for the terms "grandparent" and "visitation" as keywords. Three tabs at the top of the screen provide different information about the result. The screenshot in Figure 2-1 shows the catalog record view. This book appears in the search results be-

---

1. In a keyword search you enter any word or phrase that might appear anywhere in the online record for the item, ranging from the title of a book to the listing of the contents. A subject search enables you to find all the materials cataloged under a particular topic, such as "Visitation rights" to find materials on grandparent visitation rights. Other options are available to enhance searching which range from date restrictions to searching for titles in a series, such as the Nutshell series of study aids.

cause the record includes the table of contents, which has a section on grandparent and third party visitation. The subject terms for the item indicate that other useful materials may be found looking at the subject heading "Custody of children."

Clicking on the subject link "Custody of children" will retrieve items on that general subject even if their catalog records did not include the keywords grandparent and visitation. The fact that an item's record does not include those terms, does not necessarily mean that the item itself does not address that issue. Remember, a catalog record includes only very limited information about the item it describes. The book in Figure 2-1 would not have appeared in the search results if its table of contents was not included in the catalog. For many books, the contents are not part of the catalog record. Looking at materials on the general subject to see if they include a relevant section can help you ensure you find all pertinent items.

The catalog search results will also show the location of each item within the library. Figure 2-2 shows the item information tab for the same book shown in Figure 2-1. The location information generally includes a *call number* that reflects the subject of the book and leads the researcher to its exact location. In the example, the call number is KF 547 .N38 2005. Because other books shelved at KF 547 will be on the same subject, you may be able to find other relevant items by browsing the nearby shelves. However, browsing is not a definitive way to find all relevant books; some might be in use and some might be shelved in a different location. You can determine where to find a particular call number in the library by asking library personnel or consulting library guides, such as maps and *stack*[2] location lists.

B. Government, Organization, and Educational Websites

The web offers an abundance of legal information, some of it extraordinarily useful. However, the open nature of the web—allowing

---

2. The stacks are the area of a library in which most of the books are shelved. For example, see the location information in Figure 2-2.

Figure 2-1. Screenshot of Drake Law Library Catalog Record: Catalog Record View

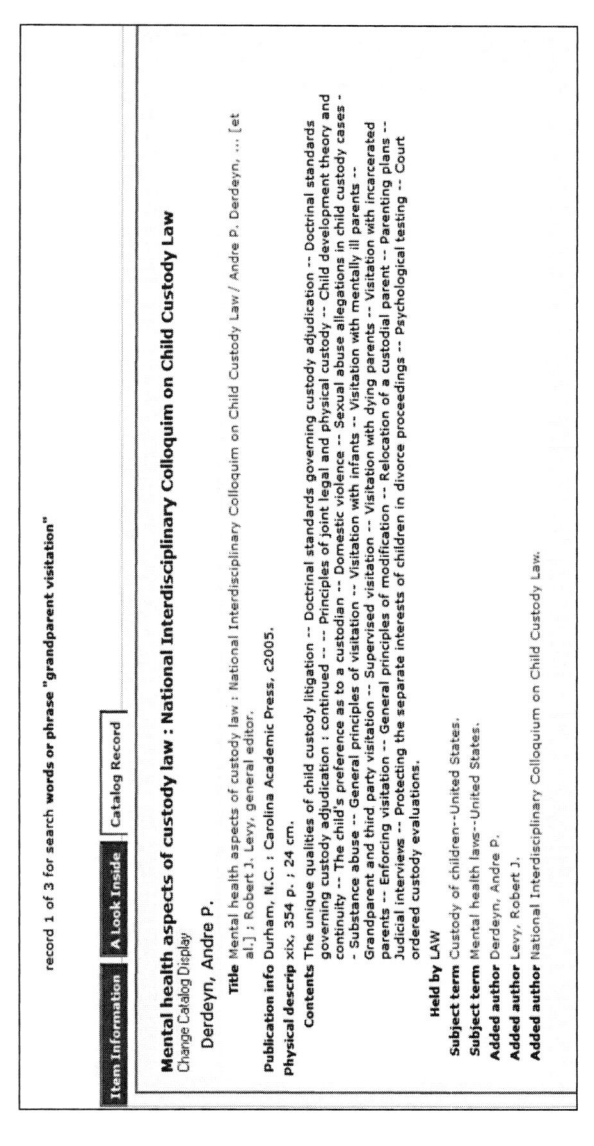

record 1 of 3 for search words or phrase "grandparent visitation"

Item Information | **A Look Inside** | **Catalog Record**

Mental health aspects of custody law : National Interdisciplinary Colloquim on Child Custody Law
Change Catalog Display
Derdeyn, Andre P.

Title Mental health aspects of custody law : National Interdisciplinary Colloquium on Child Custody Law / Andre P. Derdeyn, ... [et al.] ; Robert J. Levy, general editor.
Publication info Durham, N.C. : Carolina Academic Press, c2005.
Physical descrip xix, 354 p. ; 24 cm.
Contents The unique qualities of child custody litigation -- Doctrinal standards governing custody adjudication -- Doctrinal standards governing custody adjudication ; continued -- -- Principles of joint legal and physical custody -- Child development theory and continuity -- The child's preference as to a custodian -- Domestic violence -- Sexual abuse allegations in child custody cases - - Substance abuse -- General principles of visitation -- Visitation with infants -- Visitation with mentally ill parents -- Grandparent and third party visitation -- Supervised visitation -- Visitation with dying parents -- Visitation with incarcerated parents -- Enforcing visitation -- General principles of modification -- Relocation of a custodial parent -- Parenting plans -- Judicial interviews -- Protecting the separate interests of children in divorce proceedings -- Psychological testing -- Court ordered custody evaluations.

Held by LAW

Subject term Custody of children--United States.
Subject term Mental health laws--United States.
Added author Derdeyn, Andre P.
Added author Levy, Robert J.
Added author National Interdisciplinary Colloquium on Child Custody Law.

Source: Drake Law Library Catalog, http://www.law.drake.edu/library/catalog.html.

Figure 2-2. Screenshot of Drake Law Library Catalog Record: Item Information View

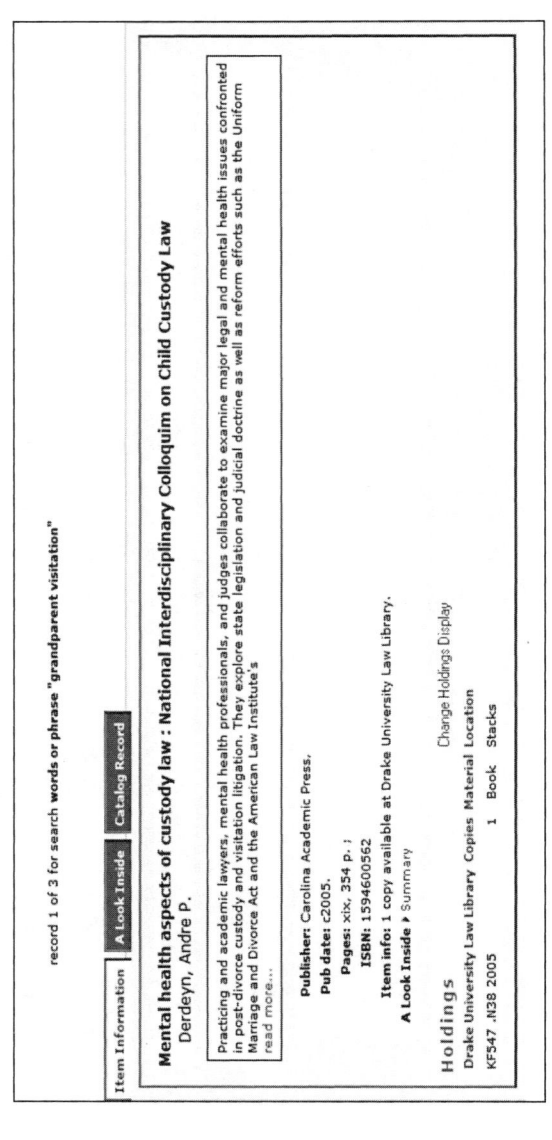

| Item Information | A Look Inside | Catalog Record |

record 1 of 3 for search words or phrase "grandparent visitation"

Mental health aspects of custody law : National Interdisciplinary Colloquim on Child Custody Law
Derdeyn, Andre P.

Practicing and academic lawyers, mental health professionals, and judges collaborate to examine major legal and mental health issues confronted in post-divorce custody and visitation litigation. They explore state legislation and judicial doctrine as well as reform efforts such as the Uniform Marriage and Divorce Act and the American Law Institute's
read more....

Publisher: Carolina Academic Press.
Pub date: c2005.
Pages: xix, 354 p. ;
ISBN: 1594600562
Item info: 1 copy available at Drake University Law Library.
A Look Inside ▶ Summary

Holdings   Change Holdings Display
Drake University Law Library   Copies   Material   Location
KF547 .N38 2005   1   Book   Stacks

Source: Drake Law Library Catalog, http://www.law.drake.edu/library/catalog.html.

almost anyone to post almost anything—means you must exercise particular caution when using the web for legal research. The Electronic Legal Information Access & Citation Committee of the American Association of Law Libraries has developed specific guidelines for evaluating law-related websites.[3] These guidelines offer multiple questions to ask in reviewing each aspect of the website. Those general areas include: jurisdiction (What law applies?), authorship (What person or organization is the source of the information?), content (How comprehensive is it?), currency (How up-to-date is the site's information?), and quality.

Although you will still want to evaluate a website yourself before relying on it, you can increase your odds of accessing high-quality sites by locating sites through research guides and directories provided by libraries, reputable associations, and official government agencies. The Iowa government sites for the judicial, legislative, and executive branches provide information that can be essential to researchers.[4] County and city sites also can be invaluable, especially for municipal codes.[5] *Research guides*, such as Drake Law Library's guide to Iowa Legal Research,[6] provide tips on researching a particular area and note sources of interest. *Directories* provide organized links of lists. For instance, sites like Cornell's Legal Information Institute, the Public Library of Law, and FindLaw, all provide an abundance of legal information arranged by topic and jurisdiction.[7]

---

3. *See* http://www.aallnet.org/committee/eliac/websiteguidelines.html.

4. The Iowa Legislature site is http://www.legis.iowa.gov, the Judicial Branch site is http://www.iowacourts.gov, and the Executive Branch site is http://governor.iowa.gov. The state government homepage, Iowa Government Online, is http://www.iowa.gov.

5. *See Iowa Municipal and County Law Research Guide* at http://drakelaw.libguides.com/IowaLocalCodes for links to those sites.

6. Drake University Law Library, Iowa Legal Research, is at http://drakelaw.libguides.com/IowaBasic.

7. Cornell's LII can be accessed at http://www.law.cornell.edu, the Public Library of Law is located at http://www.plol.org, and FindLaw is at http://lp.findlaw.com.

Specific websites will be discussed throughout this book, but one site bears mention now: The Iowa State Bar Association (ISBA) page.[8] On the public part of the site you can find ethics opinions, bar publications such as *The Iowa Lawyer*, and links to many other items. Of particular interest to lawyers and law students is the "Practice Tools" tab which provides member access to Fastcase online legal research,[9] civil and criminal jury instructions, title standards, and other materials often needed by Iowa attorneys.

C. Commercial Databases

Law libraries and law offices purchase a vast array of databases to facilitate research. Westlaw and LexisNexis are the dominant providers of computer-assisted legal research (CALR) services in the United States and are recognized by lawyers for their value-added features that facilitate research. The costs for using these services in a law firm or office can be quite high. Understanding the billing plan for the firm subscription and formulating efficient searches are imperative. Vendors such as Loislaw, VersusLaw, and Fastcase provide access to a more finite set of resources at costs that are generally lower than either LexisNexis or Westlaw. As noted, Fastcase is a member benefit for ISBA members. Many other state bar associations also offer Fastcase, or an alternative source, such as Casemaker, making these services cost-effective CALR choices for bar members.

Academic law libraries subscribe to hundreds of commercial databases that offer comprehensive information on almost every area of law.[10] The databases are often arranged by subject, such as bank-

---

8. The ISBA website is at http://www.iowabar.org.

9. Full-time law students at Drake or Iowa or Iowa residents attending another ABA-accredited law school can access those materials by becoming a student member of the ISBA by completing a form on its website. No fee is charged for student membership.

10. Go to "Electronic Databases" from the Drake page at http://www.law.drake.edu/library and go to "Electronic Resources" from the Iowa page at http://www.law.uiowa.edu/library.

ruptcy, and also by database title, such as HeinOnline.[11] In these databases, you will be able to find in-depth information on your area of research. Access to these databases is normally limited to the primary clients of a library who have passwords, e.g., currently enrolled students at an academic library. Other people may be able to access the databases if they come into the library in person; however, when you try to access these research sources outside of the library, you will likely be prompted for login credentials.

As you use CALR services and other databases, be sure to focus on developing the skills of an efficient researcher. It is easy to lose sight of how much time is being spent online and how much that time costs. Some new researchers in law firms start off on the wrong foot by accumulating thousands of dollars in search charges because they did not understand the firm's pricing plan and were used to "unlimited" searching in law school. In a law office setting, make sure you understand the costs and when CALR can be used. Starting with basic research on a lower cost or free service, such as Fastcase or LexisONE,[12] may help you refine your search strategy so you can see what terms are most effective.

III. West Key Number System

West, a Thomson Reuters business, is one of the oldest and largest publishers of U.S. legal materials.[13] They developed the key number system, a way to organize legal issues using a topic word and a key

---

11. HeinOnline provides an image-based fully searchable collection of more than 50 million pages. The basic collection includes a Law Journal Library, U.S. Supreme Court Library, U.S. Federal Legislative History Library, Treaties and Agreements Library, and Legal Classics Library. If you wanted an article from any major law review for the past century, for example, it probably is in HeinOnline at http://heinonline.org.

12. LexisONE provides free access to cases from Iowa for the last ten years at http://www.lexisone.com.

13. Some of the other large U.S. legal publishers include LexisNexis (including Matthew Bender), BNA, Wolters Kluwer (including CCH and Aspen), and Hein. Publishers may use some of the same organizational

number that represents a more specific aspect of that topic. The system was designed to help lawyers find cases addressing specific legal issues, and its chief use is still for case law. However, key numbers are also used in other West print and electronic publications to identify legal issues. Chapter 5, which covers case law, will describe the key number system in greater depth. The important thing to understand now is that the key number system is essentially an index; each topic and number identifies a legal issue and helps the researcher find materials that address that issue.

IV. Updating

The law changes as new statutes are passed, regulations promulgated, and court cases decided. To obtain the most current information, you must understand how the source you are using is updated. Many legal books are updated with a separately issued supplement that complements the main text. One of the most common mistakes a novice researcher makes is to look in the main text of the volume and base the answer on that information without also checking the supplementation. The supplement often will contain later cases, statutes, or other updates that may affect the validity and weight of what is in the original text.

The main forms of print supplementation are *pocket parts*, inserts placed in the back of the book, and supplemental pamphlets or volumes, shelved next to the main volume.[14] In electronic databases, the most recent information will be integrated into the text and notes; you should be sure to check the scope information to determine the currency of the source.

---

schemes or finding aids in many of their resources, which is one reason it can be useful to know who published a particular source.

14. Print products may also be updated as looseleafs. These are essentially ringed binders where individual pages are replaced to incorporate changes. Unless there are additional supplements, looseleaf page replacements allow a researcher to look in a single place to get the most up-to-date information.

In addition to thoroughly checking the source to make sure you are using the most current information it provides, you will also learn to update your research to ensure that the law, as stated, is still in effect. This form of updating using citators will be discussed in Chapter 9.

V. Print Search Techniques

A. Why Use Print?

One misconception novice legal researchers often have is that everything, including unlimited legal resources, is online. Although numerous materials are available in electronic form, many helpful resources are available only in print or other formats. Studies have found that only a small percentage of an academic law library collection is duplicated online.[15] Some questions can be more easily and efficiently answered in a print resource, while others are better suited for an online resource. The following sections provide tips on using print materials.

B. Indexes

The starting point for most print resources is an *index*. An index provides an alphabetical listing of key concepts and notes the pages, chapters, or sections that address these subjects. For a single-volume book, the index will be at the back of the book. For multi-volume sets, the index is often a separate volume or multiple volumes, typically shelved at the end of the set. Indexes in some multi-volume sets appear at the end of each book or in back of the final volume in the

---

15. One study assessed duplication at 15 percent. Although that percentage may be increasing, a vast amount of material is not yet in digital format. *See e.g.* Penny A. Hazelton, *How Much of Your Print Collection is Really on WESTLAW or LEXIS-NEXIS?*, 18 Leg. Ref. Servs. Q. 3 (1999); Jeri Zeder, *A New Library for the 21st Century*, 61 Harv. L. Bull. 26 (Summer 2010) (noting that Harvard is in the beginning stages of digitizing its collection).

set. For any title with pocket parts or supplements, also check these updates to see if they include revised index or table of contents listings.

An initial step in conducting research is identifying key words that describe what you plan to research. The same technique applies when using any index. Identify your key words and look for those words. If you don't find them listed, consider synonyms or other terms. For example, if one of your key words is "Automobiles" and that word is not listed, you may need to look under "Motor Vehicles."

An index normally includes an alphabetical listing of major subject headings, such as "Evidence," with more detailed subheadings, such as "Suppression of Evidence." Some listings will continue for several pages, requiring careful attention as to whether you are still looking under the initial heading or are now seeing entries under a subheading. Subheadings are normally indented and main headings should appear at the top of the page to guide you. If you were looking for treatise information on grandparent visitation, for example, you might turn to the *Iowa Practice General Index*, excerpted in Figure 2-3.[16] The main heading "Children and Minors" extends for pages and is repeated at the top of each page with an indication that it continues from the prior page, as seen in Figure 2-3. Under this heading, you find scores of subheadings, many with additional subentries, such as "Endangerment of child," as also seen in Figure 2-3. Looking down the alphabetized list,[17] you find the subheading "Grandparents' visitation rights," followed by the reference "**Methprac** § 31:34."

A table of abbreviations at the front of the index tells you that Methprac means the Methods of Practice volume. The § symbolizes section, so by getting the Methods of Practice volume and turning to section 31:34, you find a discussion on grandparent visitation rights.

Note also that the index includes cross-references. If you were researching information on illegitimate children and looked under the

---

16. This work is described more thoroughly in Chapter 10.
17. An exception to the alphabetization of subheads may be the initial subhead "Generally." This indicates places in the source that broadly discuss the topic.

Figure 2-3. Excerpt from *Iowa Practice General Index*

CHILDREN AND MINORS—Cont'd
    Endangerment of child—Cont'd
        Parental authority, **Crimlaw** § 7:16
        Penalties, **Crimlaw** § 7:18, 7:20
        * * *
        Willful deprivation, **Crimlaw** § 7:11
    Estate planning, minor distributees, **Probate** § 29:8
    Filing minor's actions, **Civillit** § 10:2, 10:4
    Grandparents' visitation rights, **Methprac** § 31:34
    Habeas corpus writ, child custody provision, **Civpracfm** § 9:21
    Illegitimate Children, this index
    Incest, this index

Source: Iowa Practice General Index. Published with permission of West, a Thomson Reuters business.

heading "Children and Minors" you would see an entry for "Illegitimate Children, this index," telling you to look for entries under that heading under the letter "I" rather than as a subheading under "Children." Other indexes may use the terminology "generally this index" to indicate the term should be searched as a main heading rather than a subheading.

C. Tables of Contents

Most research books will begin with a table of contents. The table of contents provides an outline of the chapters and coverage of the book. Reviewing the table of contents may provide a quick way to find your topic of interest. Some books first provide a summary of contents that list all of the chapter topics, followed by a more detailed outline of the contents of each chapter. In multi-volume sets, the table of contents may be fully printed in each volume or only appear in the first volume.

Figure 2-4. Excerpt from *Iowa Practice: Criminal Law*

Chapter 8 table of contents

§ 8:1.	Robbery
§ 8:2.	—Robbery in the second degree
§ 8:3.	——Specific intent to commit a theft
§ 8:4.	——Lesser-included offenses
§ 8:5.	——Shoplifting elevated to robbery
§ 8:6.	——Penalty
§ 8:7.	—Robbery in the first degree
§ 8:8.	——Serious injury
§ 8:9.	——Dangerous weapon
§ 8:10.	——Penalty

Source: *Iowa Practice: Criminal Law*. Published with permission of West, a Thomson Reuters business.

So, for example, if you were asked to research the criminal law question of when shoplifting becomes robbery, you might start with a book on the topic, such as the treatise *Iowa Practice: Criminal Law*.[18] Examining the beginning pages of the book you find a Summary of Contents listing all the chapters. At a glance, you can see that robbery is covered in Chapter 8. You can then go to the more detailed Table of Contents and examine the listing for Chapter 8 on Robbery, shown in Figure 2-4.

As you scan the Table of Contents, note that § 8:5 covers "Shoplifting elevated to robbery." You can turn to § 8:5 in the treatise where the answer to your research question appears in the first paragraph. This paragraph also cites the key Iowa Supreme Court decision on the issue.[19]

---

18. Robert R. Rigg, *Iowa Practice: Criminal Law* (West 2010).
19. The treatise explains, "When the legislature enacted the new criminal code, it expanded the time frame of the assault that created the crime of robbery. At common law, robbery occurred if fear or force was used before or concurrently with the theft. The Iowa Supreme court interpreted the statute in State v. Jordan."

Figure 2-5. Excerpt from *Iowa Practice: Criminal Law* Index

ROBBERY
    Generally, §§ 8:1–8:10
    Dangerous weapon, first degree robbery, § 8:9
    * * *
    Serious injury, first degree robbery, § 8:8
    Shoplifting elevated to robbery, § 8:5
* * *
SHOPLIFTING
    Robbery, elevation to, § 8:5

Source: *Iowa Practice: Criminal Law*. Published with permission of West, a Thomson Reuters business.

The table of contents is especially useful because it provides an outline of the topics covered in the book, giving context to the research task. While the index is also an option to find the appropriate section, it does not provide the same context. Continuing with the robbery example, Figure 2-5 shows both robbery and shoplifting are listed as index headings and either will guide you to § 8:5.

D. Understanding and Using Legal Citations

A *citation* is the marker used by legal researchers to indicate where an authority can be located. Frequently, citations will provide information based on print resources, even when the information is accessed electronically. Most legal citations will include three parts: volume or title number, publication abbreviation, and page or section

---

In Jordan, a shoplifting incident was converted into a robbery when the defendant, after having left the store with stolen articles, was accosted by security guards who had followed him into another store. A scuffle followed, resulting in defendant's arrest. The court upheld the robbery conviction, finding the assault assisted the defendant's escape." (citations omitted)
    Id. at § 8:5.

(§) number.[20] For example, in the citation *State v. Jordan*, 409 N.W.2d 184 (Iowa 1997), the case can be found in volume 409 of the *North Western Reporter, Second Series*, at page 184. Some citations omit the volume/title number. For instance, Iowa Code § 232.102 refers to the *Code of Iowa* volume containing section 232.102; the spines of the books indicate the range of code sections they contain.

Some cases or statutes may be found in more than one source. Court rules or statutes designate one source as the *official* version of the law. When preparing court documents, you should cite to the official source, which will typically be a paper source rather than an electronic version. *Unofficial* sources are also useful, as they may be easier to access, be updated more frequently, provide additional content, or offer other advantages over official sources.

Legal sources frequently provide *parallel citations*, two or more citations in a row indicating multiple places where the same case or statute can be found. Consider this citation: *Lysinger v. Hayer*, 87 Iowa 335, 54 N.W. 145 (1893). The official citation, 87 Iowa 335, is to the *Iowa Reports* and the unofficial, 54 N.W. 145, is to the *North Western Reporter*.[21] Researchers can retrieve the case using either citation. In the appendix to this book, you will find examples of citations to other types of resources, such as statutes, regulations, and treatises. For most citations, it will be clear where you need to look to find the authority. If you encounter a citation that is unfamiliar, such as Misc. 3d,[22] consult a dictionary of legal abbreviations[23] or a librarian.

---

20. *See e.g. Reading Legal Citations* at http://drakelaw.libguides.com/abbreviations.

21. Note that the official *Iowa Reports* ceased publication in 1968, so you will not have an *Iowa Reports* citation for cases after that date. An official *Iowa Reports* citation is required when a *North Western Reporter* citation is not available, according to Iowa R. App. P. 6.904. However, the long-standing practice of the Iowa appellate courts is to include both when citing Iowa Supreme Court decisions, so seeing both in Iowa legal documents is very common. Both were required by court rule until 2009 when the rules changed to permit citation only to the *North Western Reporter*.

22. This abbreviation refers to *New York Miscellaneous Reports, Third Series*.

23. *See e.g.* Mary Miles Prince, *Prince's Bieber Dictionary of Legal Abbreviations* (6th ed., W.S. Hein & Co. 2009).

Sometimes you will have a citation that is no longer accurate. An area of the law may have had considerable growth and, in a new edition or printing, the publisher may have renumbered all of the old sections to make room for new ones. If you have a citation to the old volume, you can still typically locate the relevant information. Most publishers provide a *correlation* or *conversion table* that takes you from the old numbering system to the new one. If you are not able to find the cited section you need, be sure to check the front or back for a correlation table, especially if you are looking in a newer book.

VI. Electronic Search Techniques

A. Introduction

As noted earlier in this chapter under Section II.C. Commercial Databases, legal researchers today have access to a wealth of information from various vendors in addition to what is freely available on the web. Westlaw and LexisNexis dominate the market for computer-assisted legal research service. Because of their prevalence in law offices, these services will be the focus of the discussions on CALR. The basic techniques for forming search queries for Westlaw and LexisNexis are generally applicable to other services, such as Fastcase. Note, however, the specific manner in which you create a search query may vary. Before searching, read the help screens or other introductory material to familiarize yourself with a particular product. Investing this time should make your searches more effective.

The world of electronic research is constantly evolving as vendors develop products to meet the needs of researchers. Thanks to the success of Google, new platforms being developed for legal research will likely function more like Google than prior versions.[24] The explanations that follow will cover some of the search functions that are basic to Westlaw and LexisNexis but that may also be common on other

---

24. For example, the latest Westlaw release, WestlawNext, was described as Googlizing legal research. *See e.g.* http://outofthejungle.blogspot.com/2010/01/westlaw-next.html.

systems. Vendors offer various forms of training for their systems with many training materials available on the vendor websites.[25] The following sections review some of the most basic functions.

B. Developing a Search Strategy

Formulating a search that will retrieve the most relevant documents to your problem requires thoughtful preparation. As discussed in Chapter 1, you need to first identify the key words or phrases a court, legislature, or author may have used in discussing a situation similar to yours. Those key words should then be formulated into a search strategy to find documents relevant to your issue. The research process is often one of trial and error as you try to narrow the search to retrieve a manageable number of results without excluding relevant items. In the context of the Welch example presented in Chapter 1, you might do a search for "grandparent visitation" and find more than 100 results. If you narrowed the search by adding "substance or drug abuse" you might reduce the list of documents to 15 or so and find that those focus more directly on the facts of your problem.[26] The paragraphs that follow provide more details on this process.

1. Choosing Databases

One of the initial tasks is to determine where to search. Because Westlaw and LexisNexis can be very expensive, it is imperative that you search in as narrow a database as possible. If you only need cases from Iowa state courts, you would search that database. If you want federal cases from Iowa, you would select that database. Be aware of the coverage of the database in terms of sources and years included. Often a *scope note* or source description available from the database listing provides this information. In both LexisNexis and Westlaw,

---

25. For Westlaw, go to http://www.westlaw.com or call 1-800-WESTLAW, and for LexisNexis check http://www.lexisnexis.com/ or call 1-800-543-6862.

26. As outlined in the Welch matter in Chapter 1, a parent with a history of drug abuse was preventing her mother from visiting her grandchild.

these links are indicated by the letter "i" in a button after the database name. After you decide which database to search, you then enter your search query as described later in this chapter.

Both Westlaw and LexisNexis provide a directory of databases grouped by category or subject. The Westlaw directory offers headings such as U.S. Federal Materials; U.S. State Materials; Treatises, CLEs, and Other Practice Materials; Legal Periodicals & Current Awareness; and Topical Practice Areas. LexisNexis offers similar headings with Federal Legal–U.S.; Cases–U.S.; States Legal–U.S.; Secondary Legal; and Area of Law–By Topic. You can expand each of these headings to find the exact databases you want to search. If you wanted to search for the *Drake Law Review* on Westlaw, for example, you could look under the "Legal Periodicals" heading, open Law Reviews, and select the *Drake Law Review*.

Case databases generally correspond to the structure of the courts. On the federal level, there are databases for decisions of the U.S. Supreme Court, U.S. Court of Appeals, and U.S. District Courts as well as other federal courts. Database combination options enable you to search all federal cases, cases in one federal circuit, cases in one state, etc. Select the database that best meets your research needs. In a Westlaw search, the state database name follows the two-letter postal abbreviations, so you could type "IA" in the database box to search for Iowa cases.[27]

When selecting a case database, you normally choose one limited to a particular jurisdiction and then expand to other jurisdictions, especially if you don't find supporting authorities within your jurisdiction. This approach also helps you develop a search strategy likely to retrieve the most relevant documents. For example, you normally would not start with a search of all federal cases (which in some firm billing plans would trigger added charges), especially if you were using a search strategy that you had not tried previously. The results might be more than could reasonably be reviewed or might be no cases at all. You would instead start with a more focused and finite

---

27. One exception is Nebraska, which requires the use of NE-CS. NE alone is the database name for the *North Eastern Reporter*.

database for your jurisdiction, such as "Federal District Court Cases for Iowa."

The database directories in Westlaw or LexisNexis enable you to expand headings to find the file you need. If you need U.S. Supreme Court cases, you could look under "Federal materials," then "Cases," and then "U.S. Supreme Court cases." A search box also allows you to search for the database, so you could just type "US Supreme Court" and be directed to the database. The directory shows the range of materials available including cases, statutes, administrative materials, periodicals, treatises, and many other resources. Once you know what type of authorities you want to retrieve, you can formulate a search query. The same methods of browsing headings or searching apply whether you are searching for cases or any other type of database.

2. Searching with Terms and Connectors (Boolean)

One of the most common methods of searching is to identify the key words in the problem and use them to develop a search query. Sometimes a single word can be an effective query, especially if it is unique. Searching for *admiralty* in Iowa cases, for example, retrieves only a few cases because navigable water cases are not common in the state. Using *homicide* as the search term, however, retrieves thousands of cases and would need to be combined with other terms to form an effective search query. Combining terms and connectors is often referred to as *Boolean* searching.[28]

The most common connectors are: OR (results will include at least one of the search terms), AND (results will include all of the search terms), NOT or BUT NOT (results will include the first search term but not the second search term), and " " (results will include the terms in the exact order they appear within the quotation marks). Sophisticated databases, such as Westlaw and LexisNexis, employ a wider range of operators and special characters to increase search precision. For example, both Westlaw and LexisNexis use the

---

28. The Boolean name comes from the late English mathematician George Boole. Boolean connectors establish a logical relationship between search terms.

connectors /p (in same paragraph), /s (in same sentence), and /n (within *n* words). They also both use some of the same special characters. An asterisk (*) is used as a universal character representing any letter in a word or number except the first. To find cases that mention blood or bleed you could enter *bl**d*. The exclamation point (!) is used as a root expander so that if you typed *negligen!* you would find words with that root, such as negligence, negligent, or negligently. Not all databases use the same characters and connectors, so it is important to be familiar with the search function of the database you are using. LexisNexis and Westlaw provide easy help links from the search screens to the list of connectors and explanations on how to use them.

Using connectors enables you to request that the documents retrieved have terms within a certain proximity or relationship to other terms. Doing so effectively increases the odds that the results of your search will yield relevant results. To form an effective search command, consider what terms or phrases judges, legislatures, or legal scholars might have used to describe a fact situation similar to your facts or in a comparable application of the law. Also, consider how those words or phrases might appear in relationship to each other in a document. Would they appear within five words of each other? (/5) In the same sentence? (/s) The same paragraph? (/p) If you were doing research on attorney fees you would not only want results that mention that phrase, but also those that mention fees charged by the attorney. A numerical connector would enable you to retrieve both: *attorney /5 fee*. That query would search for documents in which "attorney" and "fee" were mentioned within five words of each other.

3. *Searching with Natural Language*

From the Westlaw and LexisNexis search screens you also have the option of doing a natural language search. Little training is required to use this function because all you need do is type in a question, sentence, or fragment that includes all of your key words. The computer then develops a search query based on the terms you have included and provides results ranked by relevance, rather than with the most recent first. An example of a natural language search would be, "Must a manufacturer warn about the side effects of a drug?" The computer would focus on the key words — manufacturer, warn, side effects, drug — and display the number of results the user designates as the default in order of relevancy, as determined by the system.

Researchers who use natural language must understand its limitations. The computer will always return the default number of results regardless of whether any are relevant or many others are eliminated. Moreover, the computer's manner of determining relevancy may not be clear. While researchers often find that using Boolean searches retrieves more relevant results, they may also find it helpful to perform a natural language search. They might do so early in the process to see if relevant cases can be found, especially if a Boolean search is not retrieving the results they want, or later to be sure they haven't missed anything from their terms and connector searches.

4. *Working with Search Results*

After retrieving a list of results, review the documents to see if they are relevant. The documents normally will be displayed either in reverse chronological order with the most recent one first or by relevancy. If your search retrieves an excessive number of results, refine your search to narrow those results. From an efficiency and cost perspective, that normally involves searching within your initial results. To narrow the results, use the "Locate" feature on Westlaw and the "Focus" feature on LexisNexis. Once you have narrowed your search results, review the documents to answer your research issue. Keep in mind that even the best search query may retrieve only a fraction of the documents relevant to the issue and that many of the documents you retrieve may not be relevant at all.

For example, if you used *grandparent visitation* as your search query you would find all documents containing those two words together. However, your result might show cases in which those terms were mentioned but perhaps weren't relevant. You might retrieve an attorney discipline case that mentioned a mishandled grandparent visitation case or one in which the terms only appear once, perhaps in a parenthetical citing a case, but not in any way helpful to your research. It is very important to carefully review the results you retrieve to see if they are applicable.

Your search strategy also could be eliminating relevant results. In the example of *grandparent visitation*, changing your search to *grandparent /s visitation* might double the number of documents retrieved and find cases including the phrase "grandparents were given visitation" or "visitation with grandparents," providing relevant items that were excluded by the original search. Tweaking and refining your search strategy is an ongoing process.

5. *Using Special Features and Techniques*

LexisNexis and Westlaw offer a number of features to facilitate your research. On the same screen as your search results, both systems display additional resources that may be helpful; these features are called "Results Plus" on Westlaw and "Related Content" on LexisNexis. If you were searching for cases on sex discrimination, for example, those features would provide you with links to articles, treatises, and other materials related to that topic.

Several features make reading and citing relevant cases easier. *Headnotes* that summarize and sometimes simplify the key legal holdings of cases are included with most opinions on LexisNexis and Westlaw. The opinions also include *star pagination* that alerts you to where the page breaks are located in the print volume. Star pagination appears on Westlaw as an asterisk and a number in bold italics, such as **475* shown in Figure 2-6, and on LexisNexis as an asterisk and a number in bold with brackets, such as [*475]. If a case has parallel citations, the page numbers for each reporter will be preceded by a different number of asterisks, as shown in Figure 2-6. This allows you to provide page numbers indicating the exact location of material you cite in any of the reporters.

In the case of *McCarty v. Jeffers*, 261 Iowa 470, 154 N.W.2d 718 (1967), shown in Figure 2-6, **475* shows where the page breaks in the official printed copy of the *Iowa Reports*, so you could give a pinpoint citation if you needed to cite the official report. The ***722* refers to the page break in the *North Western 2d* reporter, so you could pro-

Figure 2-6. Westlaw Screenshot Showing Star Pagination

> **McCarty v. Jeffers**
> 261 Iowa 470, 154 N.W.2d 718
> Iowa 1967.
> December 12, 1967 (Approx. 3 pages)
>
> The contract also provided the grantee of each piece of property would be entitled to All of the growing crops on the real estate to be conveyed. This would mean plaintiff was entitled to all crops on the 225 acre tract while defendant was entitled to all crops on the 60 acre tract. Plaintiff says each year after the contract was signed he proposed the crops be divided on that basis and each year defendant refused. Although defendant denies this, both agree the crops (or the income therefrom), for both tracts operated as a whole, were divided each year on a fifty-fifty share basis. The parties made and filed partnership income tax returns at least until 1962, continued the partnership farming as to all crops to 1964 and *475 were still in partnership as to wheat, pasture and cattle at time of trial. The farm was treated as a unit for purposes of participating in government programs to date of trial. We find such **722 action to be inconsistent with continued reliance on the rights created by the written contract.

Source: Westlaw screenshot. Published with permission of West, a Thomson Reuters business.

vide a pinpoint citation for it without having to consult the bound volume of the reporter.

Both Westlaw and LexisNexis also have tools that enable you to highlight relevant text and paste it directly into a document together with the citation to that material. On Westlaw, this feature is located under "Tools" and "Copy with Ref" at the lower right hand side of the screen; on LexisNexis, you can use "Copy w/ Cite." When using these tools, be sure to correct citations to adhere to the citation system preferred by your court, office, or supervisor. Also, remember that excessive quotations and citations sometimes indicate weak analysis.

Another convenient feature allows you to save materials for later use. In addition to printing a hard copy of the documents you find, you also can download or email the results. Moreover, you may choose to print a citation list of all the documents retrieved. You can also select only certain documents to print or download.

Both Westlaw and LexisNexis save past searches, allowing you to review an earlier search: "Research Trail" on Westlaw is available for two weeks, and "History" on LexisNexis is on file for 30 days. If you need to run the same search periodically, retrieving only new additions to your original result list, you can set up a Westlaw WestClip or LexisNexis Alert. For assistance, click the "Help" link and review tutorials, request live support while you are online, or call customer support.

As will be explained in Chapter 9, citators are an indispensable tool in legal research and must be used to verify that each authority on which you plan to rely is still "good law." An authority is "good law" if no later legal authority has reversed, overruled, or otherwise diminished its value. Shepard's on LexisNexis or KeyCite on Westlaw serve that purpose by listing negative subsequent treatment of authorities. Additionally, Shepard's and KeyCite enable you to find every source that has cited your authority, providing a powerful research tool. For court decisions you can also retrieve a list of all authorities a case relied on, a feature called *Table of Authorities*. It allows you to determine the current weight of authority for the cases cited within the opinion.

Westlaw and LexisNexis continually update and enhance their products, so any list of features would soon be outdated. The vendors' web pages are good sources of information on how to use the services and their recent enhancements.[29]

C. Starting with a Citation

In addition to keyword searching, there are other approaches to searching LexisNexis and Westlaw. As noted earlier in this chapter, if you have a citation to begin your research, you have a good headstart. Both LexisNexis and Westlaw have a citation retrieval box into which you can enter the citation for the case, statute, article, or other document you want to retrieve. If the format you use is not what the system accepts, you will be guided to the correct one. For example, if you wanted to locate the case *State v. Jordan*, 409 N.W.2d 184 (Iowa 1997), in Westlaw you would enter the citation, "409 N.W.2d 184," into the "Find" search box to retrieve the case. In LexisNexis, the feature is "Get a Document." These features also allow you to find cases or briefs by party name.

D. Topic Limits

LexisNexis and Westlaw also offer a variety of options to allow you to limit your searches to particular areas of law. For example, they provide directories of subject-specific sources, called *Topical Materials by Area of Practice* in Westlaw and *Area of Law — By Topic* in LexisNexis. In addition, they both enable you to browse topics, selecting from a list of subjects the one relevant to your research and then continuing to select narrower topics from more specific subject lists or search within a select subset of materials. On LexisNexis, select the "Search" tab and then the "By Topic or Headnote" subtab to access

---

29. Westlaw's website is at http://www.westlaw.com and the LexisNexis website is at http://www.lexisnexis.com.

VII. Recording Legal Citations

A. Introduction

As you research, you need to accurately record where you find information. In formulating your legal argument, you will have to review and present many authorities.[31] When the law is presented in a legal document, it must include attribution in an accepted citation format so that the judge, senior partner, opposing counsel, and anyone else can review the sources cited. For legal researchers, the two most well-known guides are *The Bluebook: A Uniform System of Citation*[32] and the *ALWD Citation Manual: A Professional System of Citation*.[33]

Most readers cannot distinguish the citation format for a document prepared using the *ALWD Manual* versus that of one completed using the *Bluebook*. Some differences do exist, however, and the ALWD web page includes charts that illustrate those differences when they occur.[34] One significant difference is that the *Bluebook* was written primarily as a guide for preparing citations that appear in law review articles. The majority of the text is devoted to that end, and the

---

30. The key number system and its use, introduced in this chapter at III, are explained more thoroughly in Chapter 5.

31. Thorough legal research seeks not only authorities that support your client's position, but also those authorities on which the opposing party's counsel may rely. This helps you anticipate the other party's arguments.

32. *The Bluebook: A Uniform System of Citation* (The Columbia Law Review et al. eds., 19th ed., The Harvard Law Review Assn. 2010).

33. ALWD & Darby Dickerson, *ALWD Citation Manual: A Professional System of Citation* (4th ed., Aspen Publishers 2010). Local citation rules must also be followed and the *ALWD Manual* includes those in Appendix 2. *See e.g.* Iowa R. App. P. 6.904, available at http://www.iowacourts.gov/Court_Rules_and_Forms.

34. The ALWD site is at http://www.alwdmanual.com.

examples show how to cite authorities used in law review footnotes, including the use of unique typeface convention of large and small capitals.[35] The portion of the *Bluebook* most relevant to lawyers and law students is the Bluepages, which is a small grouping of pages at the beginning of the book that shows how to prepare citations for legal briefs and memoranda. The *ALWD Manual*, in contrast, provides for only one typeface convention — the same one used for court documents and legal memoranda.

B. Citation Examples

This section provides a few examples of some of the types of citations which frequently appear in Iowa court documents and legal memoranda. This listing is intended to be illustrative of a few key primary authorities. More examples and information are provided in the Appendix. For details on other citations, be sure to consult the *ALWD Manual* or the *Bluebook*.

1. Cases

A court citation includes the names of the parties, the reporter citation, and the date in parentheses. The court making the decision must be indicated, normally in the parentheses with the date. Thus, a reference to (Iowa 2010) at the end of a citation indicates that the decision was by the Supreme Court of Iowa because the state name in the parenthetical indicates it is the highest court in the jurisdiction. If the court is clear from the reporter because only one court's cases are reported there, then no court indication is included in the date parenthetical.

Iowa Supreme Court:

Harris v. Jones, 476 N.W.2d 54 (Iowa 1991). [N.W.2d became official in 1968]

---

35. For example, the *Bluebook* requires large and small caps for periodical abbreviations, e.g., DRAKE L. REV., and book citations, e.g., DEBORAH L. RHODE, JUSTICE AND GENDER.

Iowa Court of Appeals (since 1977):

Foster v. Schwickerath, 780 N.W.2d 746 (Iowa App. 2009). [*Bluebook* would be Iowa Ct. App.]

U.S. District Court for the Southern District of Iowa:

Losee v. Maschner, 113 F. Supp. 2d 1343 (S.D. Iowa 2000).

U.S. Court of Appeals for the Eighth Circuit:

Lowe v. Apfel, 226 F.3d 969 (8th Cir. 2000).

U.S. Supreme Court:

Knowles v. Iowa, 525 U.S. 113 (1998).

2. *Statutes*

A citation to a statute includes the state code, section number, and year.

Iowa Code § 232.102 (2011).

3. *Constitutions*

Constitution citations include the abbreviated name followed by the pinpoint reference. Citations to current constitutions do not require a date.

Iowa Const. art. XII, § 1.

Chapter 3

Secondary Sources

I. Introduction

People new to legal research sometimes mistakenly believe that you find the law in the same manner you would find the rules of a board game: by consulting one officially designated source that explains what is required or permitted. As explained earlier, however, there are multiple sources of law, broadly falling into the categories of constitutions, statutes, regulations, and court opinions. These sources are primary authority, and they are the goal of your research. But by starting your research with any one of these sources, you may not understand how it interacts with other sources of law or how the area of law in question actually functions.

Secondary sources—written not to make law, but to summarize, clarify, and comment on it—offer one solution to this dilemma. Knowledgeable professionals conduct substantial research to write a secondary source, which provides a narrative description and explanation of an area of law. Secondary sources may also provide useful background information, explain key concepts, or otherwise point your research in the right direction. Secondary sources address a variety of different sources of law and reference important statutes, cases, regulations, and constitutional provisions in their discussion. These references can save you time when you begin to look at primary authorities. For all of these reasons, secondary sources can be an excellent place to begin many legal research projects, especially when the area of law is unfamiliar to you or particularly complex.

Secondary sources commonly consulted by legal researchers include treatises and other books, restatements, uniform laws and model codes, legal periodicals, looseleafs and portfolios, *American Law Reports*, legal dictionaries, legal encyclopedias, and research guides. Another significant category of secondary sources, practice materials, is covered in Chapter 10. Choosing which secondary source to use to begin your research is not an exact science. Some secondary sources are better suited to certain research tasks, as described in Table 3-1. Other times several sources might work, and you may select a starting point based on availability, cost, and personal preference. By becoming familiar with how different resources are organized, you can greatly enhance your efficiency in using these sources.

Remember that secondary sources are not the law. Once you have used one or more secondary sources in your research, you will need to consult the relevant, current, and primary legal authorities. Likewise, you will not cite most secondary sources in legal documents. Some, like research guides, are strictly finding aids and should never be cited. Others, like encyclopedias, are introductory materials that would not be considered very authoritative by the court. The four types of secondary sources most likely to be cited in a legal document are treatises, law review articles, restatements, and uniform laws and model codes. The reputation of the title or author will be a primary consideration in whether a treatise is cited. Similarly, law review articles are more likely to be cited when they are written by a respected professional and published in an esteemed journal; student notes published in a law review are unlikely to be cited in a legal document. Restatements are prestigious and are cited fairly frequently. After a jurisdiction has adopted a uniform law or model code, the text and associated commentaries may be cited when the legislative intent of the adopted statute is at question. Even highly regarded secondary sources will often only be cited when relevant law cannot be found or as additional support for your argument.

Table 3-1. Secondary Source Overview

Materials	Use
Treatises and Other Books	Obtain background information, overview, analysis, and practical tips. Treatises typically offer in-depth descriptions and analyses of the law. Other types of books may introduce an area of law or help sharpen legal skills.
Restatements	Obtain in-depth, analytical treatment of broad areas of law; use as a highly regarded persuasive authority. A restatement attempts to synthesize the common law, stating rules of law or principles that the courts have applied.
Uniform Law and Model Code Commentary	When the Iowa General Assembly adopts a uniform law or model code, related commentaries can help you find cases interpreting the statutes and understand their intent.
Law Journal Articles	Law reviews: Obtain a fairly in-depth treatment of a topic with extensive footnotes to primary law and other sources of interest. Other types of journals: Obtain practical tips and sharpen legal skills.
Looseleafs and Portfolios	Obtain thorough and up-to-date information related to different practice areas. These sources are often particularly good in areas that significantly rely on administrative law, such as tax, labor, and environmental law.
ALR and ALR Federal	Find key legal issues as well as citations to and descriptions of many interpretive court cases on a narrow topic.
Legal Dictionaries	Find definitions of unknown legal terms and phrases; discover related concepts and develop a list of search terms.
Legal Encyclopedias	Obtain a broad overview of an area of law; find references to key cases, laws, and secondary sources.
Legal Research Guides	A time-saving starting point when researching a new area of law or jurisdiction, use to learn specific research tips and techniques and obtain a compilation and description of specific research sources.

II. Types of Secondary Sources

A. Treatises and Other Books

The wide range of available legal books means they can serve many purposes. Some legal books are small, single-volume works on a particular area of law, legal issue, or legal skill. Others, often called *treatises*, provide comprehensive treatment of a topic, often in multiple volumes of text. Treatises may be useful for experienced attorneys trying to answer a narrow question of law, understand a certain procedure, or otherwise gain more in-depth information on a legal topic. For instance, if you have a question on almost any aspect of copyright law, you may well find an answer in the multi-volume title *Nimmer on Copyright*. As one former Iowa law librarian describes them, such reputable, in-depth treatises are "experts, just sitting on the shelves, waiting for you to ask them a question."[1]

Some legal books may be useful for novices who want to familiarize themselves with an area of law. The Nutshell series published by West is one well-known example. It is designed to provide a condensed overview of many different legal topics, each covered in one small volume. *Hornbooks* are another type of introductory treatise. Usually written by law professors for students, hornbooks provide a narrative statement of the law in different areas with references to key cases. Other books written specifically for law students may help explain material presented in law school courses. For instance, the Examples and Explanations series published by Aspen provides an overview of an area of law and then illustrates legal principles through examples and explanations.

1. Updating Treatises

As explained in Chapter 2, it is important to know how a source is updated to ensure you are consulting the most recent version. Legal

---

1. Cheryl Gritton, former U.S. Court of Appeals Eighth Circuit branch librarian.

books are updated in three ways, each with its own means of assessment. New pages might be issued to replace content in a looseleaf treatise. With this updating mechanism, look at the bottom of each page for a date and the front of the first volume for filing instructions with a date of the last release filed into the book. Pocket parts, supplements, and replacement volumes may update treatises, particularly in multi-volume sets. In this instance, look for a date on the cover of the pocket part or supplement. Other books may only be updated through release of a new bound edition, and the copyright date at the front of the volume will reflect its currency. For books available through a database, check the database scope note or information link to see what it includes, and how current contents are.

2. *Finding Relevant Treatises*

There are two steps to using a legal text: finding a relevant book and finding the material of interest in the book. As discussed in detail in Chapter 2, you might use a law library catalog to identify a book of interest. You might also get the title of a book suitable for your information need from a reference in another source or from a recommendation from a trusted professional, such as an attorney, professor, or librarian. For instance, you may check the Georgetown Law Library legal treatise finder, which lists reputable treatises in over 50 areas of law.[2] Each title list designates the books that are introductory or *study aids*—law student class supplements—and those that are widely regarded as the preeminent treatises in the field. Increasingly, books are available online, as well as in print. Electronic sources for books include databases, such as Westlaw, LexisNexis, HeinOnline, Commerce Clearing House (CCH), and Bureau of National Affairs (BNA), and the open Web, via a source such as Google Books. Librarians at state and academic law libraries can help you determine your options for accessing legal books.

Remember, like all books, some legal books provide higher quality information than others. When evaluating a legal book, consider

---

2. The Georgetown Law Library legal treatise finder can be found at http://www.ll.georgetown.edu/guides/treatisefinder.cfm.

not only the subject and depth of its coverage, but also the credentials of its author(s), the book's purpose, and the date of last update. When determining if a book is current, look at the book itself and do not limit yourself to the library catalog record. The publication date listed in a library catalog can be misleading, as it may reflect the initial release of a treatise, but not the date of the last supplementation, or the date of the first book published in a series but not the last one. Once you have found a book of interest, you will need to find relevant sections within the book using one of the methods described in Chapter 2: searching by index, table of contents, or, for treatises available electronically, keyword.

B. Restatements of the Law

The American Law Institute (ALI) is a select group of highly regarded lawyers, judges, and law professors. Among its publications is a series called restatements of the law, which are texts that attempt to clearly state what the common law is in different areas and provide references to court cases that have cited the restatement. Some of the best known titles in the series are the *Restatement of Torts* and the *Restatement of Contracts*. The ALI does not approve, or adopt, a restatement until it has passed through a series of drafts; this process gives members opportunities to provide input and improve the text. Restatements are somewhat like treatises in that they provide extensive commentary on a particular area of law. However, restatements are considered more authoritative than most treatises, insofar as they are authored by the leading authorities on the subject and are widely cited by courts.

In fact, courts may even adopt a restatement, or section of it, as law. For instance, in a 2009 Iowa Supreme Court opinion, Justice Hecht stated, "We find the drafters' clarification of the duty analysis in the Restatement (Third) compelling, and we now, therefore, adopt it."[3] Consulting the case citations part of a restatement as well as the textual part will help you identify such adoptions.

---

3. *Thompson v. Kaczinski*, 774 N.W.2d 829 (Iowa 2009).

The textual part of the restatement begins with an introduction that explains the scope of the work. The bulk of the restatement consists of many sections, each addressing a particular legal issue. Each section includes the rule of law, comments, and the reporter's note, which includes information about the drafting of the restatement section and references to related laws and secondary sources.[4] Some sections also offer illustrations that provide examples of the application of the rule.

To use a restatement, the first step is to identify which one might cover your topic. Current restatement titles are listed in Table 3-2. To check for changes since this book was published, consult the list of restatement topics on the ALI website.[5] Note that most titles include a series designator, i.e., second or third; the ALI issues a new restatement series to expand or update its coverage in that area of law. As new volumes are slowly released, it sometimes happens that more than one series of an adopted restatement is at least partially current at the same time, such as is the case now with the *Restatement of Trusts*. Generally, you will want to start with the most recent relevant restatement. Detailed information linked from the ALI list of restatements on its website will indicate if the newest restatement has completely replaced any older restatements or if you also need to consult an earlier series in whole or part.

Each restatement has its own index, often included at the end of the last volume with restatement text. Index entries point to the restatement section for a topic. They may also pinpoint the relevant discussion more precisely, referencing a specific part of the comment (Com), reporter's note (RN), or introductory note (Intro). In addition to the index, the table of contents may help you find a pertinent section.

After reading a relevant section, check to see which courts have cited it. Case citations are listed by restatement section in supplemental material. For a recently issued restatement, most case citations

---

4. The reporter is the person in charge of the restatement project and serves as the principal drafter.
5. The ALI website is at http://www.ali.org. Click on publications.

Table 3-2. Current Adopted Restatements

Restatement of the Law Third, Agency

Restatement Second, Conflict of Laws

Restatement Second, Contracts

Restatement of the Law Third, Restatement of the Foreign Relations Law of the United States

Restatement of the Law Second, Judgments

Restatement of the Law Third, The Law Governing Lawyers

Restatement of the Law, Property (only vol. 1–3 and 6 are current)

Restatement of the Law Second, Property (Donative Transfers)

Restatement of the Law Second, Property (Landlord and Tenant)

Restatement of the Law Third, Property (Servitudes)

Restatement of the Law Third, Property (Wills and Other Donative Transfers)

Restatement of the Law Third, Property (Mortgages)

Restatement of the Law, Restitution

Restatements of the Law — Security (only part of Division I still current)

Restatement of the Law Third, Suretyship and Guaranty

Restatement of the Law Second, Torts

Restatement of the Law Third, Torts: Apportionment of Liability

Restatement Third, Torts: Liability for Physical and Emotional Harm

Restatement of the Law Third, Torts: Products Liability

Restatement of the Law Second, Trusts

Restatement of the Law Third, Trusts

Restatement of the Law Third, Unfair Competition

---

may be contained in the annual pocket part or separate softbound supplement. For older restatements, one or more bound appendix volumes may also include case citations for a particular range of years.

When using the appendix volumes, carefully read the information on the spine to see what range of years and restatement sections each includes. In addition, a separate paperback supplement, *Interim Case Citations to the Restatements and Principles of the Law*, is released twice a year to add even more recent case citations.

Restatements can also be searched through Westlaw and LexisNexis in databases that combine all restatements or only include a particular restatement. Both services include the most recent case citations available. A Westlaw result gives the restatement text first, followed by a case citations section that provides all case citations. LexisNexis has separate, but linked, databases for restatement rules and case citations. The rule document provides a link near the top to case citations, and the citations document provides a link at the top to the rule.

C. Uniform Laws and Model Codes

Sometimes organizations other than the government draft legislation that they encourage state legislatures to adopt. The Uniform Law Commission (ULC, formerly the National Conference of Commissioners on Uniform State Laws, or NCCUSL) has created hundreds of uniform laws in areas where it believes standardization among state laws is most beneficial, typically private civil law. The best-known uniform law is the Uniform Commercial Code (UCC), drafted by the ULC and the American Law Institute (ALI).

Model acts or codes are also drafted for consideration by state legislatures, often in areas where uniformity is not as significant a concern. The Model Penal Code is one well-known example. Model legislation is somewhat more likely than uniform legislation to be changed by a state, although a legislature may modify either type of proposal before adoption. The ULC and the ALI both produce model acts, as do the American Bar Association and other organizations.

Some groups specialize in drafting legislation in a specific area. For instance, the National Association of Insurance Commissioners drafts model laws and regulations related to insurance. Similarly, the International Code Council (ICC) drafts building and safety codes. Although ICC titles do not include the word uniform or model, they have no authority unless adopted by a particular state or other jurisdiction, just like a uniform law or model code.

As you assess whether a uniform law, model code, or other draft legislation applies to your research, consider the following:

- Has Iowa, or another jurisdiction of interest, adopted this law?
- If so, did Iowa adopt the law in whole or make changes to it before adopting it?
- How can I find the text of the model or uniform law if it was *adopted by reference*, wherein the full-text of the law is not reprinted in the local code? (As one example, 661-301.3 of the Iowa Administrative Code (IAC) adopts the International Building Code by reference.)
- What was the organization's intent when drafting this law?
- What court cases interpret this law?

Uniform Laws Annotated (ULA) is one of the best tools for answering all of these questions. This multi-volume work provides access to well over 100 acts and codes, categorized by area of law. The specific volume you need can be found using the annual Directory of Uniform Acts and Codes Tables-Index volume. This pamphlet provides an alphabetical listing of all acts and codes covered in the title, indicating the volume and page number on which coverage starts. (Hint: If you are looking for a uniform law, search for the first word after "uniform" in the name, but search under "model" for acts whose names begin with model.) The pamphlet also includes state tables that indicate which uniform legislation the state has adopted and provides the volume and page reference for the act's table of adoptions. Finally, the pamphlet includes a keyword index to help find relevant acts by subject.

For each piece of legislation, ULA coverage begins with very helpful preliminary matter: a table of jurisdictions where the act has been adopted, including the effective date and references to the state's code section and bill/session law number; historical notes; authorship; prefatory notes that explain the act's purpose; statutory notes that broadly discuss state derivations in adoption; and an outline of the act. Within each section of the act, ULA offers the text of the act, comments that further explain the text, specific notes on ways adopting jurisdictions have altered the original act, and references to interpreting court decisions and secondary sources, such as law review articles.

ULA is available as a Westlaw database. You can either search the full text of the title, using standard Westlaw search options, or navigate by the table of contents. The "table of contents" link is in the upper right corner; it provides a list of the acts and codes in the set. Clicking on the plus box to the left of the relevant act opens a more detailed list of contents. The "references and annotations" link provides access to the preliminary matter. Each section also includes the other ULA elements.

The *Code of Iowa* and *Iowa Code Annotated* both provide index access to the uniform and model acts that Iowa has adopted. At the back of the index volume, the official code includes a *skeleton and popular name index*, intended for quick reference. Under the heading "Uniform Laws," it lists all the uniform laws in force in Iowa and the corresponding code sections. It also lists adopted model acts, such as the Business Corporation Act, by name. In addition, the General Index of the *Iowa Code Annotated* includes the heading "Uniform Laws" and, at the end of the last index volume, has a popular name table where you can look up legislation by its commonly known name and see where it has been codified.

Other treatises and finding aids only focus on a particular uniform or model act. For instance, there are several well-known titles that explore the Uniform Commercial Code, including the *Uniform Commercial Code Reporting Service: Cases and Commentary*, the *Uniform Commercial Code Case Digest*, and *Anderson on the Uniform Commercial Code*. Such works can be found using a library catalog, as discussed in Chapter 2.

A few additional options for finding information about uniform and model laws are listed in Table 3-3.

Table 3-3. Additional Sources for Uniform/
Model Law Information

Source	Address
Uniform Law Commission Final Acts and Legislation	http://www.nccusl.org/Acts.aspx
American Law Institute (codifications and studies publications catalog)	http://www.ali.org. Click on publications.
Cornell Legal Information Institute, Uniform Laws	http://www.law.cornell.edu/uniform
Public.Resource.Org (bulk code collection)	http://bulk.resource.org/codes.gov

D. Legal Periodicals

1. Introduction

Legal periodicals are typically published more quickly than treatises, which makes them important for many research projects. Many legal periodicals are published several times a year, insuring that the articles are current and topical when published. Often, periodical articles cover a developing area of the law before books on the subject are available. Furthermore, articles are useful tools for examining present trends and recent changes in the law. However, periodical articles are not updated, so the older the publication date, the more likely the content no longer reflects the current state of the law.

This section describes the different types of legal periodicals and their general use. It then explains how to find relevant articles by either subject or citation. Finally, it considers options for locating very recently published or forthcoming articles.

2. Types of Legal Periodicals and Their Use

Published periodically by law schools, bar associations, or commercial publishers, legal journals contain articles exploring legal issues, providing law-related news, and offering practical legal information. Law school periodicals, generically called *law reviews*, and similar commercial publications typically contain analytical articles, many of which are quite lengthy and include extensive footnote references. Either "law review" or "journal" often appear in these titles, which can be general in scope, such as the *Iowa Law Review*, or focused on a specific subject, such as the *Drake Journal of Agricultural Law*. Bar association publications, often called *bar journals*, typically include shorter pieces that provide advice and information about current legal issues and events. For instance, the *Iowa Lawyer* includes a column that explores ethical issues in legal practice.

Law review articles can be an ideal starting place for legal research in a new area. They often begin with a brief summary of the evolution of the law and analyses of it, as well as describing the current state of the law. The law review standard of heavy footnoting helps the researcher identify other primary and secondary sources on the topic.

3. Finding Articles by Topic: Indexes and Full-Text Databases

Library catalogs list the titles of journals, e.g., *Drake Law Review*, but do not list the individual articles within these journals. If you want to find articles on a particular subject or by a particular author, you will use an index or a full-text journal article database. Unlike library catalogs, which are usually freely available online, most journal indexes and databases are available only in-person in the library or to the library's primary clientele, as described in Chapter 2.

Indexing and full text are two different dimensions. Sources can be indexed with or without having full-text availability. However, the kinds of searches that will be more successful in an index vary significantly from those that are better suited to searching the full text. This is primarily because an index labels articles by subject.

Indexes are compiled by people who actually read or review each article and then select the subjects covered by the article from a list of established subject descriptors, called a *controlled vocabulary*. The yellow pages of the phone book provides a simple illustration of the use and advantage of a controlled vocabulary. If you want to find a restaurant in the yellow pages, you look under the heading Restaurants, and eateries of all types are found there. You do not have to also search for words like café, drive-through, bistro, pizzeria, buffet, or any other headings that are synonyms for restaurant or represent a specific type of restaurant. The use of a controlled vocabulary can make searching journal indexes more efficient than searching an unindexed, full-text database where the searcher must try to think of the exact words that are used in the article in order to retrieve relevant results.

Further, a search in a full-text database will retrieve all articles that contain the key word(s) or phrase(s), regardless of how often the terms appear or the context in which they are used. Therefore, search results are likely to include many articles that are not relevant to your topic. In an index, the search can be limited to the subject headings, therefore yielding only results actually addressing the subject, not just mentioning the subject words. Moreover, once you find a relevant article, you can search for other articles with the same subject descriptors, which often produces other items of interest.

Full-text databases allow researchers a means of accessing articles beyond subject, title, and author searching. If you are looking for a specific article, finding it in a full-text database can save you time by combining the steps of locating citations and then locating the article text. Also, controlled vocabulary tends to change slowly. Some subjects, especially newer ones, may not have their own index terms yet, or an assigned index term may be much broader than your research interest, leading to a significant number of irrelevant articles in your research results. In these situations, you may be more likely to find relevant articles if you can search the entire article text for your specific terms and concepts. Many successful researchers move back and forth between index and full-text searching. For example, if you find a highly relevant article in a full-text source, locate the same article in an indexed database to see if that yields any useful subject terms that can be used to find more articles.

Indexes may be available in print or electronically. Print indexes are generally arranged by topic, author, title, and cases and statutes mentioned in journal articles. These tools only provide citation information, e.g., journal title, volume, page number. Some electronic indexes provide either an *abstract* (a narrative description of the article) or the full text of an article in addition to citation information. Examples of indexed databases of legal periodicals include *Index to Legal Periodicals*, *LegalTrac*, and *Index to Periodical Articles Related to Law*. Searching the electronic version of an index will almost always be more efficient than searching its print counterpart. In print, you will have to conduct the same search in multiple volumes to cover an extensive time period, whereas in an electronic index a single search can cover many years. Electronic indexes also provide more search options.

Full-text databases are only available electronically. Both Westlaw and LexisNexis offer databases containing the text of several hundred legal periodicals, some dating back to the 1980s, and others dating back to 1990s. It is possible to search in one or more selected law journal at a time or to search a combined database of all the available law journals. Also, an increasing number of law reviews are freely available in full-text format on the web. Although these articles can be found using a general search engine, it might be more efficient to use the American Bar Association's *Free Full-text Online Law Review/Law Journal Search Engine*.[6]

Whether the database you are using is indexed or not, be aware of the coverage it provides by checking the scope note, as explained in Chapter 2. Many databases do not contain older articles. Although coverage varies from title to title, often it does not extend back further than 1980. Two notable exceptions are the *Index to Legal Periodicals Retro* database, which indexes articles published between 1908 and 1979, and *HeinOnline Journals Collection*, which provides articles back to the first issue of each title included. The specific titles included in a database vary from source to source, which can mean you will get different results by searching different databases. Full-text databases usually cover fewer journals than indexes.

---

6. The ABA site is http://apps.americanbar.org.

Because the practice of law is becoming increasingly interdisciplinary, you may also need to find information about subjects that are not necessarily included in traditional legal periodicals. There are many databases for finding multi-disciplinary or non-legal articles, such as EBSCO's Academic Search Complete, OCLC's ArticleFirst, and Scopus.[7] Law school libraries will likely have access to a variety of legal and interdisciplinary indexes and full-text databases. Sometimes, these may be available through other libraries on campus. Public libraries also often offer cardholders access to one or more article databases that might be useful in legal research.

The Welch Matter

Here is an example of the research process for finding legal periodical articles by topic as it relates to the Welch matter, the hypothetical grandparents' visitation rights scenario described at the end of Chapter 1.

One approach to searching for law review articles is to search a full-text database of articles such as one available on Westlaw. To find articles that discuss grandparent visitation and include consideration of Iowa, first select a database, such as Journals and Law Reviews (JLR), which provides access to articles from U.S. and Canadian law reviews, bar journals and CLE publications.

One possible search—grandparent /3 visitation /p iowa—brings up articles that include the word grandparent within three words of visitation in the same paragraph as Iowa, as shown in Figure 3-1.

Reviewing these results shows the power and pitfalls of full-text searching. The first result is on a different topic and just mentions our search terms in passing. Other articles sound far more promising and point us to a relevant Iowa statute and case law.

Figure 3-1 also shows the "ResultsPlus" feature, which suggests potentially relevant Westlaw sources outside of the database we searched. As explained in Chapter 2, law school students cannot access anything outside their school's Westlaw plan, but this may not be the case in practice. You will want to be familiar with your database subscription agreements and read screen messages carefully to ensure that you are not incurring additional fees by clicking on these links.

---

7. For more information about these databases, see http://ebscohost.com/thisTopic.php?marketID=1&topicID=633 for Academic Search Complete, http://www.oclc.org/support/documentation/firstsearch/databases/dbdetails/details/Articlefirst.htm for ArticleFirst, and http://info.scopus.com/scopus-in-detail/facts for Scopus.

Note that by following the advice given in Chapter 2 and running the search in a smaller database, such as Iowa Law Reviews and Journals on Westlaw (IA-JLR) or Iowa Law Reviews, Combined, on LexisNexis, you may get more focused, cost-effective results. JLR was selected for this search to illustrate the way full-text searching can include irrelevant results.

Figure 3-1. Screenshot of Westlaw JLR Search Results

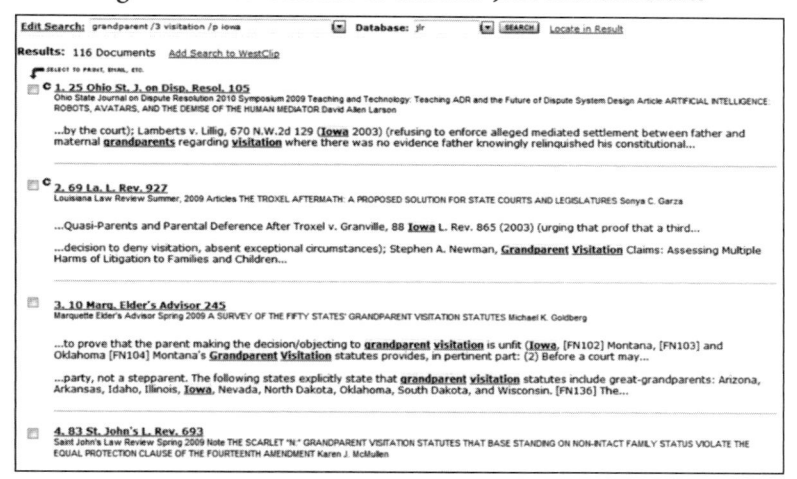

Source: Westlaw. Published with permission of West, a Thomson Reuters business.

4. Finding an Article When You Already Have a Citation

If you already have a citation to a journal article or you find one in an index that does not offer full-text, you will then need to determine where you can find the full text. (Tip: If you have a citation with a journal name you cannot decipher, look up the abbreviated name in *Bieber's Dictionary of Legal Abbreviations* or in the periodicals table of the *Bluebook* or the *ALWD Citation Manual*.) Many libraries now offer journal finders that allow you to type in the name of the journal and see which library databases provide access to the full-text of the articles in that journal. When using these tools, be sure you enter the title of the journal, not the title of the article. If your library does not have the full text of the article, you may still

Table 3-4. Finding Law Articles on the Web

American Law Sources On-line (ALSO!) Law Reviews and Periodicals

http://www.lawsource.com/also/usa.cgi?usj

This list of links to U.S. published legal periodicals uses boldface to indicate journal sites that offer the full text of articles.

Law Library of Congress Law Reviews Online

http://www.loc.gov/law/help/guide/federal/lawreviews.php

This list of links to law journals with articles online indicates the date online content begins.

State Bar Journals

http://drakelaw.libguides.com/content.php?pid=86467&sid=643483

This list provides links to state bar journals that offer at least some full-text articles online, free of charge.

---

be able to obtain it through the interlibrary loan service, where libraries lend or provide copies of materials to each other on your behalf. It can take several days or longer to obtain material from interlibrary loan, so allow yourself some extra time if you pursue this option. A variety of tools also help you check to see whether a known article is available on the web. Some of these are listed in Table 3-4. If using a search engine to find an article, try searching for the author's homepage; full articles are sometimes linked from an online profile or résumé.

5. *Locating Recent and Forthcoming Articles*

Both indexes and full-text databases have some delay before adding new content. If you are searching for something very recent, special resources can help you find recently published articles, copies of working papers, preprints, articles accepted for publication, and the like. Some of these sources are listed in Table 3-5.

Table 3-5. Resources for Locating Recent and Forthcoming Articles

Berkeley Press Legal Repository

http://law.bepress.com/repository

This database offers browsable and searchable access to many full-text, law-related research materials posted by law schools, research units, institutes, centers, think tanks, conferences, and other subject-appropriate groups (PDF format).

Contents Pages from Law Reviews and Other Scholarly Journals

http://tarlton.law.utexas.edu/tallons/content_search.html

This keyword-searchable database offers tables of contents from over 750 scholarly legal publications that the Tarlton Law Library, University of Texas School of Law, has received over the past three months.

Current Index to Legal Periodicals (CILP)

http://lib.law.washington.edu/cilp/cilp.html

This weekly index of current articles from over 500 legal publications is organized by subject. The last eight issues are also available via the Westlaw database CILP. It is compiled by the University of Washington School of Law.

Current Law Journal Content

http://lawlib.wlu.edu/CLJC/index.aspx?age=7

This database offers table-of-contents coverage of over 1,500 law journals. It contains no articles in full text, though it might contain links to the full text. This search default shows the most recent 7 days but you can change this setting if you wish. It is provided by the Washington and Lee University Law Library.

Google Scholar

http://scholar.google.com

This specialized search engine provides access to a range of scholarly literature on the web, including working papers.

SSRN/Legal Scholarship Network

http://www.ssrn.com/lsn/index.html

This database offers browsable and searchable access to abstracts and selected full-text preprints, articles, and studies. Use the "Search" command from the top menu line to retrieve papers by keyword search.

E. Looseleaf Services and Portfolios

Lawyers who specialize in an area of law will often subscribe to a print or electronic topical looseleaf service that reports and analyzes legal news, proposed statutes, and regulations and brings together cases, statutes, regulations, and other administrative law in the area. Such services are frequently updated, through issuing new pages to replace or add to the current pages, and/or by releasing newsletters that update coverage. Bureau of National Affairs (BNA), Commerce Clearing House (CCH), and Research Institute of America (RIA) are three of the largest publishers of such services.

Portfolios are similar to looseleaf services in that they specialize in a particular area of law and the print versions are updated by replacing or inserting specific pages. Portfolio series are most often published in the areas of taxation, real estate, and corporate law; BNA series are among the most recognized. They consist of a number of individual portfolios, which present practitioner-oriented explanations and analysis on the application of a fairly narrow issue of law.

If you do not know what specific title you need, it may be easiest to check for a looseleaf service or portfolio series on your area of law by asking a librarian. The library may provide access either in print or electronically, and the library catalog may not specify whether the item is a looseleaf service or portfolio. Note again that publication dates listed in the catalog can be misleading, as they may reflect the initial release of a looseleaf, but not the date of the last update, or the date of the first book published in a series but not the last one. Table 15 in the *Bluebook* (19th ed.) lists some of the more commonly used looseleaf titles and their publishers. If your library subscribes to it, you can also check the annual *Legal Looseleafs in Print*, which includes both looseleaf services and looseleaf treatises.

1. Using a Print Looseleaf Service

The key to using a looseleaf service successfully is making sure you know how it is organized. Print sources will typically have an explanation of how to use the service at the front of the first volume. Each looseleaf service is different, although some titles, especially those by the same publisher, may share similar features. The how-to-use section will show you the overall arrangement of the work. Looseleaf services often consist of a variety of parts. The main text may be subdivided by topic or organized by statutory code section. There may be separate sections for newsletters and for reported cases or statutes. Older cases may be transferred into other binders or bound volumes, and these may not even be shelved directly next to the rest of the looseleaf.

The how-to-use section will also introduce the different finding aids within the looseleaf service. There are often multiple indexes and tables, and the best one to use depends on what you need and what you already know. For instance, the decisions binder and case volumes of the *Environment Reporter* offer a topical index to find cases by subject, a classification guide that categorizes environmental law topics and assigns each a number, an index digest that presents cases by their classification number, a table of cases to find a known case alphabetically by name, and a table of cases by jurisdiction to find cases decided in a particular jurisdiction.

Finally, you will benefit from reading the how-to-use section because it will explain other anomalies of the service. For instance, looseleaf services often have page numbers, but instead of using these as references, they use paragraph references or section numbers. These numbers on the page are typically preceded by the paragraph symbol (¶) or the section symbol (§). Note that a "paragraph" may consist of many paragraphs and even run many pages. When using a looseleaf index be sure to look for a note indicating whether references are to paragraph numbers, section numbers, or page numbers.

2. Using a Print Portfolio

In print, use the separate general index volume to locate relevant portfolios by subject; statutory or administrative code sections may also be search options for some portfolios. The index citation will provide the portfolio number and the section in which that subject is discussed. Note that as portfolios are replaced, they will keep their main number but add an edition signifier after it; e.g., 659 becomes 659-2nd. Each portfolio will also have a table of contents and may begin with a scope note describing what the portfolio covers.

3. *Electronic Options*

Many attorneys now access looseleaf services and portfolios as subscription databases available separately or through more comprehensive research tools, like Westlaw and LexisNexis. The content and organization of the electronic versions is generally the same as the print source. However, online access is more up-to-date than print access, as there is no lag time while new material is mailed and filed. Electronic access also provides some user-friendly enhancements, such as automatic e-mail delivery of news and search alerts.

You can learn how to use an electronic looseleaf or portfolio set through a variety of sources. The database itself may offer help screens or other on-screen, step-by-step guidance, such as noting what search operators may be used. The publisher may provide online training sessions or training materials. Your librarian may also be able to provide training. Depending on the interface, you may find some sources easier to use in print and others easier to use electronically.

F. *American Law Reports*

American Law Reports (ALR) provides *annotations*, which are essentially articles that focus on a narrow, often unsettled, legal topic. Using one key court decision to introduce the issue, the annotation cites and describes other relevant court cases. ALRs are published in different series, each consisting of many volumes. The earliest ALRs included federal issues, but this jurisdiction later split into a series of its own: *American Law Reports, Federal* (ALR Fed). ALR is now in its sixth series, and ALR Fed is in its second series.[8] Although the basic

---

8. A recent addition to the ALR series, *ALR International*, provides citations to U.S. and foreign court cases on topics of international importance.

character of the annotations has remained largely the same over the years, specific features have changed, and the description that follows focuses on the newest series.

If you do not already have an ALR citation from another secondary source, you can look for one by using one of the index volumes found at the end of the set. Two separate, one-volume indexes include the third through sixth series of the ALRs (*ALR Quick Index*) or the first and second series of the ALR Feds (*ALR Fed Quick Index*). The multi-volume *ALR Complete Series Index* provides subject access to the annotations in all the ALR and ALR Fed series. Another multi-volume title, *West's ALR Digest*, allows you to find annotations from any of the ALR series using the West key number system.[9] You can also search for an annotation through the ALR database on Westlaw, which includes all series of both ALR and ALR Fed.

Each individual annotation begins by introducing the central issue and what the court found in a specific case. Other preliminary matter includes a table of contents showing the titles of the sections of the articles; research references to a variety of other secondary materials and West key numbers; an index to help find relevant sections within the article; and a table of cases, laws, and rules, which notes primary law cited in the annotation and the section where the law is discussed. This table is organized by jurisdiction, which makes it easy to determine whether any cases have been heard by the U.S. Supreme Court, the Eighth Circuit Court of Appeals, an Iowa court, or another jurisdiction of interest. Outside of court cases, the table only includes other types of laws that are discussed in the referenced court cases.

The text of each annotation begins with the same three sections: scope, indicating what the article includes; summary and comment, briefly describing the area of law; and practice pointers, offering guidance for attorneys representing clients on the legal topic. The annotations then continue with specific discussion of the legal issues involved in the topic and how courts have treated these. At the end of

---

9. The West key number system is introduced in Chapter 2 and described more fully in Chapter 5.

Figure 3-2. ALR Outline Excerpt

§ 4[a] Where child's parents are living apart, generally—Visitation awarded or held permissible, or remand necessary

§ 4[b] Where child's parents are living apart, generally—Visitation denied or held impermissible

* * *

§ 7[a]—Where child is adopted after divorce—Visitation awarded or held permissible, or remand necessary

§ 7[b]—Where child is adopted after divorce—Visitation denied or held impermissible

§ 8[a] Where child's biological parents are living together—Visitation awarded or held permissible, or remand necessary

§ 8[b] Where child's biological parents are living together—Visitation denied or held impermissible

Source: 71 A.L.R.5th 99. Published with permission of West, a Thomson Reuters business.

---

each volume, there is a section called "Reported Cases," which reprints the court case highlighted in each annotation's introduction. This case provides additional context for understanding the annotation. Through ALR 4th and ALR Fed volume 110, the case was reprinted directly before the annotation.

One of the most valuable features of the annotation is the presentation of authorities on both sides of an issue. Not only will you find cases supporting your client's position, but you also are given cases that support the opposite position. This enables you to review authorities to strengthen your case as well as determine how contrary authorities, which opposing counsel may cite, can be distinguished from your client's case. Figure 3-2 provides a few lines from the outline in an annotation addressing grandparent visitation rights, showing sections where you can find supporting and opposing authorities.[10] Note that under [a] you find summaries of cases in which visitation was awarded and under [b] you find those in which visitation was denied.

---

10. George L. Blum, *Grandparents' Visitation Rights where Child's Parents are Living*, 71 A.L.R.5th 99 (1999).

Unlike a law review article, annotations are updated after publication. New cases decided on the issues, new developments in the area of law, and references to newer annotations are included in annual supplements to the ALR, released in paper as either a pocket part or a separate softbound supplement. West also offers a latest case hotline where you can learn whether any additional cases have been added to an annotation after the last supplement was issued.[11] Electronically, updates are merged into the text of the annotation on a weekly basis, so if you look at an annotation on Westlaw, it will include any cases provided by the print supplements or the latest case hotline.

Sometimes a more recent annotation will replace an older one on the same topic. For instance, *Physician's or Other Healer's Conduct, or Conviction of Offense, Not Directly Related to Medical Practice, as Ground for Disciplinary Action*, 34 A.L.R.4th 609, replaced *Physician's Conviction of Offense Not Directly Related to Medical Practice as Ground of Disciplinary Action*, 12 A.L.R.3d 1213. In Westlaw, the text of a superseded ALR is replaced by a link to the new annotation. In print, starting with the third series, the supplementation provides the citation to the replacement annotation.

G. Legal Dictionaries

Legal dictionaries provide an alphabetical list of legal terms and phrases with definitions for each. They may include additional features, such as a guide to pronunciation or notes on the term's history. In explaining the meaning of a term, legal dictionaries often provide valuable context about the broader area of law into which the term falls—introducing related concepts and suggesting alternative terms that can be used to search databases, indexes, and other research resources.

Legal dictionaries may also note other primary or secondary sources which further explain the term. For instance, *Ballentine's Law Dictionary* includes references to cases, statutes, and other secondary

---

11. The latest case hotline phone number is (800) 225-7488.

Table 3-6. Selected Legal Dictionaries

Title	Audience	Electronic Access
Black's Law Dictionary	Law students; attorneys	E-book available for purchase; available on Westlaw
Ballentine's Law Dictionary	Law students; attorneys	Available on LexisNexis
Merriam-Webster's Dictionary of Law	Public; law students	http://dictionary.lp.findlaw.com
Oran's Dictionary of the Law	Paralegals; law students	Print only
Research Guide: One-L Dictionary	New law students	http://law.wlu.edu/deptimages/Library/1Ldictionary.pdf

materials. Starting with the eighth edition, *Black's Law Dictionary* includes citations to the legal encyclopedia *Corpus Juris Secundum* and West key numbers.

Legal dictionaries may offer broad coverage or specialize in a particular area of law, such as *West's Tax Law Dictionary*. Dictionaries may also be specifically written for a particular audience, whether attorneys, new law students, or members of the general public. Additional judicial definitions can be found in the multi-volume West title *Words and Phrases* and specific digests' Words and Phrases volumes, described in Chapter 5. Table 3-6 lists a few well-known legal dictionaries.

H. Legal Encyclopedias

Legal encyclopedias introduce different areas of law and refer to important primary law within each area. They may also reference other relevant secondary sources. Each area of law is discussed in its own topical article, which consists of separate sections. The topics are arranged alphabetically. Researchers primarily use legal encyclopedias to get an overview of a particular area of law.

Some encyclopedias have focused coverage. Some states have state-specific legal encyclopedias,[12] but Iowa does not. Subject-specific encyclopedias include *Encyclopedia of Environmental Health Law and Practice* and *Encyclopedia of Information Technology Law*. You would search for these encyclopedias in the same way you would search for a treatise, described in this chapter in Section II.A.2.

The two major general legal encyclopedias in the U.S. are *Corpus Juris Secundum* (CJS) and *American Jurisprudence 2d* (AmJur). Historically, the two titles had different publishers and slightly different goals. West now publishes both titles, but their differing characteristics largely remain. CJS begins each section with *black letter law*, a succinct summary of the rule of law, and strives to provide an extensive list of citations to cases related to each area of law covered. AmJur sections do not begin with black letter law, they cite only the most important cases and ALR annotations, and the notes are more likely than CJS to provide a brief summary of the relevance of cited cases. Electronically, AmJur is available through both Westlaw and LexisNexis, while CJS is only available through Westlaw. See Figure 3-3 for an excerpt from the AmJur topic Divorce and Separation.

In print, both titles are updated annually through a combination of replacement volumes, pocket parts, and supplements, so be sure to check the pocket part or separate supplement to see if there is additional information on your section. Electronically, click on the i-link, called source description in LexisNexis and scope information in Westlaw, to find the database's currency.

If you do not already have a specific CJS or AmJur reference, there are three ways to find a relevant topic, or section of a topic, in either encyclopedia. These methods, described in detail below, may differ depending on whether you are using the print or electronic version.

---

12. The following states have their own legal encyclopedias: California, Florida, Georgia, Illinois, Indiana, Kentucky, Maryland, Massachusetts, Michigan, New York, Ohio, Pennsylvania, South Carolina, Tennessee, Texas, Virginia, and West Virginia. See chart 26.1 in the *ALWD Manual* for a list of the titles.

Figure 3-3. Excerpt from AmJur

DIVORCE AND SEPARATION § 895

visitation has ended.[10]

b. Rights of Others

§ 895 Rights of grandparents and other relatives

Research References

West's Key Number Digest, Child Custody ⚖ 271, 282 to 289, 311 to 313

Grandparents' visitation rights where child's parents are living, 71 A.L.R.5th 99

Grandparents' visitation rights where child's parents are deceased, or where status of parents is unspecified, 69 A.L.R.5th 1

Grandparent Visitation and Custody Awards, 69 Am. Jur. Proof of Facts 3d 281

Am. Jur. Pleading and Practice Forms, Divorce and Separation §§ 48, 49 (Petition or application—By grandparent—For visitation rights), 50 (Affidavit—By grandparent—In support of petition for visitation rights), 330 (Judgment or decree—Provision—Visitation rights to grandparents)

The court's broad powers to determine all issues in a dissolution action have been recognized to include jurisdiction over issues of the rights of grandparents and other nonparents to visitation.[1] Grandparent visitation statutes provide a procedural mechanism for grandparents to acquire standing to seek visitation with minor grandchildren.[2] An award of visitation to grandparents ordinarily must arise out of a pending dissolution proceeding; the court normally has no jurisdiction to award visitation where there is an existing marriage.[3]

In some jurisdictions, grandparents and other relatives may have a legal right of visitation,[4] but other jurisdictions do not bestow a legal

---

[10]Breazeale v. Hayes, 489 So. 2d 1111 (Ala. Civ. App. 1986).

As to the requirement of bond, generally, see § 888.

[Section 895]

[1]Kanvick v. Reilly, 233 Mont. 324, 760 P.2d 743 (1988); In re Visitation of Z.E.R., 225 Wis. 2d 628, 593 N.W.2d 840 (Ct. App. 1999).

[2]E.S. v. P.D., 8 N.Y.3d 150, 831 N.Y.S.2d 96, 863 N.E.2d 100 (2007).

Grandparent access statute gives only a biological or adoptive grandparent, and not a step-grandparent, standing to seek access to grandchildren. In re Derzapf, 219 S.W.3d 327 (Tex. 2007).

Grandparent visitation statute was unconstitutional as applied to parents in proceeding in which maternal grandparents sought visitation with grandchildren, where no threshold finding was made, regarding whether parents were unfit or whether exceptional circumstances existed demonstrating current or future detriment to the child absent visitation from grandparents, before proceeding to determine whether allowing visitation was in the children's best interests. Koshko v. Haining, 398 Md. 404, 921 A.2d 171 (2007).

[3]Sragowicz v. Sragowicz, 603 So. 2d 1323 (Fla. Dist. Ct. App. 3d Dist. 1992); Theodore R. v. Loretta J., 124 Misc. 2d 546, 476 N.Y.S.2d 720 (Fam. Ct. 1984).

[4]Santaniello v. Santaniello, 18 Kan. App. 2d 112, 850 P.2d 269 (1992); Olson v. Olson, 534 N.W.2d 547 (Minn. 1995).

Source: 24A Am. Jur. 2d Divorce and Separation § 895. Published with permission of West, a Thomson Reuters business.

1. Using the Index to Find Encyclopedia Articles

This option, which is often the most efficient approach, works only for the print volumes where each set has a general index. Typically shelved after the main encyclopedia volumes, these indexes are released annually in multiple volumes. For detail on using indexes in general, see Chapter 2. Index entries in both titles provide the name, or abbreviation, of the topic and the section (§) number or numbers that discuss the specific indexed issue, such as Divorce § 895, shown in Figure 3-4. Both encyclopedias have a table at the front of each index volume that lists the topic abbreviations with the correspond-

Figure 3-4. Excerpts from AmJur General Index

GRANDCHILDREN AND GRANDPARENTS
Adoption of Children (this index)
Advancements, **Advance** § 22
Custody of children, intervention, **Divorce** § 213, 214
Descent and distribution, **DescentDst** § 80
Estate and Inheritance Taxes (this index)
Funeral and burial, **DeadBodies** § 22
Homesteads (this index)
In loco parentis, **Parent** § 13
Insurance, **Insurance** § 1699
Railroad Retirement Act, **Pensions** § 960
Restitution and implied contracts, **Restitutn** § 75
Search and seizure, consent to, **Searches** § 159
Social Security, child's benefits, **SocialSec** § 734
Visitation, **Divorce** § 895
Workers' compensation, death benefits, **Workers** § 186
Wrongful death, **Death** § 94

....
GRANDPARENTS
Grandchildren and Grandparents (this index)

Source: American Jurisprudence 2d. 2009 General Index. Published with permission of West, a Thomson Reuters business.

Figure 3-5. Excerpt from AmJur Table of Abbreviations

Damages	Damages
DeadBodies	Dead Bodies
Death	Death
DeclJuds	Declaratory Judgments
Dedication	Dedication
Deeds	Deeds
Deposition	Depositions and Discovery
Deposits	Deposits In Court
DescentDst	Descent and Distribution
Desertion	Desertion and Nonsupport
Dismissal	Dismissal, Discontinuance, and Nonsuit
DisordH	Disorderly Houses
DistCol	District of Columbia
Disturb	Disturbing Meetings
Divorce	Divorce and Separation
Domicil	Domicil
Dower	Dower and Curtesy
Drains	Drains and Drainage Districts
DrugsEtc	Drugs and Controlled Substances
Duress	Duress and Undue Influence
Easements	Easements and Licenses In Real Property
Ejectment	Ejectment
ElectionRm	Election of Remedies
Elections	Elections
Elevators	Elevators and Escalators

Source: *American Jurisprudence 2d*. 2009 General Index. Published with permission of West, a Thomson Reuters business.

ing full titles, e.g., "Divorce" abbreviates the full title "Divorce and Separation," shown in Figure 3-5.

With the reference to topic and section number, find the main volume(s) of the encyclopedia that includes that topic. Some topics may span more than one volume; in this case, make sure you select the volume that covers not only your topic but also the relevant section(s). Also be aware that the topic name might not appear on the spine, which only lists the first and last topics in the volume.

Open the relevant volume and go to the correct topic. The front of the volume lists all the topics it contains and the page numbers on which they start. The topic title can also be found at the top of each right-hand page. Within the correct topic, turn to the relevant section number. Section numbers appear in bold headings within the text of the topic. The number of the first section, or partial section, on the left-hand page will appear at the top of that page, and the number of the last section, or partial section, on the right-hand page will appear at the top of that page.

The back of each volume provides a partial index, covering only the topics in that volume. This index can be a handy reference when you have already put the general index away or if the general index volume you need is not available.

The Welch Matter

You can use the general index encyclopedia research process to learn about the hypothetical grandparents' visitation rights scenario.

Figure 3-4. One approach to beginning encyclopedia research is to use the general index to look up research terms. In the Welch case, logical terms include grandparents and child custody. As shown in Figure 3-4, the term Grandparents in the general index refers to the subject heading Grandchildren and Grandparents. That subject heading has a subheading "visitation," which leads to the relevant topic and section number: Divorce § 895.

Figure 3-5. To determine whether the topic Divorce was a shortened version of a longer name, check the table at the front of the set. You find that Divorce stands for Divorce and Separation. Then look at the spines of the books to locate the AmJur volume that includes Divorce and Separation § 895.

Figure 3-3. Opening the AmJur volume to the correct section, you see a number of research references to other sources that might be useful. You can also begin to read a general description of how different states handle visitation rights for grandparents and obtain case citations in the footnotes. Although there are not any Iowa cases cited, you do pick up a significant research lead that many states have statutes on this issue that the courts have interpreted.

---

2. *Using the Topic Outline to Find Encyclopedia Articles*

In each encyclopedia, the topics begin with an outline, or table of contents, that lists the main headings and subheadings of the topic. A subsequent *scope note* provides a narrative description of what the topic covers. Each title also references related topics that are covered in other encyclopedia topics. Before the narrative text begins, AmJur also offers general research references to West's key numbers (described in Chapter 5), primary law, and other secondary materials. These references can most easily be accessed electronically through the table of contents. In LexisNexis, the table-of-contents view is shown under the search box; in Westlaw, it can be accessed through the table-of-contents link in the upper-right corner. From the alphabetical list, find the topic of interest, then select the plus boxes to expand them and see the different sections of the topic outline.

3. Conducting a Keyword Search to Find Encyclopedia Articles

Keyword searching is only an option in the electronic databases. The advantage of this approach is that your search will retrieve every topic that includes a specific term of interest. Your search can also become quite sophisticated, using the many options available in Westlaw and LexisNexis, and the databases can suggest additional terms you may want to add to your search. The principal disadvantage of this approach is that it requires skill and familiarity with the terms likely to be used in the encyclopedia to construct a precise search that will only retrieve relevant items. You may get many irrelevant results with a simple keyword search, which will pick up your search term(s) anywhere regardless of how important each term is to the topic. Also, you may miss relevant topics or sections with a more complex search or a keyword search that does not use the right terms. For example, attorneys colloquially refer to "slip-and-fall" cases in which someone is injured after falling in an accident at least partially caused by unsafe conditions. However, searching either for the phrase slip-and-fall or the words slip and fall in close proximity to each other may lead to results that might miss relevant cases that would come up with broader search terms like premises liability or accidental falls.

I. Research Guides

Research guides describe available research sources and suggest search strategies. Particularly when you are unfamiliar with a certain area of law, consulting a relevant research guide can make your research more effective and efficient. Using a research guide can be akin to consulting a travel guide before going on a journey. A research guide familiarizes you with a particular area, notes sources of interest, and provides practical tips from someone who has already done research in this area. Research guides may also indicate what you will not find. For instance, as will be discussed further in Chapter 5, most opinions rendered in state trial-level cases are not published. Therefore, they will likely not be found in either the books or databases of a major law library. Knowing this before you begin a fruitless search can save you significant time and frustration.

Some research guides are simple lists of valuable sources for researching a topic. Others, like this book, are much more developed. In addition to providing in-depth descriptions of how to locate and use research sources in the field, they may provide important background information, such as explaining key concepts and structures. A federal tax research guide, for instance, may explain the various kinds of regulations issued by the Treasury Department, the regulations' numbering scheme, where regulations are published, and how they can be located.

General guides to legal research cover the field broadly and may include sections on specialized but widespread areas, such as employment law or environmental law. Other guides may have a narrower scope, focusing only on a particular area of law or jurisdiction. Still other guides consider a particular research task. For instance, attorneys sometimes want to compare state statutes on an issue. Before diving directly into all 50 states' codes, you could save a significant amount of time if you first check *Subject Compilations of State Laws*, a guide to sources that have already compiled this kind of information.[13]

Research guides are often written by librarians, lawyers, and professors. They may be formally published as books or journal articles or published on the web. Whatever source you use, be aware of the date the guide was created. For instance, in the grandparent visita-

---

13. *Subject Compilations of State Laws* is available in print volumes and as a database on HeinOnline.

tion hypothetical, you could begin your research by consulting M. Kristine Taylor Warren's *Grandparent Visitation Rights: A Legal Research Guide*. Because the book was published in 2000, you will have to update the key statutes and cases it cites. (See Chapter 9 for information about updating.) However, it will still help you understand the scope of the issue, recommend other secondary sources, and provide research tips, including the suggestion to start with a state's statutes.

Ways to access different legal sources change over time, especially as an increasing number of primary law collections become available on the open web. Legal research guides may be published on the web, as books, or as journal articles. As such, they can be found using the best corresponding search tools: a web search engine, a law library catalog, and law journal article indexes.

1. Finding Guides Using Web Search Engines

Law library web pages and other legal research sites often provide a variety of law-related guides. Table 3-7 includes examples of Internet sites for locating legal research guides. Use your favorite search engine to find more web-based guides. Using search terms like "research guide" *or* pathfinder *or* bibliography along with your subject, e.g., "environmental law," will likely return a large number of potentially valuable resources, as well as some less useful ones. To remove some of the lower quality sites, try adding the term "law library" and/or limiting the search to educational domain sites, e.g., "site: .edu" in Google.

2. Finding Guides Using Law Library Catalogs

Search the catalog of an academic law library collection, as described in Chapter 2, to locate research guides published as books or book chapters. (Hint: Use the phrase "legal research" as a subject search term along with a keyword for your topic of interest.) Issue-oriented guides range from the broad, such as Albert P. Melone's *Researching Constitutional Law*, to the very narrow, such as Amy R. Stein's *Illegal Sex Discrimination or Permissible Customer Preference?: Refusal to Hire and Employ Male Gynecologists: A Legal Research Guide*.

Table 3-7. Selected Internet Sources for Legal Research Guides

Site	Address
Drake University Law Library	http://drakelaw.libguides.com/index.php
University of Iowa Law Library	http://www.law.uiowa.edu/library/pathfinders.php
Georgetown Law Library	http://www.ll.georgetown.edu/research/browse_guides_title.cfm
GlobaLex (international, foreign, and comparative guides)	http://www.nyulawglobal.com/globalex/index.html
LLRX	http://www.llrx.com/
University of Washington Gallagher Law Library Legal Research Guides	http://lib.law.washington.edu/ref/guides.html
Zimmerman's Legal Research Guide (encyclopedia-style guide to legal research)	http://law.lexisnexis.com/infopro/zimmermans

3. Finding Guides Using Law Journal Article Indexes

Law articles can include research guides. To find these guides, search law journal indexes, described in Section II.D. Search for the area of law of interest and add the subheading "bibliography" or the keywords "research guide." For example, conduct a subject search for "Environmental Law—bibliography."

Chapter 4

The Constitution

I. Introduction

The United States Constitution serves as the country's preeminent legal authority. It establishes the three-branch form of federal government and grants powers to that government. The Iowa Constitution also creates a three-branch system of state government. However, rather than granting power to the state government, Iowa's constitution, like that of most states, imposes limitations on what the state can do.[1] The state legislature must be cognizant of constitutional requirements and avoid enacting laws not permitted under either the federal or state constitutions.

As the supreme law of the state, the Iowa Constitution may be one of the first places for a researcher to look in certain legal situations. For example, if an Iowa citizen thinks his or her rights have been abridged, a review of the provisions in the Iowa Constitution will be an essential first step for the lawyer assessing the case. The Iowa Constitution plays a key role in the development of the law, providing a lens through which the courts consider the validity of legal principles. For example, the Iowa Supreme Court was asked to review a statute setting the requirements for grandparent visitation and ruled that a

---

1. For example, the U.S. Constitution grants Congress the power to borrow money and regulate commerce (Art. 1, §8). Some limitations in the Iowa Constitution include: each branch of government is prohibited from exercising a function over another (Art. III, §1), a legislator can't have a lucrative job with the U.S. government (Art. III, §22) or be collecting public monies (Art. III, §23), the legislature cannot grant a divorce (Art. III, §27).

key provision of the statute violated Article 1 of the Iowa Constitution.[2]

Even with a number of amendments, Iowa's Constitution of 1857 remains substantially the same as it was when enacted and is one of the older state constitutions still in force.[3] As shown in Table 4-1,

Table 4-1. Articles of the Iowa Constitution

I.	Bill of Rights	
II.	Right of Suffrage	
III.	Of the Distribution of Powers	
	Legislative Department	
IV.	Executive Department	
V.	Judicial Department	
VI.	Militia	
VII.	State Debts	
VIII.	Corporations	
IX.	Education and School Lands	
	1st — Education	
	2nd — School Funds and School Lands	
X.	Amendments to the Constitution	
XI.	Miscellaneous	
XII.	Schedule	

---

2. In *Santi v. Santi*, 633 N.W.2d 312 (Iowa 2001), the Court found that Iowa Code § 598.35(7) was unconstitutional on its face because the statute authorized grandparent visits without a threshold finding that the parents were unfit or their decision to deny visits posed substantial harm to the child. The statute could not withstand strict scrutiny under Art. I, §§ 8, 9. The legislature repealed that provision and replaced it with Code § 600C.

3. For a brief history of the Iowa Constitution, see the article by Steven C. Cross, *The Drafting of Iowa's Constitution*, in the *Iowa Official Register* at http://publications.iowa.gov/135/1/history/7-6.html.

twelve articles comprise the Iowa Constitution. These are preceded by a brief preamble and description of the state's geographic boundaries.

II. Historical Context and Constitution of 1857

Over the years three constitutions have been drafted for Iowa, with two of those being adopted. In drafting each version of the constitution, Iowa legislators examined the federal constitution and the foundational documents of other states and territories. The geographic area that became Iowa had been founded under the "Organic Act for the Wisconsin Territory,"[4] so that act served as the basis for some of the initial provisions for the Iowa Constitution, including a Bill of Rights.

The first constitution of 1844 was rejected due to a disagreement regarding boundaries. The 1846 constitutional convention produced and approved a document similar in most respects to the rejected 1844 version but modified mainly to adopt the geographic boundaries of Iowa that are in effect today.[5] The 1857 constitutional convention was called to address some deficiencies apparent in the 1846 document, such as the lack of a lieutenant governor and provisions for election of judges. This 1857 version is still the Iowa Constitution, although it has been amended. In 1868 following the Civil War, for example, the first amendments to the constitution were approved by voters, striking the word "white" preceding the word male in several provisions. This change gave men of color the right to vote, something voters had rejected in 1857.

---

4. An Act Establishing the Territorial Government of Wisconsin, ch. 54, 5 Stat. 10 (1836).

5. The geographic boundaries in the 1844 version included much of what is currently Minnesota. The 1846 version adjusted the geographic boundaries to those in effect today.

III. Constitutional Amendments

As detailed in Article 10, the Iowa Constitution can be changed only by amendment initiated in the legislature and approved by voters. In establishing an amendment process in 1857, the drafters of the Iowa Constitution required that amendments first be passed by both houses of the General Assembly and then passed again by both houses in the next elected General Assembly before being submitted to the voters for approval. Because each General Assembly lasts two years, it can take several years for an amendment to reach the voters. This long and sometimes difficult method of amending the constitution may help ensure that an amendment reaching the voters has been thoroughly debated and considered. This long process also makes it possible for voters to reflect on the prior legislature's work and indicate through the ballot box who they want making constitutional decisions for the next legislative session.

Voters have approved 46 amendments, most recently in 1998 when Amendment 45 affirmed equal rights for men and women and Amendment 46 indicated when a grand jury is required. When researching the Iowa Constitution, you can choose to review the codified version with the amendments integrated into the text or the original with amendments separately listed at the end. Versions with separate amendments can be found in the *Code of Iowa* or *Iowa Code Annotated*. They present the amendments in chronological order and are helpful in understanding the historical context of the amendments. In 1988, for example, Amendment 41 provided for the joint election of governor and lieutenant governor, eliminating the possibility that these officials could be from different political parties. Voters in 1992 approved the deletion of the dueling prohibition in Article 1, § 5, which no longer seemed germane.

Interest in amending the Iowa Constitution may sometimes be spurred by hot-button issues of the day. For example, in the 2009 case *Varnum v. Brien*[6] the Iowa Supreme Court ruled unanimously that an Iowa Code provision prohibiting same-sex marriage violated the equal

---

6. 763 N.W.2d 862 (Iowa 2009).

protection clause of the Iowa Constitution.[7] Following the decision, groups lobbied the legislature to move forward on a constitutional amendment that would permit marriage only between a man and a woman.

IV. Interpreting the Iowa Constitution

When analyzing the Iowa Constitution and its interpretation by the Iowa Supreme Court, it is helpful to consider how the Iowa Court has interpreted the original intent of the drafters. The Court has emphasized the state motto, which is emblazoned on the state seal and flag and provides: "Our liberties we prize and our rights we will maintain."[8] From that statement, it should come as no surprise that the very first article of the Iowa Constitution is the Bill of Rights. As the Court has interpreted the constitution, it has been mindful of those rights. The Court explained that historical background in a recent case:[9]

> In [this court's] first reported case..., *In re Ralph* (1839), we refused to treat a human being as property to enforce a contract for slavery and held our laws must extend equal protection to persons of all races and conditions. This decision was seventeen years before the United States Supreme Court infamously decided *Dred Scott v. Sandford,* which upheld the rights of a slave owner to treat a person as property. Similarly [in 1868 and 1873], we struck blows to the concept of segregation long before ... *Brown v. Board of Education* (1954). Iowa was also the first state in the nation to admit a woman to the practice of law, doing so in 1869. Her admission occurred three years before the United States Supreme Court affirmed the State of Illinois' decision to *deny* women admission to the practice of law, and twenty-five years before the

---

7. Iowa Const. art. I, §6.
8. Iowa Code §§ 1A.1, 1B.1 (2009) (cited in *Varnum v. Brien*, 763 N.W.2d 862, 872 (Iowa 2009)).
9. *Varnum v. Brien*, 763 N.W.2d 862, 877 (Iowa 2009).

United States Supreme Court affirmed the refusal of the Commonwealth of Virginia to admit women into the practice of law. In each of those instances, our state approached a fork in the road toward fulfillment of our constitution's ideals and reaffirmed the "absolute equality of all" persons before the law as "the very foundation principle of our government."

Iowa Courts are frequently asked to determine the meaning of the Iowa Constitution. Perhaps the most notable recent exercise of that authority was the *Varnum* case, described in Section III. In that case, Justice Mark Cady discussed the court's role in interpreting the Constitution:

> The Iowa Constitution is the cornerstone of governing in Iowa. * * *
>
> A statute inconsistent with the Iowa Constitution must be declared void, even though it may be supported by strong and deep-seated traditional beliefs and popular opinion. Iowa Const. art. XII, § 1 (providing any law inconsistent with the constitution is void). * * *
>
> It is also well established that courts must, under all circumstances, protect the supremacy of the constitution as a means of protecting our republican form of government and our freedoms. As was observed ... in reference to the United States Constitution, the very purpose of limiting the power of the elected branches of government by constitutional provisions like the Equal Protection Clause is "to withdraw certain subjects from the vicissitudes of political controversy, to place them beyond the reach of majorities and officials and to establish them as legal principles to be applied by the courts." * * *
>
> In fulfilling this mandate..., we look to the past and to precedent. We look backwards, not because citizens' rights are constrained to those previously recognized, but because historical constitutional principles provide the framework to define our future as we confront the challenges of today.

Our responsibility, however, is to protect constitutional rights of individuals from legislative enactments that have denied those rights, even when the rights have not yet been broadly accepted, were at one time unimagined, or challenge a deeply ingrained practice or law viewed to be impervious to the passage of time. The framers of the Iowa Constitution knew, as did the drafters of the United States Constitution, that "times can blind us to certain truths and later generations can see that laws once thought necessary and proper in fact serve only to oppress," and as our constitution "endures, persons in every generation can invoke its principles in their own search for greater freedom" and equality. * * *

Finally, it should be recognized that the constitution belongs to the people.... While the constitution is the supreme law and cannot be altered by the enactment of an ordinary statute, the power of the constitution flows from the people, and the people of Iowa retain the ultimate power to shape it over time. *See* Iowa Const. art. X.[10]

V. Researching the Iowa Constitution

As the supreme law of the state, the Iowa Constitution is the definitive source in many areas of the law. The Iowa Constitution's twelve articles outline the rights of the people and the structure of government. If a topic of law you are investigating could be governed by the constitution, you need to know that early in the research process.

The first article contains the Bill of Rights and includes many provisions also found in the U.S. Constitution. Table 4-2 notes which Iowa provisions correspond to those in the federal constitution. This table can be helpful as you look for cases interpreting a provision.

---

10. *Varnum*, 763 N.W.2d at 875–76.

Table 4-2. Iowa Bill of Rights and Corresponding U.S. Constitutional Provisions

Article 1. Iowa Bill of Rights	U.S. Constitution
§1. Rights of persons.	Amendments 1, 5, & 14 §1
§2. Political power.	
§3. Religion.	Amendment 1
§4. Religious test—witnesses.	Article 6, clause 3
§5. Dueling. [Repealed]	
§6. Laws uniform.	Amendment 14 (equal protection); Article 4 §2 (privileges and immunities)
§7. Liberty of speech and press.	Amendment 1
§8. Personal security—searches and seizures.	Amendment 4
§9. Right of trial by jury—due process of law.	Amendments 5 & 1 §1 (due process); Amendment 6 & Article 3 §2 (jury trial)
§10. Rights of persons accused.	Amendments 7 (jury trial) & 6 (speedy trial)
§11. When indictment necessary—grand jury.	Amendment 5
§12. Twice tried—bail.	Amendment 5 (double jeopardy)
§13. Habeas corpus.	Article 1 §9
§14. Military.	Article 1 §8; Article 6 §1 et seq.; Amendment 2
§15. Quartering soldiers.	Amendment 3
§16. Treason.	Article 3 §3; Article 4 §3
§17. Bail—punishments.	Amendment 8
§18. Eminent domain—drainage ditches and levees.	Amendments 5 (just compensation) & 14 §1 (limits on state power)
§19. Imprisonment for debt.	
§20. Right of assemblage—petition.	Amendment 1
§21. Attainder—ex post facto law—obligation of contract.	Article 1 §§9–10
§22. Resident aliens.	Article 6 (treaties are supreme law of the land)
§23. Slavery—penal servitude.	Amendments 13–14
§24. Agricultural leases.	
§25. Rights reserved.	

The Iowa Constitution can be found in a number of sources in print and online. Annotated versions are among the most helpful because they include a court's interpretation of constitutional provisions and other explanatory materials. The following sections will explain those sources.

A. Print Sources for the Iowa Constitution

1. Iowa Code Annotated

An excellent starting point for researching the Iowa Constitution is West's *Iowa Code Annotated* (ICA), which includes the constitution in the first volume (labeled as volume 1, 2). The ICA includes the current constitution and its amendments with annotations of cases interpreting the constitution. It also provides twelve historical documents, including the 1846 and 1857 Constitutions as originally enacted.

The comprehensive index in the back of the constitution volume directs you to relevant provisions. When you look for a topic, such as freedom of speech, the index will refer to the provision that is applicable, such as Const. Art. 1, §7. Retrieve the provision and carefully read the actual language of the text. Then consult the annotations, which will help you understand the way the text has been applied. Figure 4-1 illustrates a single section of the Iowa Constitution in ICA, followed by its annotations as explained below.

As illustrated in Figure 4-1, following the original text is an *historical note* helping identify the origin of the section and *cross references* to related sections of interest. The heading for *law review and journal commentaries* is next with a list of articles on the topic, primarily from Iowa-based periodicals, such as the *Drake Law Review* and the *Iowa Law Review*. *Library references* then indicate where to find similar information in other West resources, such as using the topic and key number in a digest or on Westlaw or consulting legal encyclopedias such as *Corpus Juris Secundum* (CJS). For the Bill of Rights sections, there also may be a heading for the *United States Code Annotated* (USCA) noting the corresponding sections in the United

States Constitution volumes of the USCA. The following heading may be of related decisions by the United States Supreme Court.

The final heading, called *Notes of Decisions*, is one of the most important sections in the annotations. Here you find annotations for relevant cases interpreting that section of the constitution. The notes begin with a table of contents of the decisions showing their organization by subject. As an example, assume a church and its members are disputing who owns the church property. You check the Iowa Constitution and find that Section 3 of the Bill of Rights covers religion. When you look under that section, as illustrated in Figure 4-1, one of the entry headings is "Church property disputes" followed by the number 12. You could then skim through case summaries in the notes until you see the bold-faced heading for **12 Church property disputes**, which would have annotations of the key cases on the topic. Figure 4-2 provides an example of a case annotation.

After finding a case that appears to be helpful, retrieve the full text of the case. Read the entire case to ensure that the editorial summary accurately reported the decision and to fully understand and analyze the wording of the court. See Chapter 5 for more detailed information on researching and analyzing case law.

As with other ICA volumes, the constitution volume is supplemented by an annual pocket part in the back of the volume and an interim pamphlet between the annual publication dates. Checking that supplementation is essential to make sure new cases or changes are not overlooked. See Chapter 6 for more detailed information about publication formats and research information on the *Iowa Code Annotated*.

2. Code of Iowa

The official *Code of Iowa* is published by the state and includes the codified 1857 Constitution as well as the original 1857 Constitution and the amendments presented separately. However, the *Code of Iowa* does not contain the case annotations, cross-references, law review citations and other tools found in the ICA. Thus, it is a less helpful research tool.

Figure 4-1. Excerpt of Iowa Constitution from *Iowa Code Annotated* v. 1, 2

Iowa Constitution Art. 1, § 3. Religion

The General Assembly shall make no law respecting an establishment of religion, or prohibiting the free exercise thereof; nor shall any person be compelled to attend any place of worship, pay tithes, taxes, or other rates for building or repairing places of worship, or the maintenance of any minister, or ministry.

HISTORICAL NOTE

Prior Constitution: Const.1846, Art. 1, § 3.

CROSS REFERENCES

Bible not to be excluded from public school or institution, see § 280.6.

Children not to be required to read Bible contrary to wishes of parent or guardian, see § 280.6.

* * *

LAW REVIEW AND JOURNAL COMMENTARIES

Attorney's right to religious freedom: A critical look at the clerical collar. 61 Iowa L.Rev. 899 (1976).

Contempt—enforcement of divorce decree—duty to raise child in particular religion. 42 Iowa L.Rev. 617 (1957).

* * *

LIBRARY REFERENCES

Constitutional Law 84.

Westlaw Topic No. 92.

C.J.S. Constitutional Law §§ 513 to 517.

UNITED STATES CODE ANNOTATED

Freedom of religion, see U.S.C.A. Const. Amend. 1.

UNITED STATES SUPREME COURT

Charitable tax deductions, payments for religious auditing and training services, see Hernandez v. C.I.R., 1989, 109 S.Ct. 2136, 490 U.S. 680, 104 L.Ed.2d 766.

Colleges and universities, funding of student newspapers with Christian editorial viewpoint, see Rosenberger v. Rector and Visitors of University of Virginia, 1995, 115 S.Ct. 2510, 515 U.S. 819, 132 L.Ed.2d 700.

* * *

NOTES OF DECISIONS

Burden of proof, government aid 2.7
Church property disputes 12
Construction and application 1
Defamation 13

* * *

Source: Iowa Code Annotated. Published with permission of West, a Thomson Reuters business.

Figure 4-2. Sample Case Annotation from ICA

12 Church property disputes

Where provisions of constitution of hierarchical church gave hierarchical church exclusive ultimate control of uses and disposition of local church property, ... hierarchical church could properly take over local church government to control use and disposition of local church property after local church disaffiliated itself from hierarchical church. Fonken v. Community Church of Kamrar, 1983, 339 N.W.2d 810.

Source: Iowa Code Annotated. Published with permission of West, a Thomson Reuters business.

B. Free Online Sources of the Iowa Constitution

Several websites provide access to the Iowa Constitution free of charge. The Iowa General Assembly website[11] is one of the easiest to use. The constitution and historical information can also be found in the *Iowa Official Register* at the Iowa Publications Online website.[12] Copies of the original constitution also can be found in books that have been digitized to the web, such as Shambaugh's *Constitution of the State of Iowa*.[13] The state also has digitized the *Debates of the Constitutional Convention*, so those documents are easily accessible.[14]

C. The Iowa Constitution in LexisNexis and Westlaw

1. Finding Relevant Provisions

Westlaw and LexisNexis provide ready access to the Iowa Constitution. In most instances, you would choose the annotated version of the database to also access cases interpreting the Iowa Constitution. In Westlaw, the Iowa Constitution is found in the statutory databases

---

11. The legislature's website provides access to the Constitution on its Iowa Law page at http://www.legis.iowa.gov/IowaLaw/Constitution.aspx.

12. The address is http://publications.iowa.gov/4074. Print editions of the *Official Iowa Register* are referred to as the "Redbook."

13. See Google Books for several of these works on the Iowa Constitution at http://books.google.com/books.

14. The address is http://www.statelibraryofiowa.org/services/law-library/iaconst.

and includes an unannotated version and an annotated one corresponding to the print *Iowa Code Annotated*.[15] The scope note for the database listing indicates how to use Find by Citation to retrieve a specific section of the constitution (e.g., use "ia const art 1 s 1" for Const. Art. 1, §1.) The Table of Contents feature allows you to expand headings and find sections and subsections of the Constitution. You can also search the entire database but restrict your results to just the Constitution by using "pr (constitution)" in your search query so that Westlaw retrieves only documents with the word constitution in the preliminary field.

In LexisNexis, the database listing for Iowa includes the LexisNexis Iowa Annotated Constitution. That database also can be found by using Find a Source and entering "Iowa Constitution." Once that database is selected, a Table of Contents with checkboxes is provided to help you easily narrow your search to particular articles or sections. Otherwise, you can search the entire constitution.

2. Using a Citator

You always want to make sure that you find the most current authorities interpreting the Iowa Constitution. Citators provide cases and other authorities citing the Iowa Constitution and can be used to make sure any cases you find are still good law. Some researchers find it helpful to use a citator early in their research once they locate a relevant provision of the constitution. Doing so gives them a quick overview of the authorities interpreting that part of the constitution. Chapter 9 provides more details on using citators—Shepard's on LexisNexis and KeyCite on Westlaw. After searching for cases interpreting the Iowa Constitution, whether via citator or otherwise, you may want to look for federal cases on the topic; as shown in Table 4-2 some provisions are similar in both constitutions.

---

15. The database identifier is IA-ST for the unannotated version and IA-ST-ANN for the ICA.

> **The Welch Matter**
>
> As noted in Section I, the Iowa Supreme Court declared unconstitutional a prior statute regarding grandparents' visitation rights. In the Welch hypothetical introduced in Chapter 1, you are representing a client on such a matter. As such, you may want to research the Iowa Constitution to understand the provisions the court believed the earlier law violated.
>
> If you start in Westlaw's IA-ST-ANN database, the *Iowa Code Annotated* equivalent, you might run this search: grandparent /3 visitation. The first two results are citations to the Iowa Constitution (Sections 8 and 9 of Article I). Those documents reference the aforementioned Iowa case involving grandparent rights: *Santi v. Santi*, 633 N.W.2d 312 (Iowa 2001). You can read that case to learn what the constitutional issues were with that Iowa statute and with one mouse click you find the current statute on grandparent visitation.

VI. United States Constitution

The United States Constitution can be found in the same volumes of the *Code of Iowa* (v. 1) and *Iowa Code Annotated* (v. 1, 2) as the Iowa Constitution. An index to the U.S. Constitution follows the index to the Iowa Constitution in the back of the ICA. Researching the U.S. Constitution is perhaps best approached using an annotated version which includes cases interpreting the provisions. The *United States Code Annotated* (USCA) and *United States Code Service* (USCS) provide coverage in their initial volumes. Comparable versions can be found online on Westlaw (USCA-CONST) and LexisNexis (USCS). Table 4-3 details some reliable websites that provide access to the U.S. Constitution.

Table 4-3. Selected Websites Providing Access to the U.S. Constitution

Cornell's Legal Information Institute	http://topics.law.cornell.edu/constitution
—offers an annotated constitution	
FindLaw	http://www.findlaw.com/casecode/constitution
—features extensive annotations and hyperlinks	
GPO Access	http://www.gpoaccess.gov/constitution/index.html
—analysis and interpretations includes case annotations	
Emory Law School	http://library.law.emory.edu
—provides links to various constitution sites, such as Justia, from law student subject guides	

Chapter 5

Judicial Opinions, Reporters, and Digests

I. Introduction

The United States and individual states, including Iowa, operate under the *common law system*, in which established court decisions help determine future court decisions.[1] In contrast, the *civil law system* is primarily based on legislation. The common law system originated in England and spread to those countries England settled or controlled. The civil law system, based on Roman law, predominates in continental Europe and other Western countries.[2]

Case law refers to the body of prior court decisions.[3] In the common law system, previously decided cases have *precedent*, meaning prior courts' decisions on similar questions or issues influence how current courts rule on those same issues. Note, however, that not all decisions become precedent. Only cases a court designates for publication become binding authority for the jurisdiction in which the case was decided.[4] The researcher can be fairly confident precedent will be upheld due to the doctrine of *stare decisis*, which compels courts to

---

1. Common law is defined as: "a judge-made rule as opposed to a statutory one." *Black's Law Dictionary* (Bryan A. Garner ed., 9th ed., West 2009).
2. Note that Louisiana developed under French rule and operates under a mixture of civil and common law.
3. Case law is defined as "the law to be found in the collection of reported cases that form all or part of the body of law within a given jurisdiction." *Black's Law Dictionary* (Bryan A. Garner ed., 9th ed., West 2009).
4. "Opinions designated 'not for publication', even though available on Lexis and Westlaw, are not binding precedents or even persuasive authority."

abide by or adhere to previously decided cases. This doctrine also allows the court system to be fairly confident that people in similar situations are treated the same under the law.

Although most legal research projects typically require an examination of case law at some point in the process, researchers do not often begin the research process with case law, beginning instead with secondary sources, as discussed in Chapter 3. This is especially true in situations when the researcher is not familiar with the applicable area of law.

This chapter describes the structure of the state and federal court systems and the organization of published court opinions in reporters. It also explains how to find relevant cases on a legal issue using print digests, LexisNexis and Westlaw, and the open web as well as how to analyze cases.

II. Court Systems

To find case law effectively, a researcher must first understand the structure of the court system both in Iowa and in the United States. Whether at the federal or state level, the basic court structure moves from the trial court level to the intermediate court of appeals, and finally to the ultimate appellate court, often called the "supreme" court. The *jurisdiction* of the trial court—the authority of the court to issue decisions—may be based on geography (e.g., U.S. District Courts on the federal level or county courts on the state level) or subject (e.g., U.S. Tax Courts, state family courts, or probate courts).

A. Iowa Courts

Iowa's trial courts are known as district courts. Iowa has two appellate courts: the Court of Appeals and the Supreme Court. The

---

Neil Duxbury, *The Nature and Authority of Precedent* 6 n. 12 (Cambridge University Press 2008).

website for the Iowa judiciary[5] contains a great deal of information, including a map of Iowa's judicial districts; links to courts maintaining websites, which include judicial opinions; an explanation of jurisdiction of state courts; court rules and forms; and information about jury service.

1. Iowa District Courts

In Iowa, trial courts are called district courts. There is one district court in each of Iowa's 99 counties; the counties are organized into eight judicial districts for administrative purposes.[6] Each of the eight judicial districts has a chief judge who is appointed by the Iowa Supreme Court. District courts have *general jurisdiction*, authorizing them to hear all civil and criminal cases.[7] District Courts have divisions for Juvenile Court, Probate Court, and Small Claims. Different types of judges in the district court system have varying amounts of jurisdiction. District Judges have general jurisdiction over all types of cases in the district courts. Judicial officers with more *limited jurisdiction*, authorizing them to hear only certain types of cases, include District Associate Judges, Associate Juvenile Judges, Associate Probate Judges, and Judicial Magistrates.

2. Iowa Court of Appeals

The Iowa Court of Appeals is an intermediate appellate court that consists of nine judges who are appointed by the governor and confirmed to six-year terms by election after they have served for one year. The Court of Appeals typically hears cases in Des Moines in

---

5. The website for the Iowa Judicial Branch is http://www.iowacourts.gov.
6. A map of the districts is available at http://www.iowacourts.gov/District_Courts.
7. District courts have jurisdiction over all matters unless specifically accorded by the legislature. Iowa Code § 602.6101 (2009) (noting that "[t]he district court has exclusive, general, and original jurisdiction of all actions, proceedings, and remedies, civil, criminal, probate, and juvenile, except in cases where exclusive or concurrent jurisdiction is conferred upon some other court, tribunal, or administrative body").

panels of three judges. Cases come to the Court of Appeals from the Iowa Supreme Court, which transfers certain district court cases that have been appealed. The majority of district court appeals are decided by the Court of Appeals, and its decisions are final unless reviewed by the Iowa Supreme Court on grant of further review. Some of the opinions of the Iowa Court of Appeals are published and become precedent for subsequent cases.

3. Iowa Supreme Court

The Iowa Supreme Court is an appellate court consisting of seven justices who are appointed by the governor and confirmed to eight-year terms by judicial election once they have served for one year. The Iowa Supreme Court hears cases *en banc*—with all justices present—typically in Des Moines. The *court of last resort* in Iowa, it hears the final appeals of cases in the state, and its opinions are binding on all other Iowa state courts. The court also admits attorneys to practice in Iowa and is responsible for prescribing rules on attorney conduct and for disciplining attorneys. The court promulgates rules of procedure and practice used in the state court system. It also has supervisory and administrative authority over the judicial branch and its officers and employees.

B. Federal Courts

Trial courts in the federal judicial system are called United States District Courts. There are 94 federal judicial districts, including at least one district in each state, as well as the District of Columbia and Puerto Rico. Some states are subdivided into smaller geographic regions, while others are not. The entire state of Minnesota, for example, makes up the federal District of Minnesota. Iowa, in contrast, has two federal districts. The United States District Court for the Northern District of Iowa[8] has jurisdiction over fifty-two of Iowa's ninety-nine counties. It is headquartered in Cedar Rapids, with satel-

---

8. The website for the United States District Court for the Northern District of Iowa is http://www.iand.uscourts.gov.

lite facilities in Fort Dodge and Sioux City. The United States District Court for the Southern District of Iowa[9] has jurisdiction over forty-seven of Iowa's ninety-nine counties. It is headquartered in Des Moines, with satellite facilities in Council Bluffs and Davenport. Cases from both the Northern and Southern District of Iowa are appealed to the United States Court of Appeals for the Eighth Circuit.

United States Courts of Appeals are the intermediate appellate courts in the federal system. A court of appeals hears appeals from the district courts located within its circuit, as well as appeals from decisions of federal administrative agencies. The 94 judicial districts are organized into 12 regional circuits,[10] each of which has a United States court of appeals. There is also a thirteenth federal circuit, called the Federal Circuit, which has nationwide jurisdiction to hear appeals from district courts in all other circuits in specialized cases, such as patent law and cases decided by the Court of International Trade and the Court of Federal Claims. Iowa is in the Eighth Federal Circuit which also includes Arkansas, Minnesota, Missouri, Nebraska, North Dakota, and South Dakota.[11]

The United States Supreme Court is the highest court in the federal system. It stands at the head of the judicial branch of government and provides the ultimate interpretation of the U.S. Constitution and federal statutes, although not on matters of state law as stated in Chapter 1. The website for the federal judiciary contains much useful information such as maps, addresses, definitions, and more.[12]

C. Courts of Other States

While the court systems of many states follow the three-tier system of Iowa and the federal judiciary, some deviate from this struc-

---

9. The website for the United States District Court for the Southern District of Iowa is http://www.iasd.uscourts.gov.
10. There are eleven numbered circuits covering all the states as well as a twelfth circuit for the District of Columbia. A map of the circuits is available at http://www.uscourts.gov/court_locator.aspx and may also be found at the front of bound volumes for both the *Federal Supplement* and the *Federal Reporter*.
11. The website for the Eighth Circuit is http://www.ca8.uscourts.gov.
12. Their website is www.uscourts.gov.

ture. Some states, such as Rhode Island and South Dakota, do not have an intermediate appellate court.[13] In New York and Maryland, the highest court is the Court of Appeals; also in New York, the "supreme" court is the trial level court. In Maine and Massachusetts, the highest court is the Supreme Judicial Court.

When working with an unfamiliar jurisdiction, verify the court structure and hierarchy. Court websites and citation manuals are both excellent references for locating this information, as discussed in Chapter 1.

III. Published Case Law

When appellate courts decide cases, they usually write opinions that summarize the facts of the case, detail existing laws, and explain how and why they resolved the case.[14] More specifically, opinions usually contain the following information, although not necessarily in this order: an introduction to the case where the court may briefly discuss key facts and issues; a statement of the case, which includes the facts of the case and its procedural history; a statement of the issues the court will address; the applicable law, which may also include previously decided cases; an analysis of the case; and the disposition of the case, which includes the court's resolution of the case and how that may affect other courts in its jurisdiction.

If the opinion is written by a majority of judges it will be referred to as a *majority opinion.* Judges who do not share the majority opinion may write a *concurring* or *dissenting opinion.* A concurring opinion means that the judge agrees with the decision but for different

---

13. Iowa did not have an intermediate appellate court until 1977.

14. Trial courts may also issue such detailed opinions. However, particularly at the state level, trial courts may also issue decisions in an abbreviated form that does not include detailed analysis of how the court came to its conclusion but simply reports the jury verdict or judge's findings.

reasons than those stated in the majority opinion. A dissenting opinion means a judge does not agree with the majority.

Significantly, the vast majority of court cases are unpublished, in the sense that they are not printed in case reporters or available as precedent even if found online.[15] This is especially true of state trial court cases. If you want to read the decision of a highly publicized trial, there is likely no "published" decision as such. There may be a brief court order or memorandum in the case file. A trial transcript may or may not be included in the case file. You must contact the court clerks directly to find out whether they will allow you to copy or view the file. Docket information—the official schedule of proceedings in a court of law—may be available in federal cases through PACER,[16] which may also provide access to court documents, and in Iowa through Iowa Courts Online.[17]

Cases that are published are released in three stages: slip opinions, advance sheets, and reporters. These are explained more fully in the following sections.

A. Slip Opinions

A case first appears as a *slip opinion*. These are individual pamphlets issued directly by the court that are published as a single opinion per pamphlet. Slip opinions are often freely available from court websites but do not have any editorial information that can help the researcher determine the court's intent or highlight the legal issues addressed. Slip opinions can also be difficult to cite because they do not have final page numbers and may be referred to by their *docket number*.[18]

---

15. Although unpublished opinions are not binding authority, they can still be cited in a brief. Barry A. Lindahl, *Iowa Practice: Civil and Appellate Procedure* § 45:5 (2010 ed.).

16. PACER's website is http://www.pacer.gov.

17. Iowa Courts Online can be accessed at www.iowacourts.state.ia.us.

18. A docket number is a unique number that identifies a specific case on the court's calendar.

B. Advance Sheets

Slip opinions released for publication are compiled into a softcover book called an *advance sheet*. Advance sheets contain multiple decisions and are published weekly or bi-weekly, generally in chronological order. Page numbers of advance sheets mirror the page numbers of bound reporters so, if you cite to a case in an advance sheet, that citation will also be accurate for the reporter. The cases from several consecutive advance sheets will comprise a volume and the pagination will be continuous within that volume. Advance sheets contain some of the same additional information as individual bound reporters, e.g., Words and Phrases, Table of Cases Reported.

C. Reporters

The contents of multiple advance sheets are compiled into a bound *reporter*. Once the reporter has been published, most libraries and law firms discard the advance sheets. Reporter volumes are consecutively numbered. When the volumes of a reporter reach an arbitrary number, such as 300, the publisher starts over with volume 1, second series. Some reporters are now in their third or later series. Reporters include editorial features that make it easier to find and understand the decision. See Section III.C.1 for an example.

Two types of reporters are published: official and unofficial. *Official reporters* are published by state and federal governments. However, there can be a large time delay between when a case is decided and when the decision is officially published. To remedy this situation, in the 1880s the West Publishing Company began publishing *unofficial reporters* that cover the state and federal courts in the United States. These publications comprise the National Reporter System. Sometimes decisions are published in both official and unofficial reporters; other times a state may give up publishing its own reporter and designate a commercial source as its official reporter. For instance, Rules 21.25 and 21.30 of the Iowa Court Rules designate

West[19] as the publisher of the official opinions of the Iowa Supreme Court and Iowa Court of Appeals.

Unlike official reporters published by a state and only covering that state, the National Reporter System divides the fifty states into seven regions. Under the reporter system, each region has a separate reporter that contains opinions from the states' highest court and courts of appeals.[20] The seven regions are: Atlantic, North Eastern, North Western, Pacific, Southern, South Eastern, and South Western. See Table 5-1 for the states included in each region. Note that the coverage of each regional reporter is not the same as the composition of the federal circuits. For example, Michigan and Wisconsin are included with Iowa in the *North Western Reporter* but are not in the same federal circuit as Iowa. Iowa is in the Eighth Circuit while Michigan and Wisconsin are in the Sixth and Seventh Circuits, respectively.

To find a case in a reporter, you must have a citation, e.g., 484 N.W.2d 864.[21] See Table 5-1 for a list of regional reporter abbreviations. In order to locate a case without a citation, you can begin your research with a digest, as described in Section IV.

1. Features of a Reported Case

A case printed in a reporter, or available through a database such as Westlaw, contains the text of the court opinion. However, it also contains editorial enhancements that can aid researchers. Some of the information is gathered from court records while other information is written by the publisher's editorial staff.

---

19. The publisher is known as West, a Thomson Reuters business.

20. In California and New York intermediate appellate cases have separate reporters. The *Pacific Reporter* contains Supreme Court opinions from California, but the *West California Reporter* has both the California Supreme Court and California intermediate appellate court opinions. The *North Eastern Reporter* contains decisions for the Court of Appeals (the state's highest court) from New York, and the *New York Supplement* has both the New York Court of Appeals opinions as well as the opinions of New York's intermediate appellate courts.

21. As explained in Chapter 2, 484 is the volume, N.W.2d refers to the *North Western Reporter* 2d series, and 864 is the page number.

Table 5-1. West's National Reporter System

Regional Reporter	Abbreviations	States Included
Atlantic Reporter	A., A.2d, A.3d	Connecticut, Delaware, District of Columbia, Maine, Maryland, New Hampshire, New Jersey, Pennsylvania, Rhode Island, and Vermont
North Eastern Reporter	N.E., N.E.2d	Illinois, Indiana, Massachusetts, New York, and Ohio
North Western Reporter	N.W., N.W.2d	Iowa, Michigan, Minnesota, Nebraska, North Dakota, South Dakota, and Wisconsin
Pacific Reporter	P., P.2d, P.3d	Alaska, Arizona, California, Colorado, Hawaii, Idaho, Kansas, Montana, Nevada, New Mexico, Oklahoma, Oregon, Utah, Washington, and Wyoming
South Eastern Reporter	S.E., S.E.2d	Georgia, North Carolina, South Carolina, Virginia, and West Virginia
South Western Reporter	S.W., S.W.2d, S.W.3d	Arkansas, Kentucky, Missouri, Tennessee, and Texas
Southern Reporter	So., So. 2d, So. 3d	Alabama, Florida, Louisiana, and Mississippi

The following description refers to the *North Western Reporter 2d*. It may be helpful for you to consult a volume while reading this description. Figure 5-1 shows a case as it appears in N.W.2d (the numbers in boxes in Figure 5-1 correspond to the bracketed numbers below). Figure 5-2 shows the same case as it appears in Westlaw. Editorial enhancements will be different, and sometimes absent, in official reporters and in non-West publications and databases; however, the text of the opinion will be identical.[22]

---

22. In the rare case that a discrepancy does exist between the text of a case in an official reporter and an unofficial reporter or database, the official reporter is the final authority.

5 · Judicial Opinions, Reporters, and Digests

Figure 5-1. Case Excerpt from *North Western Reporter 2d*

> **IN RE MARRIAGE OF HOWARD** — Iowa **183**
> Cite as 661 N.W.2d 183 (Iowa 2003)
>
> after the settlement will be free from a claim of indemnity by the employer or its insurer.
>
> **V. Conclusion.**
>
> We conclude a settlement under section 85.35 bars an employer's or insurer's statutory right to indemnification under section 85.22(1). We reverse the judgment of the district court and remand the case for entry of judgment for Stanley.
>
> **REVERSED AND REMANDED.**
>
> All justices concur except CARTER, J., who takes no part.
>
> [KEY NUMBER SYSTEM]
>
> In re the MARRIAGE OF Charitie S. HOWARD and Dennis M. Howard, Jr.
>
> Upon the Petition of Charitie S. Howard, Appellant,
>
> and
>
> Concerning Dennis M. Howard, Jr., Respondent,
>
> Dennis Howard, Sr., and Connie Howard, Intervenors–Appellees.
>
> No. 02–0211.
>
> Supreme Court of Iowa.
>
> May 7, 2003.
>
> Ex-wife appealed from decision of the District Court for Polk County, George W. Bergeson, J., granting paternal grandparents visitation. The Supreme Court, Cady, J., held that section of the grandparent visitation statute permitting a petition for grandparent visitation when the parents of a child are divorced failed on its face to comport with the due process clause.
>
> Reversed and dismissed.
>
> **1. Child Custody** ⟪4
>
> Supreme Court would apply strict scrutiny analysis when determining if section of grandparent visitation statute, permitting a petition for grandparent visitation when the parents of a child are divorced, was unconstitutional. I.C.A. § 598.35, subd. 1.
>
> **2. Child Custody** ⟪4
>
> Because section of grandparent visitation statute permitting a petition for visitation when the parents of a child are divorced interfered with a fundamental interest, a compelling interest of the State had to be demonstrated for the section to withstand constitutional scrutiny. I.C.A. § 598.35, subd. 1.
>
> **3. Parent and Child** ⟪1
>
> Divorce can alter the decision-making ability of parents to a point that may generate a sufficient state interest to intervene in areas not affecting fundamental rights, or to invoke the need for special considerations to protect children.
>
> **4. Child Custody** ⟪8
>
> Divorce, by necessity, permits the State to intervene to resolve immediate and direct disputes that arise between parents over custody and visitation.
>
> **5. Child Custody** ⟪8
>
> Divorce is not the sine qua non of a compelling state interest when non-parents seek to challenge parental decision-making; instead, a compelling state interest arises when substantial harm or potential harm is visited upon children.

Source: *In re Marriage of Howard*, 661 N.W.2d 183, 185 (Iowa 2003). Published with permission of West, a Thomson Reuters business.

Figure 5-1. Case Excerpt from *North Western Reporter 2d*, continued

---

IN RE MARRIAGE OF HOWARD
Cite as 661 N.W.2d 183 (Iowa 2003)

tion of fitness to parents rendered it unconstitutional on its face. I.C.A. § 598.35, subd. 1.

West Codenotes

Held Unconstitutional
I.C.A. §598.35(1).

Recognized as Unconstitutional
I.C.A. §598.35(7).

---

[7]

Anjela A. Shutts of Whitfield & Eddy, P.L.C., Des Moines, for appellant.

Eric R. Eshelman, Des Moines, for appellees.

CADY, Justice. [8]

In *Santi v. Santi*, 633 N.W.2d 312 (Iowa 2001), we determined that at least one subsection of the Iowa grandparent visitation statute was unconstitutional on its face. In this appeal, we revisit the question of the statute's constitutionality to determine whether the section of the statute permitting a petition for grandparent visitation when the parents of a child are divorced is also unconstitutional. We conclude that it is unconstitutional on its face, and we reverse the decision of the district court and dismiss this petition for grandparent visitation.

I. Background Facts and Proceedings.

Delainey Howard (Delainey) was born on April 28, 1999. Her parents, Charitie Howard (Charitie) and Dennis Howard, Jr., (Dennis) were in the process of dissolving their marriage. The pending dissolution prompted Dennis' parents, Connie and Dennis Howard, Sr., (Howards) to file a petition for grandparent visitation to establish their right to visitation with Delainey. *See* Iowa Code § 598.35(1) (permitting a petition for grandparent visitation when "[t]he parents of the child are divorced."). A final decree was issued in the dissolution action on February 16, 2000. One of the issues decided by the decree was the visitation arrangement under which Dennis and the Howards were to have subsequent contact with Delainey. The district court granted Dennis joint legal custody and unsupervised visitation, but made the exercise of his visitation right contingent on his resumption of drug treatment and counseling. The court did not grant the Howards independent visitation, choosing instead to allow them visitation through their son.

Unfortunately, Dennis failed to pursue drug treatment and counseling as ordered. In March 2000, Charitie filed an application to alter his visitation privileges. In response, the Howards filed a motion for intervention, requesting again that they be granted visitation independent of their son. The district court ordered Charitie and Dennis to participate in mediation to settle on an agreeable revised visitation schedule.[1] When Dennis failed to show for the mediation, the court put in place its own supervised visitation schedule that again did not provide for independent visitation for the Howards. The visitation alteration made no real difference to Dennis—his

---

1. At this point in the proceedings, Charitie had already appealed from the court's original decree order. Therefore, the court concluded it no longer had jurisdiction to rule on the Howards' request for enhanced visitation because they sought to intervene in a matter that was the subject of a pending appeal. Charitie eventually dismissed her appeal, at which time the Howards filed an application for modification of the decree of dissolution as it related to grandparent visitation.

5 · Judicial Opinions, Reporters, and Digests 115

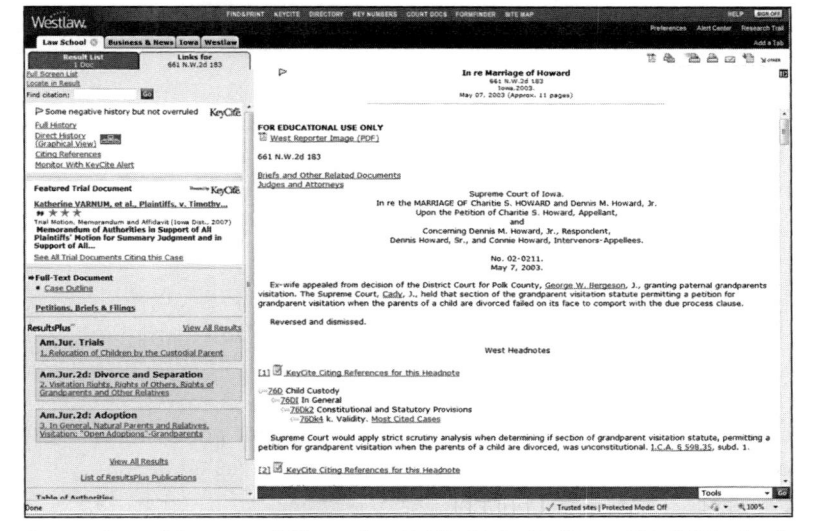

Figure 5-2. Case Excerpt from Westlaw

Source: *In re Marriage of Howard*, 661 N.W.2d 183 (Iowa 2003)(Westlaw). Published with permission of West, a Thomson Reuters business.

Citation information. {1} Above the text is the title of the case along with citation information. You need this citation information to refer to the case in legal documents.

Parties and procedural designations. {2} At the beginning of the case, all parties are listed with their procedural designations.

Docket numbers. {3} The number assigned to a case by the court is called a docket number. Docket numbers can aid in locating briefs, court orders, and other documents related to the case. Sometimes these materials are available in online databases; other times you need to contact the court directly. When citing to a published case, you do not cite the docket number, but rather the reporter citation.

Court and date information. {4} The name of the court that decided the case as well as the date it was decided appear below the docket number.

Background. {5} This is a brief synopsis of the case as written by the editors at West. As this information is not from the court, you should never cite or quote to background information as primary authority.

Holdings. This is another West editorial addition that is not always present. For instance, there are no holdings in Figure 5-1. A *holding* is the legal principle or principles derived from the opinion. In a reporter, West may summarize these holdings in a bullet point or number format. The same citation warning for background information applies here as well.

Headnotes. {6} A headnote is a sentence or short paragraph that sets out a single point of law in a case. The headnote is then assigned a preexisting West topic and key number (explained in Section IV.A.1) that enables researchers to easily find cases on that point of law. Most cases will have more than one headnote.

Attorney Information. {7} The names of the attorneys who argued the case are listed before the official opinion of the case.

Opinion. {8} The name of the judge who wrote the opinion is followed by the official text of the case as originally reported by the court. This text is primary authority and can be cited as such.

The Welch Matter

As noted in Chapter 4, in the *Santi* case, the Iowa Supreme Court declared unconstitutional part of an Iowa statute on grandparents' visitation rights. A few years later the court revisited the issue in *Howard*, which effectively overturned Iowa Code § 598.35. Figures 5-1 and 5-2 illustrate this seminal decision. 5-1 shows the decision as it is printed in the *North Western Reporter*, while 5-2 shows the case as it appears in Westlaw.

---

2. *Other Features of a West Reporter*

Beyond the editorial enhancements of individual cases, each reporter contains other useful information, such as Parallel Citation Tables,[23] if applicable; Table of Cases Reported; Table of Cases Arranged by States; Words and Phrases; and Key Number Digest. Of these, Words and Phrases and the Table of Cases are the most useful because they give you a succinct list of key terms defined by the court and a list of cases you will find in the volume. Both are explained in full in Sections IV.A.3 and IV.A.4. In a reporter, Words and Phrases and the Table of Cases are only applicable to that volume. However, both are published in full as part of the reporter's respective digest.

D. Reporters for Iowa Cases

Iowa appellate court case decisions from 1879 to 1942 are reported in the *North Western Reporter,* cited as N.W. Cases from 1942 to the present are published in the *North Western Reporter, Second Series,* cited as N.W.2d.

From 1855 to 1968, *Iowa Reports* was the official reporter of Iowa Supreme Court opinions. In 1968, the Iowa Supreme Court designated West Publishing Company as the official reporter of Iowa decisions. Cases prior to 1968 may contain a parallel citation to *Iowa Reports.*

Cases published prior to the reporter system can be found in the reports of Bradford (1838–1841), Morris (1839–1846), and Greene (1847–1854). Prior to the systematic official publication of Iowa case law, various individuals privately published court decisions compiled from their observations and notes. These early publications are referred to by the names of those who published them and are called *nominative reporters.* If at an Iowa law library, these volumes can be found with *Iowa Reports* and the *North Western Reporter.*

E. Other Sources for Finding Iowa Cases

Court decisions are available from the Iowa Supreme Court website. The full text of cases from 1998 to the present is available for

---

23. Reference Chapter 2 for information about Parallel Citation Tables.

118   5 · Judicial Opinions, Reporters, and Digests

both the Iowa Supreme Court[24] and the Iowa Court of Appeals[25] in the form of slip opinions.

F. Reporters for Federal Cases

Federal reporters are similar in many respects to Iowa reporters. Table 5-2 lists the federal courts and their respective reporters and the reporters' abbreviations.

Table 5-2. Reporters for Federal Court Cases

Court	Reporter Name	Reporter Abbreviation
U.S. Supreme Court	*United States Reports* (official) *Supreme Court Reporter* *United States Supreme Court Reports, Lawyers' Edition* *United States Law Week*	U.S. S. Ct. L. Ed., L. Ed. 2d U.S.L.W.
U.S. Courts of Appeal	*Federal Reporter* *Federal Appendix* (unpublished cases)	F., F.2d, F.3d Fed. Appx.
U.S. District Courts	*Federal Supplement* *Federal Rules Decisions*	F. Supp., F. Supp. 2d F.R.D.

---

24. Iowa Supreme Court opinions are located at http://www.iowacourts.gov/Supreme_Court/Opinions_Archive.

25. Iowa Court of Appeals opinions are at http://www.iowacourts.gov/Court_of_Appeals/Opinions_Archive/index.asp.

1. United States District Courts Cases

Originally, the *Federal Reporter* covered decisions of both district and circuit courts. In 1932, West began the *Federal Supplement*, which publishes selected U.S. District Court decisions, leaving the *Federal Reporter* to cover U.S. Court of Appeals decisions.

In 1940, West began publishing *Federal Rules Decisions*. This series contains a limited number of U.S. District Court decisions dealing with procedural issues under the Federal Rules of Civil Procedure and the Federal Rules of Criminal Procedure.

LexisNexis and Westlaw contain district court opinions back to the beginning of the court system in 1789. Some district court cases are also available online outside of subscription databases, as shown in Table 5-3.

2. United States Court of Appeals Cases

Cases decided by the federal intermediate appellate courts are published in the *Federal Reporter*. The decisions of all thirteen circuits are available in this source. In general, a decision is published if it lays down a new rule of law or alters an existing rule, criticizes existing law, resolves a conflict of authority, or involves a legal issue of public interest. From 2001 to the present, West's *Federal Appendix* has published U.S. Court of Appeals decisions that are not released for publication in the *Federal Reporter*. Opinions are included from all circuits except for the 5th and 11th, which do not provide their "unpublished" opinions to any publisher.

As with district court opinions, Federal Court of Appeals decisions are available via LexisNexis and Westlaw from the beginning of the court system in 1789. While not as ubiquitous as Supreme Court cases, Court of Appeal decisions are also available online. Table 5-3 provides a selected list of free websites. Note that decisions are also often available through the website of each individual circuit court.

Table 5-3. Selected List of Free Internet Sources Containing Court of Appeal and District Court Decisions

Source	Address	Content
Cornell's Legal Information Institute	www.law.cornell.edu/federal/districts.html	District Court and Bankruptcy Court Decision
FindLaw: District Courts	http://www.findlaw.com/10fedgov/judicial/district_courts.html	A list of U.S. District Court websites with descriptions of their content.
FindLaw: Federal Courts of Appeals	http://www.findlaw.com/casecode/courts/	U.S. Courts of Appeals decisions from 1996–present.
Google Scholar	http://scholar.google.com/advanced_scholar_search	State appellate and supreme court cases since 1950 as well as federal district, appellate, tax, and bankruptcy court cases since 1923.
LexisOne	http://www.lexisone.com	The most recent five years of U.S. Court of Appeals decisions.
Open Jurist	http://openjurist.org	First, second, and third series of the *Federal Reporter* (1880–1993).
U.S. Courts site	http://www.uscourts.gov/courtlinks	Access to specific circuit courts (some contain material back to 1995).

3. *United States Supreme Court Cases*

Cases decided by the U.S. Supreme Court can be found in numerous places. The official reporter of the Supreme Court is *United States Reports*. However, after a case is decided it can take upwards of two years for the official reports to appear in bound volumes, although the advance sheets are available much sooner. Two unofficial reporters publish decisions in a more timely fashion: *Supreme Court Reporter*, published by West, and *United States Supreme Court Reports, Lawyers' Edition*, published by LexisNexis.

Many online sources offer access to Supreme Court opinions. The website of the Supreme Court[26] publishes slip opinions as soon as they are decided. The website may also include supplementary material, such as court briefs which provide the parties' written arguments in the case. LexisNexis and Westlaw both have Supreme Court databases. In addition, HeinOnline contains the full text in PDF format of *United States Reports* from volume 1 to the present. Table 5-4 lists some of the other Internet sites that make court opinions freely available.

Table 5-4. Selected List of Free Internet Sources of Supreme Court Opinions

Source	Address	Dates
Cornell's Legal Information Institute	http://www.law.cornell.edu/supct	1990–present; selective coverage prior to 1990
FindLaw	http://www.findlaw.com/casecode/supreme.html	1893–present
Google Scholar	http://scholar.google.com/advanced_scholar_search	1791–present
Justia.com	http://supreme.justia.com	1790–present
LexisOne	http://www.lexisone.com	1790–present
Open Jurist	http://openjurist.org	1790–present
Oyez	http://www.oyez.org	1995–present (audio recordings of oral arguments); 1955–1995 (selected audio)

---

26. The U.S. Supreme Court site is located at http://www.supremecourt.gov.

IV. Digests

Case research can be difficult because the courts issue numerous opinions each year, and cases are published chronologically as they are decided, not by subject matter. You can use electronic databases to search for specific terms, as described in Section V.A.1., but that will not locate all of the relevant cases unless you use the exact terms that the court used in deciding each case. For instance, if you search Westlaw or LexisNexis for the term "children" you may miss cases in which the court used the term "juvenile" or "minor." An effective way to overcome this problem is to use a digest to search for cases.

This discussion will focus on the West digest system, as it is the most widely used and well known. However, the same basic arrangement and research principles apply to any published print digest.

A digest arranges each case's points of law by subject categories and provides summaries of cases that discuss the law on that subject. When using a digest, determine the jurisdiction for which you need to find cases, and then consult a digest that covers that jurisdiction. See Table 5-5 for a list of digests and jurisdictions. Always work with the narrowest jurisdiction possible so you are not searching through irrelevant information.

North Western Digest and *North Western Digest 2d* contain information about cases published in the *North Western Reporter* and *North Western Reporter 2d*, respectively. Remembering the states included in the *North Western Reporter*, this means that the *North Western Digest* will contain information about state and federal cases from Iowa, Michigan, Minnesota, Nebraska, North Dakota, South Dakota, and Wisconsin. *Iowa Digest*[27] contains summaries of points of law in Iowa cases published in *Iowa Reports*, *North Western Reporter*, and *North Western 2d*, as well as Iowa cases decided in the Supreme Court of the United States, U.S. Court of Appeals, and U.S. District Courts.

---

27. *Iowa Digest* is published by West Publishing.

Table 5-5. West Digest System

Court or Jurisdiction	Reporter	Digest
United States Supreme Court	*United States Reports*	*West's United States Supreme Court Digest*
Federal Courts	*West's Federal Reporter* *West's Federal Supplement*	*West's Federal Practice Digest*
State Courts		All states except Delaware, Nevada and Utah. Virginia Digest covers Virginia and West Virginia. Dakota Digest covers North Dakota and South Dakota.
Regional	*Atlantic Reporter*	*Atlantic Digest*
	North Eastern Reporter	*West's Illinois Digest, West's Indiana Digest, West's Massachusetts Digest, West's New York Digest, West's Ohio Digest.* (N.E. Digest is no longer published.)
	South Eastern Reporter	*South Eastern Digest*
	Southern Reporter	*West's Alabama Digest, West's Florida Digest, West's Louisiana Digest, West's Mississippi Digest.* (So. Digest is no longer published.)
	South Western Reporter	*Arkansas Digest, West's Kentucky Digest, West's Missouri Digest, West's Tennessee Digest, West's Texas Digest.* (No S.W. Digest exists.)
	North Western Reporter	*North Western Digest*
	Pacific Reporter	*Pacific Digest*
Combined State & Federal		*General Digest*, 11th Series (2005–present); *Decennial Digest*, Century through Eleventh (1658–2004)*

* Note that, as most academic law libraries have access to Westlaw in which to search all jurisdictions, many libraries no longer carry recent *Decennial* and *General Digests*.

A. Digest Features

West's digests contain four key features, which are discussed below. See Figures 5-3 and 5-4 for examples from the *North Western Digest*.

Figure 5-3. Example of the Analysis Outline from the *North Western Digest*

CHILD CUSTODY

SUBJECTS INCLUDED

Child custody rights pending or following divorce or dissolution of marriage

Visitation rights of parents, grandparents, and others

Extent of custody rights

Geographical limitations imposed on custodians

Enforcement of custody rights

Interstate and international custody disputes

SUBJECTS EXCLUDED AND COVERED BY OTHER TOPICS

Custody and access to dependent, neglected, abandoned, or delinquent children, see INFANTS

Issues peculiar to children born out-of-wedlock, see CHILDREN OUT-OF-WEDLOCK

Issues peculiar to custody of Native American children, see INDIANS

Parent and child relationship generally, rights of parents to control their children, and duty of parents to protect and supervise their children, see PARENT AND CHILD

For detailed references to other topics, see Descriptive-Word Index

Analysis

I. IN GENERAL, ⚖1-9.

II. GROUNDS AND FACTORS IN GENERAL, ⚖20-88.
    (A) IN GENERAL, ⚖20-37.
    (B) FACTORS RELATING TO PARTIES SEEKING CUSTODY, ⚖41-68.
    (C) FACTORS RELATING TO CHILD, ⚖75-88.

Source: 4D *North Western Digest 2d* 1 (Thomson/West 2004). Published with permission of West, a Thomson Reuters business.

Figure 5-4. Example from the *North Western Digest 2d*

⬥279 CHILD CUSTODY 4D N W D 2d—32

For later cases, see same Topic and Key Number in Pocket Part

In habeas corpus proceedings by a father to obtain the custody of his infant children, it was admitted on the trial that he was not a fit person, and it appeared that the mother was of good character and, although in straitened circumstances, was industrious and able to care for them. Held, that it was a wise exercise of discretion to refuse to take them from their mother in order to give them to their paternal grandfather, who was wealthy, although it further appeared that the mother had at times been passionate and profane of speech under provocation of shameful misconduct on the part of her husband, and that her mother, with whom she lived, was a person of coarse and vulgar speech and conduct.

Johnston v. Johnston, 62 N.W. 181, 89 Wis. 416.

⬥280. —— **Abandonment by parent or custodian.**

Iowa 1966. Where 12-year-old boy had lived for last 10 years with paternal grandparents, and mother had visited boy only about six times during that period, and boy desired to remain with grandparents and did not wish to live with mother, best interests of boy required that grandparents retain custody; Wooley v. Schoop, 234 Iowa 657, 12 N.W.2d 597 overruled. 58 I.C.A. Rules of Civil Procedure, rule 344(f), par. 15.

Halstead v. Halstead, 144 N.W.2d 861, 259 Iowa 526.

Iowa App. 1986. Best interests of child, whose mother died suddenly, who had no contacts with father for seven years, and who had close relationship with maternal grandparents, would be served by awarding custody to maternal grandparents rather than to father.

Thompson by Thompson v. Collins, 391 N.W.2d 267.

N.D. 1976. Grandparents who raised six-year-old child in their home from birth were entitled to custody, as against father, divorced and remarried, who abandoned child and provided little support or care even when contact was reestablished. NDCC 27-20-1, et seq., 27-20-30.

In Interest [Custody] of D. G., 246 N.W.2d 892.

⬥281. —— **Failure to support or provide for child.**

For other cases see earlier editions of this digest, the Decennial Digests, and WESTLAW.

⬥282. Grandparent visitation and access to child.

Rights following adoption, see ⬥313.

⬥283. —— **In general.**

not the mere marital status of parents, and thus, if grandparent visitation is to be compelled by the State, there must be a showing of harm to the child beyond that derived from the loss of the helpful, beneficial influence of grandparents; the problem with a divorce standard is that it either assumes harm occurs in all families touched by divorce when there is no grandparent visitation or it embraces a standard short of harm, and both approaches are rejected. I.C.A. § 598.35.

In re Marriage of Howard, 661 N.W.2d 183.

If grandparent visitation is to be compelled by the State, there must be a showing of harm to the child beyond that derived from the loss of the helpful, beneficial influence of grandparents, and, although the statutory requirement of an established substantial relationship between child and grandparents fails to specify any harm or potential harm to the child, when a grandparent has established a substantial relationship with a grandchild, as required under grandparent visitation statute, an emotional bond can be created that, if severed, can inflict harm on the child. I.C.A. § 598.35, subd. 1.

In re Marriage of Howard, 661 N.W.2d 183.

Divorce is, alone, insufficient to establish a compelling state interest for the State to intervene into the issue of grandparent visitation, and similarly, the best interests of a child requirement is insufficient. I.C.A. § 598.35.

In re Marriage of Howard, 661 N.W.2d 183.

Iowa 1997. Grandparent visitation can be granted when it is authorized by statute, when it is ordered in a guardianship in the best interests of the child, and when it is ordered by a juvenile court as a part of its dispositional or permanency hearing. I.C.A. § 598.35.

McMain v. Iowa Dist. Court for Polk County, 559 N.W.2d 12.

Iowa 1995. Statute designating under what circumstances grandparents may petition for visitation may limit grandparent's visitation rights, but statute does not limit statutory authority of juvenile court to decide grandparent's petition for visitation with child placed in custody of court-appointed guardians. I.C.A. §§ 232.61, 598.35.

In Interest of K.R., 537 N.W.2d 774.

Iowa 1986. Jurisdiction is vested in a district court to award grandparents visitation rights in connection with a dissolution of marriage action. I.C.A. §§ 598.2, 598.21, subd. 8, 598.35, 598.35, subd. 1.

Source: 4D *North Western Digest 2d* 32 (Thomson/West 2004). Published with permission of West, a Thomson Reuters business.

1. Topic and Key Numbers

The entire system of West reporter and digest publications rests on the topic and key number system. West's editors read cases and identify relevant points of law. They place each point into a broad subject-heading category referred to as a *topic*. They then assign a more specific *key number* that serves as a subheading, narrowing the area of law into very specific issues. For instance, the topic Antitrust and Trade Regulation is broken into 1000 distinct key numbers, each representing a different legal issue. To make it easier to find a relevant number, each topic categorizes its key numbers under subtopics. Antitrust and Trade Regulation provide 29 subtopics ranging from attempts to monopolize to unfair competition. As you can see from this example, the system is very robust and currently comprises over 400 topics.

Topics are listed alphabetically in the digest system. At the beginning of each topic entry is an explanatory section detailing which subjects are included under that topic and which topics are excluded and covered by other topics. After that there is a listing of the key numbers assigned to the topic. Once you know the appropriate topic and key number for the specific point of law in which you are interested, you can look up information on your issue in any West digest by consulting the topic and key number. For example, in the hypothetical Welch case, the point of law of interest is Grandparent Visitation and Access to Child under topic and key number Child Custody 282;[28] you would find similar cases digested under that topic and key number in the *Iowa Digest*, *Minnesota Digest*, or any other West digest, or on Westlaw.

Remember that when consulting a case on your point of law in a reporter, the topic and key number are included in the summary headnotes at the beginning of the case. You can use these to jump to the part of the case dealing specifically with that issue. Note that the numbers occasionally change; the most recent outline of the West key

---

28. More specific subdivisions of this general topic follow at key numbers Child Custody 283–289, including ones that address this issue in general (283), conduct or status of child's parent or custodian (285), and objections of parent (286).

number system can be found in the latest edition of *West's Analysis of American Law*, a West publication. In Westlaw, clicking the "Key Numbers" tab at the top of the screen will take you to an option to browse through the entire West Key Number System.

2. Headnotes

The digests are based on headnotes from reported decisions. The editorial staff selects important parts of the case and summarizes each at the beginning of the opinion. These headnotes are labeled with the relevant topic and key number. Digests arrange the headnotes under each topic and key number according to the court that decided the case. In a state digest, federal cases are listed first, followed by state cases. Within each system, cases are listed according to hierarchy so cases from the final appellate courts are listed first, followed by the decisions from the intermediate appellate courts and finally trial court cases. Cases are listed in reverse chronological order within each level of court, so the most recent cases of a court will appear first.

3. Words and Phrases

Some headnotes are reprinted in the digest's Words and Phrases volume. Headnotes are included in Words and Phrases if they refer to an instance in which a court has defined or interpreted a legally significant term. To determine if a court has defined a term, refer to the Words and Phrases volumes at the end of each digest. Headnotes interpreting the words or phrases from cases reported in the entire West National Reporter System are also included in a master set titled *Words and Phrases*, which is a multi-volume set providing judicial definitions in cases going back to 1658. Entries in both sets are arranged alphabetically and can be invaluable if you need to know the meaning of a term in a particular jurisdiction.

Entries in *Words and Phrases* refer to cases that provide judicial definitions of terms, while the entries under topics and key numbers in the main digest volumes refer to cases that discuss, explain, and possibly define a term.

Figure 5-5. Example from Words and Phrases

> **GRANDPARENTS**
>
> Wis. 1992. Paternal grandparents continued to be considered "grandparents" who could seek visitation with their deceased son's child even following child's adoption by stepfather. W.S.A. 48.92(3), 880.155.—Matter of C.G.F., 483 N.W.2d 803, 168 Wis.2d 62, reconsideration denied H.F. v. T.F., 490 N.W.2d 26, certiorari denied 113 S.Ct. 408, 506 U.S. 953, 121 L.Ed.2d 333.—Child C 313.

Source: 39 *Words and Phrases, North Western Digest 2d* 530. Published with permission of West, a Thomson Reuters business.

As with most West products, *Words and Phrases* is also a database in Westlaw. See Figure 5-5 for an example from the *North Western Digest* version of Words and Phrases.

4. Table of Cases

The *Table of Cases* is just what the name implies: an alphabetical list of all the cases reported in that digest's respective reporter, i.e., the *North Western Digest Table of Cases* lists only those cases that appear in the *North Western Reporter*. This table is another multi-volume set that is appended to West digests. The *Table of Cases* can be invaluable if you know the name of either the plaintiff, the defendant, or both but do not have a case citation. In that situation, you can look up the parties in the *Table of Cases* and the entry will list the reporter citation.

B. Digest Research

There are three basic strategies for researching case law using digests. One is to begin with a relevant case. A second is to start your research in the Descriptive-Word Index. The third is to begin with the topic analysis. All are outlined below including the pros and cons for each approach. Regardless of which method you choose, always update your research, as discussed in Section VI.

1. Beginning with a Relevant Case

One of the easiest strategies for digest research is to begin with a relevant case that you found through other methods, such as using secondary sources, speaking with a colleague, or finding relevant enacted law.

Once you have located a citation to a case that appears to be relevant, locate and read the case in its respective West reporter or on Westlaw and refer to the case headnotes. This step verifies that the case is on point and provides citations to cases upon which the judge relied when writing the opinion and that may also be applicable to your issue. Because all West reporters use standardized West topics and key numbers, once you have found a relevant case, the topic and key number covering the key points of law in that case may be used to locate additional cases. Look up the topic and key number in the West digest for your jurisdiction to find headnote summaries of other relevant cases. However, never rely upon headnotes, digest paragraphs, or references alone; always read a case completely and update it before relying on it.

Once you have a topic and key number, refer to the appropriate digest volume. Topics are arranged alphabetically and noted on the spines of the volumes, so you can simply pull the correct volume. Because key numbers can change, you may want to start with a recent case. Otherwise, you may have to use a conversion table to translate the old key number into the new one.

2. Beginning with the Descriptive-Word Index

Unless you already have a citation to a case, the Descriptive-Word Index is where you will likely begin the majority of your case research. This method allows you to find the most relevant topics within the key number/topic system and locate on-point cases.

To find a relevant case using the Descriptive-Word Index, you must first identify words or phrases that describe your topic. Using

Table 5-6. Outline for Digest Research with the Descriptive-Word Index

1. Develop a list of research terms using the journalistic or TARPP approach as discussed in Chapter 1.
2. Find the research terms in the Descriptive-Word Index, which will list topics and key numbers relevant to those terms. (Remember to check the pocket part.)
3. Review each topic and key number in the main volumes of the digest. (Remember to update your digest research by checking pocket parts, supplements, and digests contained in the reporter's advance sheets.)
4. Read all of the relevant cases your research reveals.

the journalistic or TARPP methods discussed in Chapter 1, think about the parties, places, objects, acts, omissions, defenses, and relief that may be relevant. Sometimes you may find a relevant term quickly. However, if you are having trouble finding on-point information, think about other terms or synonyms that might be used. Indexes have been developed by people examining cases and assigning terms that describe legal issues and facts. Often a concept can be expressed in many different ways. It is the job of the indexer to choose one term and put all the derivations of the term under the standard heading.

To find cases on your topic, identify the jurisdiction(s) relevant to your research and use the corresponding digest(s). Look for the terms you've identified in the Descriptive-Word Index, located in a volume at either the end or beginning of the digest set. This index will direct you to the topics and key numbers covering your issue. To use the Descriptive-Word Index, look up the subjects you want to research. The subjects will be followed by abbreviations indicating the topics and key numbers relevant to each subject. See Figure 5-6 for an example from the *North Western Digest 2d Descriptive-Word Index.*

The topic headings are arranged alphabetically in the main volumes; within each topic the key numbers appear sequentially. Once

Figure 5-6. *Descriptive-Word Index* Excerpt from *North Western Digest 2d*

GRANDPARENTS AND GRANDCHILDREN

CHILD custody. See heading **CHILD CUSTODY, GRANDPARENTS.**

CHILDREN out-of-wedlock,
  Support, duty to, **Child** ⇔ 21
  Visitation rights, **Child** ⇔ 20

DEATH actions,
  Grandchild rights, **Death** ⇔ 31(8)

DESCENT and distribution,
  Entitlement and shares, **Des & Dist** ⇔ 28, 36

SUPPORT, duty to,
  Children out-of-wedlock, **Child** ⇔ 21

VISITATION, **Child C** ⇔ 283-289
  Following adoption, **Child C** ⇔ 313

VISITATION rights,
  Children out-of-wedlock, **Child** ⇔ 20

WILLS. See heading **WILLS, GRANDCHILDREN.**

WORKERS' compensation,
  Dependency and relationship, **Work Comp** ⇔ 483-485
  Burden of proof, **Work Comp** ⇔ 1486
  Death, marriage, or other change of condition, **Work Comp** ⇔ 505
  Evidence,
    Sufficiency, **Work Comp** ⇔ 1486

Source: 34 *Descriptive-Word Index, North Western Digest 2d* 554 (Thomson/West 2001). Published with permission of West, a Thomson Reuters business.

you have found the topic and key number, read the case abstracts that summarize the legal issues involved. The case name and citation are located beneath the summary. If you are unfamiliar with the abbreviations used in the citation, consult the list of reporter abbreviations located at the front of the digest volume. Make sure you refer to the reporter and read the full case for each citation you think is relevant; do not rely on the abstract alone. In the digests, the statement "See topic analysis for scope" directs you to the analysis section that appears at the beginning of each broad topic. This analysis indicates other topics that may be relevant to the issue.

The Welch Matter

The explanations and figures in this chapter illustrate the digest research process beginning with the Descriptive-Word Index as it relates to the hypothetical grandparents visitation rights scenario.

Figure 5-6. When beginning case research on a topic, first go to the Descriptive-Word Index to look up research terms. In this case, logical terms include grandparents and child custody. As you see, the term Grandparents in the Descriptive-Word Index has a subheading "visitation" which leads to the topic and key numbers that appear on point: Child Custody 283–289.

Figure 5-5. To determine whether the term "grandparent" had been defined in any special way, a quick look at the Words and Phrases section of the *North Western Digest* shows that the one definition of grandparent is not relevant to our fact pattern.

Figure 5-4. With the relevant topic and key number, locate the *North Western Digest* volume that covers Child Custody and contains key number range 283–289. Looking through the cases under key number 283, you will find an Iowa case that seems on point, *In re Marriage of Howard*.

Figures 5-1 and 5-2. Going to the *North Western Reporter* volume, or online via Westlaw,[29] look for the citation noted in the digest citation: 661 N.W.2d 183. Read the text of the case to see if it is in fact relevant to the hypothetical situation.

---

29. Note that if you are performing this research through LexisNexis, the topics will not necessarily be the same as those in Westlaw.

3. *Beginning with the Topic Analysis*

Sometimes you can bypass the Descriptive-Word Index and go directly to the West topic that is most relevant to your problem. Digests are arranged alphabetically by topics, which are printed on the spine of each volume. So, if your topic is related to Navigable Waters, you could proceed directly to the digest volume that contains that term. Once in the correct digest volume, you can browse the beginning of the relevant entry to determine which key number best fits your topic. After you have found a topic and key number, look through the entry to determine which cases are relevant to your research. From there, locate each case in its respective reporter.

One advantage of this method is that, in browsing the topic, you can see all the related key numbers. This overview can provide a broader context for your issue and perhaps allow you to identify other issues you might not have considered. A disadvantage to this method is that it can be very time-consuming if you do not have enough knowledge to know which topic is relevant to your research.

V. Online Topic Searching

LexisNexis and Westlaw can also be used to research case law. However, your methodology will vary from the print digest strategies outlined in Section IV.B. These approaches are different if you are searching the open web. Both scenarios are discussed below.

A. LexisNexis and Westlaw

1. *Known Keywords*

Using keywords as noted in Table 5-6 is useful in LexisNexis and Westlaw in constructing a search query to search the full text of cases in databases containing Iowa cases. Be mindful of synonyms. For example, your search may be for children but the court may be referring to juveniles. Just as you choose the narrowest reporter and digest when conducting print research, so with electronic research pick the narrowest database possible so that your search does not return numerous irrelevant results.

2. Known Topic

The Topic Analysis method for print digest research can also be applied to searching LexisNexis and Westlaw, although each database has a different topic system for case research. Via Westlaw, you can search the West topic and key number system online by clicking "Key Numbers" in the header at the top of the screen. Note, however, that topics and key numbers are referenced differently in print versus online. For example, if you have Divorce (the topic) and 183.5 (the key number), in print, the information in the headnote would be written as Divorce followed by a drawing of a key and then the number 183.5. In contrast, on Westlaw that topic and key number would be expressed as 134K183.5. When searching online, replace the topic with its numerical equivalent, in this example 134, and add it to the key number separating the two with a "k." In Westlaw, the correct search for Divorce 183.5 would be 134k183.5.

In LexisNexis, search "by Topic or Headnote" to find topics and subtopics related to your research. LexisNexis does not use the West key number system and, although some terms may be similar, you cannot simply replicate your Westlaw search in LexisNexis. Even though LexisNexis has editors who assign topics, the database also uses an automated algorithm to determine topics so results may not be as accurate as the results obtained through Westlaw.

3. Known Case

If you already have a citation to a relevant case obtained, for instance, by finding topical secondary sources, as described in Chapter 3, you can use this case to find other relevant cases. Enter the case's citation in the appropriate search box: "Get a Document" in LexisNexis or "Find by citation" in Westlaw. After you have read the case to verify its relevancy, click on headnotes to find additional cases addressing that area of law.

B. Internet Research

Searching for case law on the open web is different from searching via LexisNexis and Westlaw. A modified keyword approach can be used to search the full text of documents, and, as with Westlaw and LexisNexis you would want to be in as narrow a database as possible to avoid retrieving an overwhelming number of results, many of which may be irrelevant, but for different reasons. In Westlaw and LexisNexis, choosing the narrowest database saves money. On the open web, the narrowest database saves time. Using a general search engine, e.g., Google or Yahoo, would be a very ineffective way to perform case law research as your results could number in the millions. A better approach would be to go to sites that you know contain case law in the jurisdiction you are researching. See Tables 5-4 and 5-5 for sites containing federal case law. Even then, free sites will not use the West or LexisNexis topics, so you will need to think of all the possible terms that might be used in the full text of the case. Also, some sites only provide links to cases; while the full text is accessible, it is not searchable from the main site.

The known-topic approach is very difficult on the open web as most searching is done through keyword searches of the full-text document. Remember that topics, subtopics, and key numbers are editorial enhancements by West and LexisNexis and are not present in the original court opinion. Some freely accessible legal websites do categorize their material into general practice areas, e.g., family law, real estate law, etc., but these tend not to provide the depth of classification found in subscription databases.

The known-case approach is also difficult on the open web for the same reasons as the known-topic approach. The topic systems of subscription databases that enable you to identify legal issues within a case and find other cases that address those issues are just not available on free sites. If, however, you have a citation to a case, you can usually find it online if you use a site you know contains cases from the correct jurisdiction and time frame.

VI. Updating Your Research

The final step of case law research, whether done in print or online, is to update your research. Updating fulfills several important purposes. It tells you whether a case is still good law. It indicates the treatment the case has received in subsequent opinions, e.g., whether the opinion has been questioned, explained, etc. It provides citations to cases that have cited your case and may therefore also be relevant to your issue. Refer to Chapter 9 for complete information about updating with citators.

Although updating can still be done in print, online updating is more prevalent and advantageous. Databases are more up-to-date than their print equivalents and more efficient to use, as explained below.

Via LexisNexis consult Shepard's or use Westlaw's KeyCite. To Shepardize, enter your citation into the box at the top left of the LexisNexis home page, click the Shepardize radio button and click "Go." To KeyCite in Westlaw, enter the citation into the "KeyCite this citation" box in the left-hand column or click "KeyCite" in the top header bar. If you already have your case on the screen, you only need to click the Shepard's or KeyCite icon.

If updating in print, check the same topic and key number in the pocket part of the digest volume you consulted to find your case. If there is an interim pamphlet available, check it for the same topic and key number. Check the closing table in the most recent update to the volume, i.e., the pocket part or pamphlet, to find the number of the last bound volume of the case reporter that the update covers. Then check the digest section of each bound reporter volume and advance sheet that has been published after that volume.

When using Shepard's in print, note that there are different Shepard's for different jurisdictions. You need to choose the appropriate jurisdiction in order to properly update your research. As you can see, it is much simpler to plug a case citation into the online Shepard's or KeyCite than to remember to check all the locations where an update might be. In addition, the print version is only as up-to-date as its publication date. In many cases, it is simpler to go online from the beginning to update your research.

VII. Reading and Analyzing Cases[30]

Finding a case is only the first step in the process of case law research. Once a case has been located, you must then read it, understand it, and analyze its potential relevance to the problem you are researching. Novices may spend hours reading and re-reading a single case in order to understand the details. This reading may also include frequent stops to consult secondary sources for definitions or background information.

It can sometimes be difficult to determine if a case is relevant to your research or client situation. If the case concerns the same principles of law as the client's situation, it is likely relevant. If the case contains the same legally significant facts it is also likely relevant. Legally significant facts are those that affect the court's decision.

The problem lies in the fact that research rarely reveals a case that addresses a fact pattern that exactly mirrors that of your client. Instead, several cases may have elements that are similar, but that also differ in some respect from that of your client's. It is your job to determine whether the facts are similar enough for the court to apply the law in the same way and reach the same decision.

After you have located binding cases involving similar doctrine and facts, you next need to synthesize the cases to state and explain the relevant legal rule, then decide how the rule applies to the client's facts and determine your conclusion.

As you read cases, the following strategies may help you understand them more quickly and thoroughly:

- Review the synopsis to determine if the case appears to be on point. If it is, skim the headnotes to find the particular portion of the case that is relevant. Remember that as one case may discuss several issues of law, only one or two headnotes may interest you. Go to the portion of the case identified by the relevant headnote and decide whether it is important for your research.

---

30. This part is drawn from Suzanne E. Rowe, *Oregon Legal Research* (2d ed., Carolina Academic Press 2007).

- If the headnote is important, skim the entire case to get a feeling for what has happened and why, focusing on the portion of the case identified by the relevant headnote.
- Read the case slowly and carefully. However, you may skip the parts that are obviously not relevant to your situation.
- As you finish reading each paragraph, try to summarize what you just read. If you are unable to do so, read it again.
- The next time you read the case, take notes. These will help you better understand the essential concepts of the case.[31]
- Remember that skimming is often not sufficient for you to fully understand the case.

---

31. For guidance on taking notes on cases, see Chapter 12, Section III.E.2.

Chapter 6

Statutes, Court Rules, and Ordinances

I. Introduction

A statute is a law written[1] and enacted by a legislature. Statutes are mandatory authority and binding on a court in the jurisdiction of the legislature. However, courts have the ultimate authority in interpreting a statute and determining its constitutionality. When evaluating a legal problem, you should always consider whether there is a statute applicable to the client's situation. When there is an applicable statute, you will need to consider all case law interpreting the statute and may also need to investigate the legislative history of the statute.[2]

In United States law, researchers most frequently encounter state and federal statutes. There are also local — city or county — statutes, usually called ordinances. This chapter will discuss state and federal statutes, and then address ordinances. This chapter will also address the laws governing the courts, known as court rules.

II. Session Laws and Codification

Usually, U.S. statutes are published in three basic versions both at the state and federal levels. The first version of a newly enacted statute

---

1. Sometimes legislative counsel or interested groups may write the laws.
2. For a more detailed explanation of the structure of the Iowa legislature and for information about researching legislative history, refer to Chapter 7.

Table 6-1. Research Strategy for Statutory Research

1.	Identify keywords or terms relevant to your research using the journalistic or TARPP methods discussed in Chapter 1.
2.	In print, use the index volume(s) for the applicable code (e.g., state or federal) to locate those terms. Online, search the index for your terms. If an index is not available, search the full-text for your terms.
3.	Once you identify a code section you think is relevant, go to that section to read and analyze the statute.
4.	Refer to an annotated version of the statute to find citations to cases that interpret or apply the statute.
5.	Read and analyze relevant cases.
6.	Apply the statute to the facts of your client's particular situation.

is a *slip law*. Traditionally, each law was issued by itself on a single sheet or as a pamphlet with separate pagination. Neither state nor federal slip laws are widely distributed in print now, but access is generally available online.

Next are the *session laws*. Statutes are arranged by date of passage and published in separate volumes for each legislative term. Official session laws are generally published only in bound volumes after a session has ended, but advance session law services provide the texts of new laws either online or in pamphlet form more quickly.

The third publication format is the *statutory compilation* or *code* (codification). Codes collect current statutes and arrange them by subject. Statutes are grouped into broad subject topics, usually called titles; within each title, statutes are divided into chapters and then numbered sections. Because of this subject arrangement, codes are often the starting point for statutory research.

III. Iowa Statutory Publications

The session law and codification process discussed above applies to Iowa statutes, whose publication formats are discussed below.

A. Iowa Slip Laws

Iowa slip laws are freely available online through the Iowa General Assembly Site.[3] On this site, slip laws are presented as bills. Be careful in using this site because it includes both enacted and pending legislation; only enacted statutes are slip laws. Print versions of the slip laws are cumulated in supplementation to the *Iowa Code Annotated* through the *Iowa Legislative Service*. This pamphlet service by West publishes the laws during and immediately after each session of the General Assembly.

B. Iowa Session Laws

Session laws are published as *Acts and Joint Resolutions* by Iowa's Legislative Services Agency.[4] The volumes contain enacted bills and resolutions arranged chronologically, by date enacted, and sequentially, by chapter number assigned upon enactment. One volume is published for each session of the General Assembly.[5] Iowa session laws

---

3. Current slip Laws are found at http://www.legis.iowa.gov/IowaLaw/statutoryLaw.aspx.

4. Researchers can use the *Acts* to help determine legislative intent. The process of researching legislative history is discussed in depth in Chapter 7.

5. "A General Assembly is a legislative period that consists of two regular legislative sessions. The first session of a General Assembly is held in odd-numbered years and lasts for approximately 110 calendar days. The second session is held in even-numbered years and lasts for approximately 100 calendar days." http://www.legis.iowa.gov/DOCS/Resources/gaguide.pdf.

Table 6-2. Titles in the *Code of Iowa*

I.	State Sovereignty and Management	IX.	Local Government
II.	Elections and Official Duties	X.	Financial Resources
III.	Public Services and Regulation	XI.	Natural Resources
IV.	Public Health	XII.	Business Entities
V.	Agriculture	XIII.	Commerce
VI.	Human Services	XIV.	Property
VII.	Education and Cultural Affairs	XV.	Judicial Branch and Judicial Procedures
VIII.	Transportation	XVI.	Criminal Law and Procedure

are freely available online through the Iowa General Assembly site.[6] LexisNexis and Westlaw also contain Iowa session laws.

C. Iowa Statutes

After the Iowa legislature has enacted statutes, the portions of enacted bills intended as permanent laws are codified into the *Code of Iowa*. The Code consists of 16 titles, each on a particular subject. The titles are listed in Table 6-2. Each title is then divided into subtitles and then further divided into chapters. For instance, Title IV: Public Health, has three subtitles:

 1: Alcoholic Beverages and Controlled Substances
 2: Health-Related Activities
 3: Health-Related Professions

Each subtitle is broken into chapters: Chapters 123–127 are under Subtitle 1; Chapters 135–146 are under Subtitle 2: and Chapters

---

6. Session Laws are found at http://www.legis.iowa.gov/IowaLaw/statutoryLaw.aspx.

147–158 are under Subtitle 3. (Note: in Iowa, the citation includes the chapter and section, for instance § 123.10. Numbers and letters after the decimal point indicate the specific section or subsection of the chapter.)

In print, the code is a multivolume set with a separate index volume. Code sections are consecutively numbered throughout the volumes; the number ranges on the spine of each volume refer to the range of code sections contained within that volume. The index volume contains many additional features. A Popular Name Index allows you to find the citation to a statute when you know its common name. A Table of Internal References helps you determine where else in the code a particular chapter number was cited. The index also contains Conversion Tables of Senate and House Files and Joint Resolutions to Chapters of the *Acts of the General Assembly* for the previous two years which can aid you in correlating the original senate or house file with its eventual publication in the acts; Tables of Disposition of Iowa Acts to Code Supplements that allows you to connect the code section to its original publication in the acts; and a Table of Corresponding Sections of the Previous Code to the Code Supplement for the Current Code which will tell you if the number of a code section has changed allowing you to trace its history.

The official version of the *Code of Iowa* is published by the State of Iowa biennially. It is updated each year it is not published (i.e., every other year) with a supplemental volume. Due to this publication schedule, the print version is not always the most up-to-date version, although it is the official version. The online version of the code provided through the Iowa legislature's site contains the same content as the print version, but is not official.

West publishes an unofficial annotated code, *Iowa Code Annotated*. Updated with pocket parts, this version is more current than the official version. The annotated code can be an excellent resource as it provides citations to state and federal cases that have interpreted each statute. The *Iowa Code Annotated* also contains historical and statutory notes, cross references to other relevant code sections, and references to law review and journal commentaries. Refer to Figures 6-1

Figure 6-1. *Code of Iowa* Example

> **598.35 Grandparent — great-grandparent — visitation rights.** Repealed by 2007 Acts, ch 218, § 208. See § 600C.1.

Source: Iowa Code § 598.35 (2009).

and 6-2 for examples of the differences between content in the unannotated and annotated versions of the Iowa code.

Online, an unannotated version of the *Code of Iowa* is freely available through the General Assembly site mentioned earlier.[7] Both LexisNexis and Westlaw maintain unannotated and annotated versions of the code. See Table 6-3 for online locations of Iowa Statutes.

IV. Iowa Statutory Research

Iowa statutory research follows the process outlined in Table 6-1. This section will more specifically discuss this process for both print and online sources and then explain how to update statutory research.

A. In Print

You should first develop a list of research terms by identifying keywords or terms relevant to your research. Use the journalist or TARPP methods discussed in Chapter 1 or another method of your choice; make sure you have considered the problem thoroughly so that you generate a complete list of terms.

Use the index volume for the *Code of Iowa* to locate those terms. You may have to check many entries to locate relevant chapters. Even if you find an entry that seems on point, do not stop researching before you have looked for all your keywords.

---

7. The Iowa General Assembly site is at http://www.legis.iowa.gov.

6 · Statutes, Court Rules, and Ordinances 145

Figure 6-2. *Iowa Code Annotated* Example

DISSOLUTION OF MARRIAGE/DOMESTIC RELATIONS §598.35
Note 1

of the child is the grandparent of the father of the child", and inserted "or the great-grandparent of the child is the grandparent of the mother of the child"; in subsec. 7, inserted "or great-grandparent", and added the second sentence relating to application of the subsection; and in unnum. par. 2, inserted "or great-grandchild" and inserted "or great-grandparent".

The 1998 amendment rewrote subsec. 6 which prior thereto read:

"6. The paternity of a child born out of wedlock is judicially established and the grandparent of the child is the parent of the father of the child or the great-grandparent of the child is the grandparent of the father of the child and the mother of the child has custody of the child, or the grandparent of a child born out of wedlock is the parent of the mother of the child or the great-grandparent of the child is the grandparent of the mother of the child and custody has been awarded to the father of the child."

Law Review and Journal Commentaries

Constitutional questions regarding grandparent visitation and due process standards. 60 Mo.L.Rev. 195 (1995).

Grandparent visitation law grows up: The trend toward awarding visitation only when the child would otherwise suffer harm. Joan Catherine Bohl, 48 Drake L.Rev. 279 (2000).

Library References

Child Support ⇐282.
WESTLAW Topic Nos. 76D.
Comments.
 Dissolution of marriage: grandparent visitation, see Volz, 2 Iowa Practice § 31.34 (2d ed.).

Forms.
 Petition for grandparent visitation, see Smith, 6 Iowa Rules Civil Procedure § 25.26 (3d ed.).

United State Supreme Court

Grandparent visitation rights, substantive due process rights of parent to make decisions regarding child's best interests, see Troxel v. Granville, 2000, 120 S.Ct. 2054.

Notes of Decisions

Adoption 2
Attorney fees 12
Best interests of children 3
Brothers and sisters 5
Construction and application 1
Custodial rights 7
De facto relationships 6
Denial of visitation 9
Excessive visitation 10
Guardians and wards 8
Parents of custodial parent 4
Review 13
Substantial relationship 11

---

1. Construction and application

The grandparents of a child have only statutory rights of visitation; no such right exists at common law. In re Hough, App.1999, 590 N.W.2d 556.

In order to seek visitation, grandparents must meet one of the established statutory established criteria. In re Hough, App.1999, 590 N.W.2d 556.

Grandparent visitation can be granted when it is authorized by statute, when it is ordered in a guardianship in the best interests of the child, and when it is ordered by a juvenile court as a part of its dispositional or permanency hearing. McMain v. Iowa Dist. Court for Polk County, 1997, 559 N.W.2d 12.

Grandparents are not entitled to visitation under grandparent visitation statute unless they fit in one of specific situations listed in statute. Graves v. Eckman, App.1996, 550 N.W.2d 470.

Statute designating circumstances under which grandparent may petition for visitation with grandchildren was enacted to ease harshness of common law in situations where grandparents could not seek derivative visitation rights from parent who is their child. In Interest of K.R., 1995, 537 N.W.2d 774.

Statute designating under what circumstances grandparents may petition for visitation may limit grandparent's visitation rights, but statute does not limit statutory authority of juvenile court to decide grandparent's petition for visitation with child placed in custody of court-appointed guardians. In Interest of K.R., 1995, 537 N.W.2d 774.

Only exception to common-law rule that custodial parents have veto power over visitation between child and all other third parties except noncustodial parent is statutory one that allows grandparents visitation under limited circumstances. Petition of Ash, 1993, 507 N.W.2d 400.

Source: Iowa Code Ann. § 598.35 (West 2001). Published with permission of West, a Thomson Reuters business.

Table 6-3. Iowa Legislature General Assembly Online Resources for Iowa Statutes

Publication	Address	Date Range
Slip Laws	http://www.legis.iowa.gov/IowaLaw/statutoryLaw.aspx	Current
	http://www.legis.iowa.gov/Archives/search.aspx Use Advanced Document Find for Legislative Archives	1993–present
Session Laws	http://www.legis.iowa.gov/IowaLaw/statutoryLaw.aspx	1993–present
Code of Iowa	http://www.legis.iowa.gov/IowaLaw/statutoryLaw.aspx	Current
	http://www.legis.iowa.gov/IowaLaw/statutoryLaw.aspx	1995–present

Each entry will have a number, or numbers, after it. These numbers refer to chapters of the Iowa Code. For example, "Grandchild visitation rights, granting to grandparents" is addressed at § 600C.1. If your search term appears but has no numbers after it, you need to look up the referenced term to determine the code sections. As shown in Figure 6-3, if you were researching "Grand Juries," you would need to turn to the "Juries and Jurors" entry in the index to learn the code chapter numbers that relate to your keywords. Figure 6-3 also shows that, in the grandparent visitation scenario, you should also follow

Figure 6-3. Sample from *Code of Iowa* Index

GRAND JURIES

See JURIES AND JURORS

GRANDPARENTS

See also FAMILIES

Dependent care expenses, income tax deductions for, 422.9(2e), 422.12C

Grandchild visitation rights, granting to grandparents, 600C.1

Inheritance of intestate estates, 633.210–633.226

Support of poor persons, liability for, 252.5

Source: Iowa Code Index (2009).

the "See also FAMILIES" reference to ensure you have fully researched all possible headings.

Once you have a list of code sections, go to the volume of the code that contains the relevant chapter; as noted earlier, each volume has printed on its spine the chapters that are included. Then read and analyze the statute. Do not rush through this step. A careful reading of the statute will allow you to determine if it is relevant to your research. Because statutes are often complex and the wording of statutes is so important, you may need to read the statute several times to understand it. You may also need to read the statutes that precede and follow your statute in order to understand your specific provision. For instance, many Code chapters contain a definitions section that pertains to the entire chapter, such as Chapter 256B (Special Education) of which 256B.2 is entitled Definitions—Policies—Funds.

After finding and carefully reading relevant statutes, you need to find citations to cases that interpret or apply the statute. Once you have found a relevant code section in the official, unannotated code, you can look up that same chapter number in the annotated code. Chapter 9 explains another way to find relevant cases, using a citator.

The Welch Matter

As you recall, the Welch matter, regarding grandparent visitation rights, has been addressed by statute. Careful research in Iowa statutes, e.g., following the relevant *Code of Iowa* index entry shown in Figure 6-3, leads you to Iowa Code § 600C.1. To thoroughly understand the development of this issue in Iowa you would want to read cases that interpret this statute. In the annotations for § 600C.1, you see references to *Santi v. Santi*, 633 N.W.2d 312 (Iowa 2001), a case decided by the Iowa Supreme Court in which a portion of the prior grandparent's visitation statute, Iowa Code § 598.35(7) (1999), was held unconstitutional. You also see references to *In re Marriage of Howard*, 661 N.W.2d 183 (Iowa 2003), in which another portion of the statute was held unconstitutional. Following *Howard*, § 598.35 was repealed by the 82nd Iowa General Assembly and replaced by Iowa Code § 600C.1. The Iowa legislature replaced the law again in 2010, which underscores the need to make sure you have the most current law.

Iowa Code § 598.35 is a prime example of how vitally important updating is to legal research. If you had started with this statute, e.g., from a reference from a secondary source, failed to check to see if this statute was

> still good law and based your analysis on this statute, your case would fail. However, if your research included an examination of Iowa Code § 598.35, *Santi*, *Howard*, and the latest changes, you would likely have a more sophisticated understanding of the new Iowa grandparent visitation statute, Iowa Code § 600C.1, and how it might apply to the Welch matter.

The final steps are to read and analyze relevant cases you have found[8] and apply the statute to the facts of your client's particular situation.

B. Online

Online, the process of researching statutes varies slightly from the process in print. However, even if you are beginning your research online, you should review the information in the preceding section as it explains the process in more detail. Regardless of which research medium you choose, the first step, developing a list of research terms, operates the same.

The second step is reviewing an index for your terms. At the General Assembly site, you can browse a PDF version of the index[9] to locate your terms, which makes the process similar to print research. You can also search the site for keywords but because the search engine is not very sophisticated, this can be a difficult way to look for your terms. On Westlaw, the index to the code is available under the "Iowa Statutes Annotated" database via the "Statutes Index" link. On LexisNexis, the database "Statutory Table of Contents, All States—Legislation—Practice Materials" will allow you to retrieve code sections by navigating through the topics of the code under which the documents are organized. Both LexisNexis and Westlaw may also be searched using keywords. See Chapter 2 for general information about electronic search techniques.

The next step is to find, read, and analyze the statute. If you have a citation to a code section, the General Assembly site is easy to nav-

---

8. Chapter 5 covers case law research.
9. The PDF index is located at http://www.legis.iowa.gov/IowaLaw/tablesIndex.aspx.

igate; simply enter your citation into the appropriate box, e.g., 600C.1. You can also expand the table of contents to find the relevant statute. LexisNexis and Westlaw also permit you to retrieve a statute by citation or use the tables of contents to identify relevant code sections.

Once you have located relevant statutes, you need to find cases that have addressed the statute. Annotated codes on LexisNexis and Westlaw provide references to cases, as do their citator services, which are explained in Chapter 9. If you do not have access to these services, visit a law library to access the annotated code in print or determine whether a public-access version of Westlaw or LexisNexis is available.

Finally, read and analyze the cases that interpret the statute as explained in Chapter 5 and apply the statute to the facts of your client's particular situation.

C. Updating Your Research

As a final step to any statutory research, remember to update your research to ensure you have the most current text of the statute as well as the most up-to-date list of cases that interpret the statute. If you are researching the code in print, check the pocket parts or supplements for each volume you use. If you are researching online through the Iowa legislature site or subscription databases LexisNexis or Westlaw, you should be reading the most up-to-date version as these services are updated regularly. However, it is wise to check any site or database for information on when it was last updated.[10]

Whether researching in print or online, always Shepardize or KeyCite statutes[11] to determine if there have been any changes since the source was published and to ensure that the statute has not been declared unconstitutional. If the General Assembly is in session, typically from January to April, you may also want to separately check to see if any pending legislation could affect your statute.[12]

---

10. In LexisNexis and Westlaw, the date the information was updated is usually listed at the bottom or the top of the page.
11. This is explained in Chapter 9.
12. This process is explained in Chapter 7.

V. Interpreting Statutes

As discussed in Section IV, statutory research involves reading and analyzing the text of a statute and any related statutes, analyzing any cases that have applied the statute, and applying the statute to the facts of your client's particular situation. This analytical work can be difficult if the statute is vague or if the application of the statute to the client's situation is not clear. Sometimes ambiguities exist because the statute was badly drafted, other times because of the give and take that is a natural part of the legislative process. A great deal of case law revolves around the meaning of statutes, and you cannot properly evaluate how a statute might apply to your client's facts without examining how it has been interpreted by courts.

The *Code of Iowa* provides guidance to issues related to statutes as well as the construction of statutes. Chapter 3, "Statutes and Related Matters," addresses the forms of bills, bill drafting instructions, and detailed information about the acts including effective dates. Chapter 4, "Construction of Statutes," includes, among other things, information about terminology, prospective statutes, and interpreting ambiguous statutes.[13] A helpful authoritative treatise on the subject of statutory construction is Norman J. Singer & J.D. Shambie Singer, *Statutes and Statutory Construction* (7th ed., West 2007).

In Iowa, statutes are not strictly construed according to the rule of the common law[14] except when the statute is ambiguous.[15] Rather, statute provisions are liberally construed "with a view to promote its objects and assist the parties in obtaining justice."[16] To determine the statute's purpose, Iowa courts first consider the language of the statute, using definitions provided in the code or the plain meaning of the words.[17] Courts attempt to interpret the statute as a whole, where the language of the provision interpreted should be consistent

---

13. Iowa Code §4.6, addressing the interpretation of ambiguous statutes, is discussed in more detail in Chapter 7.
14. Iowa Code §4.2.
15. Iowa Code §4.6(4).
16. Iowa Code §4.2.
17. *See e.g. Miller v. Marshall County*, 641 N.W.2d 742 (Iowa 2002).

with the rest of the statute. When the language is ambiguous or conflicting, the court follows the rules of construction established by both Iowa statutes and case law.[18]

VI. Statutes of Other States

Statutory research in other states is similar to that in Iowa. Each state publishes session laws. Many states have both official and unofficial codes. Like the *Code of Iowa*, the majority of official codes are unannotated. The most useful unofficial codes are often the annotated versions, but not always. For example, in Montana the state-published code is the only annotated version available. In any statutory research, you must determine which code is official for citation purposes; it may not be the annotated code used for research. Other states' codes may also be arranged differently than Iowa. Iowa uses numbers to denote code chapters, but other states do not. Several states, such as California and Texas, divide the codified statutes into a number of named codes.[19]

Almost all states now publish their state codes online where they are freely available to the public. Like Iowa, though, many online codes are not official versions.[20] Cornell's Legal Information Institute and Find-Law contain lists of links to state codes.[21] LexisNexis and Westlaw both contain unannotated as well as annotated versions of state codes. A good general rule is that the publisher of the print annotated version will provide the most current and up-to-date version electronically as well. In Iowa, this publisher is West Publishing, which provides Westlaw.

---

18. Iowa Code § 4.6, further discussed in Chapter 7, outlines the factors courts should consider in such cases.

19. For example, you may see code names such as the California Penal Code or the Texas Water Code.

20. The American Association of Law Libraries has published a state-by-state report detailing whether online legal resources are official or unofficial. See links to original 2007 report and 2009 updates at http://www.aallnet.org/summit.

21. Cornell's site is located at http://www.law.cornell.edu/statutes.html while FindLaw can be found at http://www.findlaw.com/11stategov/indexcode.html.

Sometimes it is necessary to compare statutes among several states, and there are resources that can make this research easier. In print, the main compilation of state laws is the *National Survey of State Laws* (6th ed., Thomson Gale 2008). It digests state law in close to fifty areas and is arranged by topic, rather than state. Electronically, it is available on Westlaw. For a more complete list of sources that contain collections of state statutes, see the bibliography *Subject Compilations of State Laws* (Greenwood Press 1981–present), which is also available through HeinOnline. In addition, the Cornell Legal Information Institute contains a freely accessible topical index to state statutes.[22]

VII. Federal Statutes

Federal statutes follow the three-tiered publication schedule discussed in Section II. Federal statutes enacted during a session of the United States Congress are known as either a *public law* or a *private law*. Public laws are designed to affect the general public, while private laws are passed to meet the needs of an individual or small group. Although both types are passed in the same way and appear in the session laws, only public laws become part of the statutory code.

A. Slip Laws

Public laws are first printed as slip laws published by the Government Printing Office. Each public law is cited by the session of Congress and number of the chronological order of enactment. For example, Pub. L. No. 109-11 was the 11th public law of the 109th Congressional session. All slip laws are only intended to be used on an interim basis until they are replaced by session laws.

After slip laws, the first print publication of federal statutes is in two advance session law services: *United States Code Congressional*

---

22. Cornell's index of state statutes is at http://topics.law.cornell.edu/wex/state_statutes.

and Administrative News (USCCAN) and *United States Code Service Advance* (USCS Advance).[23] Both services issue monthly pamphlets, publishing new federal statutes within a couple of months of enactment. USCCAN is published by West and is also available via Westlaw. The second advance session law service, USCS Advance, is published by Lexis and available via LexisNexis. These pamphlets are intended to be used only until they are replaced by bound volumes of the USCS.

B. Session Laws

The *Statutes at Large* (Stat.) set supersedes slip laws and serves as the permanent official publication for federal laws. A numbered volume is issued for each session of Congress. The volumes arrange the laws chronologically according to their public law numbers and *Statutes at Large* citation. *Statutes at Large* are cited by volume, page number, and year. For instance, Pub. L. No. 109-11 is 119 Stat. 229 (2005) in the *Statutes at Large*. Publication of the *Statutes at Large* is usually delayed by about two years. However, slip laws on government sites include the *Statutes at Large* pagination within a few weeks of enactment.

USCCAN serves as an unofficial version of the *Statutes at Large* and is available in print and on Westlaw. Electronically, LexisNexis and Westlaw contain the full text of statutes from volume one until the present, and HeinOnline provides the full text of statutes starting with volume one but not including statutes from the most recent years available.

Although for research purposes you may gravitate towards the annotated versions of the United States Code, which are discussed in Section VII.C., the *Statutes at Large* play an important role in statutory research. While sections of a public law may be spread among several code titles, the *Statutes at Large* provides the complete text of each act of Congress.

---

23. Both USCCAN and USCS Advance also contain information such as Presidential proclamations and select administrative regulations. In addition, USCCAN publishes excerpts of selective legislative history materials.

C. Codified Statutes

The *United States Code* (USC) is the final iteration of statutes and is arranged by subject rather than chronologically. Published by the government, the USC is the official codification of federal statutes and the preferred source to cite. It is arranged into 50 subject titles, with chapter and section subdivisions. A citation to the USC includes a title and section number, for example, 28 U.S.C. § 1331, where 28 is title 28, not volume 28.

The USC is not annotated although it has an extensive index and includes historical notes, cross references, and parenthetical references following each section that note the public law and *Statutes at Large* references. Other important features of the USC include the Popular Name Table, which lists statutes by their commonly used names and provides their official citations, and the Parallel Reference Table, which provides the code section corresponding to the session law number and helps you determine if a law is still in force.[24]

The USC is published only every six years with cumulative bound supplements issued between editions. Publication usually runs several years behind. To update, check the annual bound supplement for changes. HeinOnline contains the comprehensive full text of the USC. For a list of free websites providing the federal code, see Table 6-4.

There are two unofficial annotated versions of the code. One advantage to these unofficial commercial versions of the code is that they are updated much more frequently. *United States Code Annotated* (USCA) is published by West and available on Westlaw. The print version is updated through annual pocket parts and noncumulative quarterly pamphlets. USCA uses the same title, chapter, and section format as the USC but offers additional information that can aid the researcher, such as annotations for related court decisions and references to secondary sources that may help in interpreting code sections. *United States Code Service* (USCS), which is published by Lexis and available on LexisNexis, is another unofficial annotated

---

24. Examine Figure 6-4 for an example of the index to the USC and Figure 6-5 for an example from the code itself.

Figure 6-4. Sample of *United States Code* Index

GRANDPARENTS AND GRANDCHILDREN
Appropriations, housing, demonstration projects or programs, 12 § 1701q note
Caregiver, grants, 42 § 3030s et seq.
Census, 13 § 141 note
Child support, 42 § 666
Definitions,
  Housing, 12 § 1701q note
  Longshore and harbor worker's compensation, 33 § 902
Demonstration projects or programs, housing, 12 § 1701q note
Foster Grandparent Program. National Senior Volunteer Corps, this index
Generation-Skipping Transfers, generally, this index
Grants, caregiver, 42 § 3030s et seq.
Housing, 12 § 1701q note; 42 § 3535
Housing and Urban Development Department, training, 42 § 3535
Income tax, controlled corporations, shares and shareholders, 26 § 1563
Living Equitably: Grandparents Aiding Children and Youth Act of 2003, 12 § 1701q note; 42 § 3535

Source: U.S.C. General Index B-G p. 1356 (2006).

code. It contains the same editorial advantages of the USCA, though the information provided in the two is not identical. One difference between the two sets is that the USCA attempts to provide comprehensive coverage of all relevant decisions, while the USCS focuses on the best decisions and tries to weed out obsolete or repetitive information.

Researching federal statutes follows the same general principles of Iowa statutory research, as discussed in depth in Section IV. Refer to Table 6-1 for a flowchart of the general statutory research process. Note that in conducting print research, the volume numbers on the spine of each bound book are different from the title numbers that

Figure 6-5. Sample Entry in *United States Code*

§ 3030s. Definitions

(a) In general

In this subpart:

(1) Child

The term "child" means an individual who is not more than 18 years of age or who is an individual with a disability.

(2) Grandparent or older individual who is a relative caregiver

The term "grandparent or older individual who is a relative caregiver" means a grandparent or stepgrandparent of a child, or a relative of a child by blood, marriage, or adoption, who is 55 years of age or older and—

 (A) lives with the child;

 (B) is the primary caregiver of the child because the biological or adoptive parents are unable or unwilling to serve as the primary caregiver of the child; and

 (C) has a legal relationship to the child, as such legal custody or guardianship, or is raising the child informally.

(b) Rule

In providing services under this subpart—

(1) for family caregivers who provide care for individuals with Alzheimer's disease and related disorders with neurological and organic brain dysfunction, the State involved shall give priority to caregivers who provide care for older individuals with such disease or disorder; and

(2) for grandparents or older individuals who are relative caregivers, the State involved shall give priority to caregivers who provide care for children with severe disabilities.

(Pub. L. 89–73, title III, §372, as added Pub. L. 106–501, title III, §316(2), Nov. 13, 2000, 114 Stat. 2254; amended Pub. L. 109–365, title III, §320, Oct. 17, 2006, 120 Stat. 2551.)

AMENDMENTS

2006—Pub. L. 109–365 designated existing provisions as subsec. (a) and inserted heading, inserted "or who is an

Source: 42 U.S.C. §3030s (2006).

Table 6-4. Free Online Resources for Federal Statutes

Publication	Source	Address	Date Range
Slip Laws	Government Printing Office (includes Private Laws)	http://www.gpo.gov/fdsys/browse/collection.action?collectionCode=PLAW	1995–present
	GPO Access	http://www.gpoaccess.gov/plaws	1995–present
	THOMAS	http://thomas.loc.gov	1989–present
Statutes at Large (Stat.)	Government Printing Office	http://www.gpo.gov/fdsys/browse/collection.action?collectionCode=STATUTE	2003–present
	Library of Congress	http://memory.loc.gov/ammem/amlaw/lwsllink.html	1789–1875
United States Code (U.S.C.)	U.S. House of Representatives Internet Library	http://uscode.house.gov	1988–present
	Cornell's Legal Information Institute	http://www.law.cornell.edu/uscode	Current

appear in a citation. Thus, a statute in Title 42 of the USC might not be in volume 42 of the USC.

VIII. Court Rules

Court rules govern all stages of litigation, from filing an action through the completion of appeals. Failure to comply with these rules may result in the dismissal of a case, so it is important to know what they are, where they are located, and how to follow them.

A. Iowa Court Rules

The Iowa Supreme Court is "responsible for prescribing all rules of procedure, pleadings, practice, evidence, and the forms of process, writs and notices, for all proceedings in the state courts."[25] Items governed by court rules range from the Rules of Probate Court to Rules for Involuntary Commitment or Treatment for Chronic Substance Abusers.

In print, Iowa court rules are published by the Legislative Service Agency of the Iowa legislature, through commercial publisher West, under the direction of the Iowa Supreme Court. The West print version of the rules is entitled *Iowa Rules of Court: State*, which is published yearly and updated periodically with pocket parts. *Iowa Court Rules* are freely available online through the Iowa legislature's site, the Iowa judicial branch's site, and from the sources listed in Table 6-5. They also are accessible through LexisNexis and Westlaw.

Many local courts also have their own rules, which supplement and need to be consistent with the state rules. Check with the individual court to make sure there are not other rules that need to be applied beyond those at the state level. For example, the Third Judicial District has a rule on the numbering of exhibits in civil and criminal cases. Most courts list the rules on their websites.

B. Federal Court Rules

Primary federal court rules are the Federal Rules of Civil Procedure, Federal Rules of Criminal Procedure, Federal Rules of Appellate Procedure, Federal Rules of Bankruptcy Protection, and Federal Rules of Evidence. Court rules are included in the USCA and USCS; as for the statutory sections, both provide annotations for the rules.

As with local courts, individual federal courts may also have local rules. These are usually available on the court's website, from the clerk's office for the court, or in specialized publications, e.g., *Supreme Court Rules* for the U.S. Supreme Court, published by BNA. Local rules of the U.S. District Courts for the Northern and Southern Districts of Iowa, rules and procedures for the Eighth Circuit and more are in *Iowa Rules of Court: Federal*, which is published yearly by

---

25. Iowa Judicial Branch, "Iowa Court Rules and Forms," http://www.iowacourts.gov/Court_Rules_and_Forms.

West and updated with pocket parts. For local rules of Iowa-related federal courts, see Table 6-5. Always remember to check the currency of your source when consulting court rules.

IX. Local Ordinances

Just as there are statutes at the state and federal levels, so too are there statutes at the county and city level, usually called ordinances. Individual ordinances at the municipal level are similar to slip laws at the state and federal levels. Municipal codes are the codification of these ordinances. County and municipal ordinances usually deal with issues such as animal control, building regulations, city land use, emergency services, housing, parking, streets and sidewalks, traffic, and zoning.

A. Finding Local Ordinances

Local ordinances can be some of the hardest statutes to locate. Even with the enormous amount of information available on the web, many counties and cities are simply too small (or understaffed) to be able to maintain their ordinances online. Some county and city governments put their codes of ordinances and zoning ordinances on the web. Others post only specific ordinances, such as those requiring clearing the sidewalks after snow. Many counties do not post any local ordinances online. Some municipalities publish new or revised ordinances in the local newspaper.

For Iowa county and city ordinances, a few online resources have compiled lists of available sites. The Drake Law Library maintains a regularly updated list of links to Iowa municipal codes and county ordinances.[26] FindLaw and *American Law Sources Online* also both maintain partial lists of Iowa ordinances.[27]

---

26. Drake Law Library's list of municipal and county ordinances is at http://drakelaw.libguides.com/IowaLocalCodes.

27. FindLaw's site is http://www.findlaw.com/11stategov/ia/laws.html while *ALSO* is located at http://www.lawsource.com/also.

Table 6-5. Free Online Resources for Iowa Court Rules and Iowa-Related Federal Courts

Court/Document	Address
Iowa Court Rules	http://www.legis.iowa.gov/IowaLaw/CourtRules.aspx
	http://www.iowacourts.gov/Court_Rules_and_Forms
Iowa First Judicial District	http://www.iowacourts.gov/District_Courts/District_One/Local_Rules
Iowa Second Judicial District	http://www.iowacourts.gov/District_Courts/District_Two/Local_Rules
Iowa Third Judicial District	http://www.iowacourts.gov/District_Courts/District_Three/Local_Rules
Iowa Fifth Judicial District	http://www.iowacourts.gov/District_Courts/District_Five/Local_Rules
Iowa Seventh Judicial District	http://www.iowacourts.gov/District_Courts/District_Seven/Local_Rules
Iowa Eighth Judicial District	http://www.iowacourts.gov/District_Courts/District_Eight/Local_Rules
U.S. District Court Southern District of Iowa	http://www.iasd.uscourts.gov/index.php?option=com_content&view=article&id=154&Itemid=91
U.S. District Court Northern District of Iowa	http://www.iand.uscourts.gov/e-web/home.nsf/home (Clerk of Court > Local and Federal Rules)
Eighth Circuit	http://www.ca8.uscourts.gov/newcoa/publs/publs.htm

If a county or city does not make its ordinances available online, contact the city or county government directly. If you can go to the offices, you can simply ask to see the ordinances. If you cannot go in person, however, ask to have a copy of the ordinance in question sent to you. Local ordinances can be quite long, so it may not be feasible for the entire document to be sent to you. It is always better to have an ordinance number on hand in case you are only able to request a limited number of pages. Websites of the Iowa League of Cities and Iowa State Association of Counties contain much useful information about local government.[28]

B. Updating Ordinances

As with all legal research, it is critically important to ensure you are citing to the most current version of an ordinance. Even if the ordinance is available online, it is good practice to contact the city or county directly to verify that you have the most up-to-date material.

---

28. Iowa League of Cities is at http://www.iowaleague.org and Iowa State Association of Counties is at http://www.iowacounties.org.

Chapter 7

Legislative History

I. Introduction

In addition to researching Iowa laws as codified in the *Code of Iowa*, you will sometimes need to look to the law-making process to determine how a statute might apply to your client's situation. When a statute's meaning is ambiguous and has not already been clarified by earlier court decisions, you will investigate its legislative history to try to persuade the court that the statutory intent favors your client. You may also need to track current legislation to see if proposed or recently enacted bills might affect one of your clients. Both instances require a basic knowledge of the legislative process in Iowa, and this chapter begins with that introduction. The chapter then builds on this understanding to discuss the specific research tools and strategies involved in locating legislative history or tracking current legislation.[1]

II. Iowa Legislative Process

The state legislative body in Iowa is called the General Assembly (G.A.). It is composed of two chambers: the House of Representatives, whose members serve two-year terms, and the Senate, whose members serve four-year terms. Each G.A. is numbered consecutively

---

1. Thanks to Cory Quist and Mandy Easter of the Iowa State Law Library, Meaghan McCarthy and Jeffrey Dawson of the Iowa State Archives, and Valerie Hansen and Jonetta Douglas of the Legislative Services Agency for their guidance in researching this chapter.

and consists of two *regular sessions*, together spanning two years. The first session is held at the beginning[2] of the odd-numbered year. The second is held at the beginning of the even-numbered year. For instance, the 83rd G.A. began in 2009 (first session) and ended in 2010 (second session). Some General Assemblies may have additional sessions, called extraordinary sessions.

The two general forms of Iowa legislation are bills and resolutions. Most proposals of law take the form of a *bill*. A special kind of bill, called a *study bill*, is sponsored by a committee, the governor, or a state agency. The objective of a study bill is to get a sense of how the legislature will respond to the proposal. If a study bill earns committee approval, it will then be introduced as a regular bill. The second form of Iowa legislation, a *resolution*, is often used to address rules of legislative operation or ceremonial matters, such as issuing a congratulatory message. Resolutions may also be passed to issue a temporary law.

Iowa legislation must be sponsored by one or more legislators or a legislative committee. The legislative sponsor submits a bill request form to the Legal Services Division of the nonpartisan Legislative Services Agency (LSA).[3] Consulting with the sponsor as needed, an LSA drafter will then write a bill that, if passed, would enact the proposal. The sponsor reviews the bill draft and may send it back to the LSA for further revision. The sponsor may choose to introduce the legislation by filing the bill with the chamber's chief administrative officer, either the Secretary of the Senate or the Chief Clerk of the House. Typically the draft is assigned a bill number beginning with SF for Senate file or HF for House file. In the case of a study bill, the draft is assigned a number beginning with SSB for Senate study bill, or HSB for House study bill.

The remainder of the legislative process is similar to that of most states and the federal government. See Figure 7-1, Iowa Legislative

---

2. Sessions typically run from January into April.
3. The Legislative Services Bureau performed legislative drafting until a reorganization, effective April 14, 2003, created the new Legislative Services Agency. *See* 2003 Iowa Acts 44.

Figure 7-1. Iowa Legislative Process Flowchart

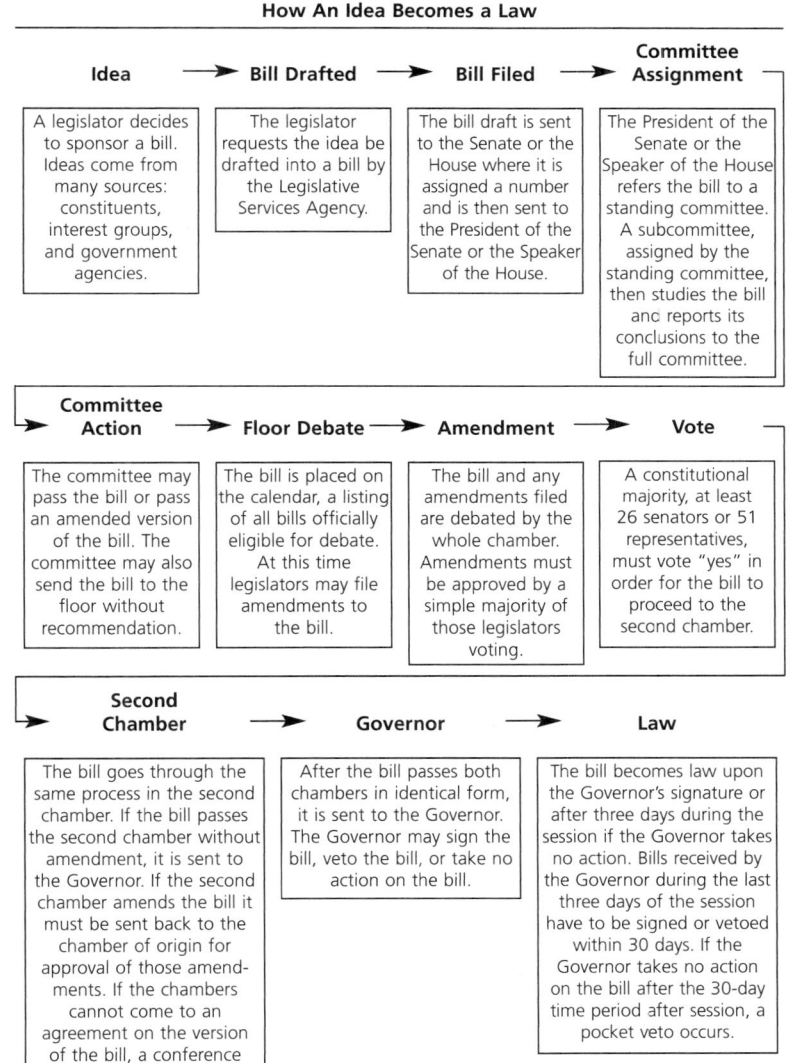

How An Idea Becomes a Law

Idea
A legislator decides to sponsor a bill. Ideas come from many sources: constituents, interest groups, and government agencies.

Bill Drafted
The legislator requests the idea be drafted into a bill by the Legislative Services Agency.

Bill Filed
The bill draft is sent to the Senate or the House where it is assigned a number and is then sent to the President of the Senate or the Speaker of the House.

Committee Assignment
The President of the Senate or the Speaker of the House refers the bill to a standing committee. A subcommittee, assigned by the standing committee, then studies the bill and reports its conclusions to the full committee.

Committee Action
The committee may pass the bill or pass an amended version of the bill. The committee may also send the bill to the floor without recommendation.

Floor Debate
The bill is placed on the calendar, a listing of all bills officially eligible for debate. At this time legislators may file amendments to the bill.

Amendment
The bill and any amendments filed are debated by the whole chamber. Amendments must be approved by a simple majority of those legislators voting.

Vote
A constitutional majority, at least 26 senators or 51 representatives, must vote "yes" in order for the bill to proceed to the second chamber.

Second Chamber
The bill goes through the same process in the second chamber. If the bill passes the second chamber without amendment, it is sent to the Governor. If the second chamber amends the bill it must be sent back to the chamber of origin for approval of those amendments. If the chambers cannot come to an agreement on the version of the bill, a conference committee is appointed.

Governor
After the bill passes both chambers in identical form, it is sent to the Governor. The Governor may sign the bill, veto the bill, or take no action on the bill.

Law
The bill becomes law upon the Governor's signature or after three days during the session if the Governor takes no action. Bills received by the Governor during the last three days of the session have to be signed or vetoed within 30 days. If the Governor takes no action on the bill after the 30-day time period after session, a pocket veto occurs.

Source: Flowchart derived from Iowa Legislature General Assembly website: http://www.legis.iowa.gov/Docs/Resources/HowAnIdeaBecomesALaw.pdf.

Process Flowchart, for a flowchart representation. Proposed legislation is debated and amended in committee. If the bill is approved by the committee, it will be debated and amended on the floor of the chamber that introduced it. If approved in that chamber, the bill then goes to the other chamber and follows the same process. If the second chamber amends the bill, the amendments are considered by the first chamber. If the two chambers cannot pass an identical bill, a conference committee will meet to try to resolve the differences. After both the House and Senate have passed the same version of a bill, it is *engrossed*, a process that incorporates all the approved amendments into the bill text. Then the bill is certified by the chief administrative officer of the chamber in which it originated. The certified, engrossed bill is sent to the governor, who can sign it, veto it, or take no action on it.

If the governor signs the bill, it becomes law. Unless otherwise specified in the bill, the effective date is July 1 or August 15, if signed by the governor after July 1. If the governor vetoes the bill, it is sent back to the legislature if it is still in session; the veto can be overridden with at least two-thirds of the members of each chamber voting for it. A bill with an overridden veto also becomes law, effective July 1 of that year unless otherwise specified in the bill. If the governor takes no action on a bill received before the last 3 days of the session, it will become law after the passage of 3 days. If the governor does not take action for 30 days on a bill received during the last 3 days, it fails to become law, a result known as a *pocket veto*.

III. Iowa Legislative History Research

A. Introduction to Iowa Legislative History Research

As discussed in Chapter 6, a statute must be read carefully to understand its meaning. In fact, a meticulous reading of the words of the statute and surrounding sections, such as definitions, is the first step in determining legislative intent. However, when a statute can be construed in more than one way, courts may look beyond the language of a statute to try to determine the legislature's intent in en-

Figure 7-2. Iowa Code § 4.6

If a statute is ambiguous, the court, in determining the intention of the legislature, may consider among other matters:

1. The object sought to be attained
2. The circumstances under which the statute was enacted
3. The legislative history
4. The common law or former statutory provisions, including laws upon the same or similar subjects
5. The consequences of a particular construction
6. The administrative construction of the statute
7. The preamble or statement of policy

Source: Code of Iowa 2009. Des Moines: Legislative Services Agency, General Assembly of Iowa, 2008.

acting it. The tools a court may consider are outlined in Iowa Code § 4.6, shown in Figure 7-2.

If court cases have already interpreted the statute, you will want to read these opinions to better understand its application. If the courts have not already interpreted the part of the statute related to your legal issue, or considered its legislative history, you will want to look at the statute's history to learn more about its purpose. You will identify the bills that enacted and amended the statute, analyze how these proposals changed the law, and assess the objectives of these changes.

Iowa, like many states, has available only a limited amount of documented legislative history.[4] Be aware when you begin your research that you will not likely find vast quantities of information. However, if you search systematically, as outlined in Table 7-1 and explained in Section III.B., you will find the available information and, possibly, something useful.

---

[4]. For a guide to legislative history sources in other states, see *State Legislative History Research Guides on the Web*, compiled by Jennifer Bryan Morgan, Documents Librarian, Indiana University School of Law Library–Bloomington at http://www.law.indiana.edu/lawlibrary/research/guides/state legislative/index.shtml.

B. Sources of Iowa Legislative History

1. Overview

To follow the legislative history process outlined in Table 7-1, you will consult several sources. Some of these sources will allow you to complete several steps, while others may only allow you to complete part of a single step. The rest of this section presents these key sources in the order in which they are first consulted when following the research process.

2. Compiled Legislative History: Annotated Codes and Index to Legal Periodicals

An efficient first step in legislative history research is to determine whether others have already examined the legislative history of your statute in a published article or book. Relatively few Iowa legislative histories have been published, so you often will not find anything relevant. However, if an analysis of the history of your code section does exist, you will save a great deal of time by beginning your research with this source. Moreover, such analyses may be persuasive to a court, so you will want to review one if it exists.[5]

Published legislative histories for a particular statute should be cited in an annotated code. You can also check for one using the tools for searching by subject for treatises and law reviews, described in Chapter 3. If you use an index, be aware that the term "legislative history" will probably not appear in the subject field and may well not be in the title, either. You will want to search by the act or code name. In addition, the *Index to Legal Periodicals* database[6] allows searching by the field statute. This method allows you to enter the Iowa code citation to see if any journal articles have examined it.

---

5. In one Iowa decision, the court established legislative history by referencing two law review articles. *See Richardson v. City of Jefferson*, 257 Iowa 709, 134 N.W.2d 528 (1965). In *Richardson*, when the court turns to legislative history, it notes, "For legislative history see "'Home Rule' For Iowa Cities and Towns?" 13 Drake Law Review 53; and "Municipal Home Rule in Iowa: House File 380," 49 Iowa Law Review 826." *Id.* at 532.

6. *See* http://www.hwwilson.com/databases/Legal.cfm.

Table 7-1. General Process for Researching Iowa Legislative History

1. Determine whether a legislative history analysis already exists for the code section.
2. If there is no compiled analysis, read the history information below the code section to note the acts that created and changed the section.
3. Examine each act to ascertain what changes were made and whether the changes are relevant to your issue.
4. If the act is relevant, note the *file number* at the top of the act.
5. Consult the *bill book* to determine how the bill changed from introduction to enrollment. If it was originally a study bill, also consult that file.
6. Examine the explanation at the end of the introduced bill and, if relevant, at the end of the study bill.
7. If the bill is neither a Ways and Means nor Appropriations measure but has a significant effect on the state's finances, determine whether a fiscal note is attached to the bill.
   * *At this point, you have likely already found most of what will be influential to the courts in determining intent. However, you can continue searching to be completely thorough and to obtain additional background or other contextual information.*
8. Determine whether there is a compiled bill history to review what actions each chamber took on the bill. If a compilation does not already exist, compile your own, using the House and Senate *journals*.
9. Check *committee minutes*.
10. Determine whether any relevant *reports* have been filed.
12. Examine the original *bill drafting file*.
13. Search for newspaper articles discussing the legislation.

3. Code Section History

If you do not find a published legislative history analysis for your code section, you will want to examine the legislative history references (or credits) as well as historical and statutory notes found in the *Iowa Code Annotated*, published by West.[7] See Figure 7-A in the chapter appendix for an example of these notes. The references list the acts that created and changed the code section and any prior section numbers where the law was previously codified. The historical and statutory notes briefly explain the changes made by each act. The notes can help you determine whether the change was relevant to your situation and which session laws you need to consult.

If you do not have access to the *Iowa Code Annotated*, you can find the legislative history citations at the end of the code section in the *Code of Iowa* in print or online. However, in the print or online versions of the *Code of Iowa*, you will not get references to court cases that have interpreted the statute or notes on how new laws may have changed the statute. See Chapter 9 for an explanation of how to find these references using citators.

4. Session Laws

Both the *Iowa Code Annotated* and the *Code of Iowa* reference individual acts that have affected a code section by providing their session law citations in this form: [year] Acts [chapter and section number]. For instance, 2009 Acts 52 refers to the act with the heading Chapter 52 in the 2009 Iowa session laws. As noted in Chapter 6, Iowa session laws are published in the *Acts and Joint Resolutions of the General Assembly*.

Acts in the session laws are printed in order by chapter number. When reviewing your referenced act, you will see a heading that includes chapter number, title, and legislation number (probably SF or HF for Senate file or House file). This heading is followed by a brief

---

7. The LexisNexis Iowa Annotated Statutes database provides most of this information, as well. However, it does not give the session law references for the acts that created and changed the code section; it provides only references to the years the code section changed.

summary that describes the act. Courts have occasionally referenced this summary in interpreting intent.[8] Next, examine the text of the act to note any changes made to the code, shown via special formatting. Underlining indicates new text; strikeouts indicate deleted text. If entirely new sections are being added, only the words New Section or New Subsection will be underlined. Note that some acts include a section entitled "LEGISLATIVE INTENT," indicating what the legislature wants to accomplish in enacting the law. Record the legislation number from the heading of the act, the G.A. number, and the session year, in case you decide to delve deeper into the bill's history. See Figure 7-B in the chapter appendix for an example of an act published in the session laws.

5. Bill Books

a. Bill Versions

Bill books include the introduced bill with all its amendments. Print sources use a color-coded system, as seen in Table 7-2.

Table 7-2. Iowa Bill Book Color Coding

White	Bill as introduced
Blue	Senate amendment
Yellow	House amendment
Pink	Bill with amendments passed by originating chamber
Green	Senate study bill
Salmon	House study bill

Tracking the changes made to a piece of legislation from introduction to enrollment can provide insight into legislative intent and has oc-

---

8. *See e.g. State v. Lathrop*, 781 N.W.2d 288 (Iowa 2010). *The Lathrop* court cited the specific language of the summary to determine the legislative intent in enacting a special sentence of lifetime parole for sex offenders.

casionally been considered by the courts.[9] If a bill started out as a study bill, that number will be indicated near the top of the original bill, and you will want to look back at the study bill, too, to see how the legislation evolved.

b. Bill Explanations

As noted earlier, the Legislative Services Agency drafts Iowa bills in response to a request from a legislator or legislative committee. Starting with the 49th G.A. (1941), House rules require an explanation to accompany most bills.[10] The Senate adopted a similar rule starting with the 63rd G.A. (1969).[11] Written by the drafter, the bill explanation is based on the information conveyed by the legislator in conversation with the drafter or on the bill request form. Some explanations are lengthy, but many are brief. Iowa courts have used these explanations fairly frequently in interpreting legislative history.[12] Within the bill book, the explanation is found at the end of the original version of the bill and preceded by the heading EXPLANATION. See Figure 7-D in the chapter appendix for an example of an original bill with explanation from the bill book.

c. Fiscal Notes

If legislation other than Appropriation or Ways and Means measures will have a significant financial effect on the state's revenues, expendi-

---

9. *See e.g. Chelsea Theater Corp. v. City of Burlington*, 258 N.W.2d 372 (Iowa 1977). In *Chelsea*, the court noted that a Senate amendment struck the phrase "to minors" from the version originally passed by the House. The court explains, "[t]he deletion of the phrase 'to minors' by both the House and Senate before enactment of § 725.9 lends support to our conclusion that the statute prohibits local governments from regulating the availability of obscene materials generally, and not just with respect to minors." *Id.* at 374.

10. For the current iteration, see Rule 27 in the House Rules: http://www.legis.iowa.gov/DOCS/ChamberRules/HouseRules.pdf.

11. For the current iteration, see Rule 29 in the Senate Rules: http://www.legis.iowa.gov/DOCS/ChamberRules/SenateRules.pdf.

12. *See e.g. City of Waterloo v. Bainbridge*, 749 N.W.2d 245, 248 (Iowa 2008) (directly quoting from and citing to the bill explanation in noting why the legislature enacted the statute).

tures, or fiscal liability, the Fiscal Services Division of LSA attaches an explanatory fiscal note.[13] This note indicates how the bill will affect the state's finances, specifies the projected dollar amount of this effect over the law's first five years, and details how resources will be allocated. The note also indicates the factual assumptions LSA made in drafting the note. Fiscal notes are included in the bill book and are also available on the Iowa legislature's site back to the 79th G.A.[14] Iowa courts have sometimes looked at fiscal notes in determining legislative intent.[15]

d. Sources of Bill Books and Older Bill Text

In print, Iowa's State Law Library offers bill books from 1937 to the present. Online, bill books are available in one of three locations, depending on the time period covered:

- 55th–81st G.A., 1953–2006 (more recent years will be added): Iowa Legislature Heritage Digital Collections.[16]
- 2nd session of 80th G.A., 2004, to last G.A.: in the General Assembly archives link to Advanced Document Find then Legislation Archives.[17]
- Current G.A.: "Track Legislation" section of the General Assembly website.[18]

---

13. *See* Joint Rules of the Senate and House, Rule 17, which notes how it is determined whether a bill will require a fiscal note. The website is http://www.legis.iowa.gov/DOCS/ChamberRules/JointRules.pdf.

14. *See* http://www.legis.iowa.gov/LSAReports/fiscalNotes.aspx.

15. *See e.g. State v. Dohlman*, 725 N.W.2d 428 (Iowa 2006). In *Dohlman*, the court considers evidentiary requirements to establish wrongful imprisonment. The court notes first that, on its face, the statutory language requires "clear and convincing evidence." *Id.* at 432. The court further assesses the plaintiff's evidentiary burden as fairly strict in quoting one of the assumptions of the fiscal note indicating that cases that meet the bill's requirements would occur less than once a year. *Id.* at 432.

16. The Iowa Legislature Heritage Digital Collections are available at http://www.legis.state.ia.us/heritage/index.htm.

17. The General Assembly archives are available at http://www.legis.iowa.gov/Archives/search.aspx.

18. The Track Legislation section of the current General Assembly site is available at http://www.legis.iowa.gov/Legislation/BillTracking/billTrackingTools.aspx.

If earlier bills are needed, bill text for 1868–1980 can be found at the State Law Library. Bills are in their original, unamended form, and include an explanation if one is available. They are arranged chronologically and then alphabetically by broad topic. The top of the first page of each bill has a note indicating what happened to it.

e. Navigating Bill Books

Each online bill book source works a bit differently. Tips on successfully using each follow.

Iowa Legislature Heritage Digital Collections

<u>Advanced search</u>

1. Under "Select specific collections:" click on the G.A. session you want and the "add >>" button to move it to the box labeled "Selected collections:"

2. Search by keyword. If you know the bill number, input it, preceded by HF or SF, without periods, in the box labeled "The exact phrase." (Hint: If this search retrieves no results, try adding one or more zeros in front of your file number so it contains four digits. See Figure 7-C in the chapter appendix for an illustration.)

3. Click on "search."

<u>Browse collections</u>

If the advanced method fails, try browsing for a known bill number. Use the drop-down menu to select the desired G.A. number, and click on "Go." Use the page number navigation on the upper right to find your information. Within the session laws, bills are listed in numerical order, with House bills and resolutions first, followed by Senate legislation.

General Assembly Archives: Bills and Amendments

1. Click on the plus box to the left of Legislation Archives in the Advanced Document Find feature.

2. Continue navigating the archives with the plus boxes to select the G.A. session you want, then bill version, and chamber. Click on the file number you want.

3. To find the explanation, be sure to select the introduced folder. After you click on the right Chamber and file number, scroll to the end of the introduced bill.

General Assembly: Track Legislation page

1. Click on the "BillBook" link near the top of the page.

2. Select the bill you want to examine by entering the file number and type under "Quick Find," then clicking on the "Go" button. You can also browse by clicking on "Display Bill Lists."

3. Use the links on the left to find information on the bill. To find the explanation, click on Print Options and select "Introduced Version." Click "Print Bill" to bring up window with complete text, and scroll to the end of the introduced bill.

6. *General Assembly Actions: House and Senate Journals*

The *House Journal* and the *Senate Journal* record actions taken in the specified chamber. They include information like motions made and how legislators voted. Typically they provide little to no detail about debate on bills or amendments. Using the journals to outline the path of a piece of legislation through the G.A. may provide additional context for your understanding of a bill.

Journals from 1995 to the present can be accessed online from the General Assembly site. Select the legislation tab and then the Senate & House Journals link on the left for a variety of access options. All journals, including those published before 1995, can be found in print in any one of Iowa's three major law libraries.[19]

For bills from 1995 or later, you should be able to find a compiled list of relevant journal entries by bringing up the bill on the G.A. website. Although the interface has changed somewhat over the years, all bills on the website will include a link called either "Current Bill History" or "Complete History." The information at this link includes the name of the sponsor, a brief description of the bill, and a list of all

---

19. Iowa's three major law libraries, described further in Chapter 2, are Drake University Law Library, the State Law Library of Iowa, and the University of Iowa Law Library.

the actions taken on it with links to the pages of the House or Senate journal that document each action.

LexisNexis and Westlaw also offer databases with limited compiled Iowa legislative history. LexisNexis's Iowa Legislative Bill History (IALH) began coverage in 2002, and Westlaw's Iowa Legislative History (IA-LH) began coverage in 1999. Both databases can be searched by keyword or bill number. Like the G.A. site, both databases note who introduced a bill or amendment, list all the actions taken on it, and cite the pages of the House or Senate journal that document each action. In LexisNexis, this information is provided under the "Retrieve Bill Tracking Report" link. LexisNexis also includes a "Retrieve Bill Text Report" link that has the text of some related documents (e.g., LSA Notes on Bills and Amendments, which are prepared for Appropriations bills) and governor's messages.

If you need to find journal entries for an older bill, you can also search the print *Index to House and Senate Journals.* This title includes a Senate-House companion bill table and brief histories of bills, with references to the journals. Indexes back to 1995 are also available via the G.A. site.[20]

7. *Committee Minutes*

Legislative committee minutes are available, but they also tend to be very limited in their coverage. They note who attended the meeting and what bills were considered. They record votes, but do not typically document the points made in discussion. The minutes might mention if someone spoke or distributed materials to committee members.

The G.A. website is beginning to include committee minutes. From the committee information page,[21] click on the committee you want and then on the "meetings" link. Click on the date to determine whether minutes are available. To search an earlier G.A. session, go to the current list of committee meetings. Look in your web browser's address bar and change the end of the URL so that the number after

---

20. *See* http://www.legis.iowa.gov/Legislation/journals.aspx.
21. *See* http://www.legis.iowa.gov/Schedules/committees.aspx.

"ga=" is the number of the General Assembly you want and the number after "s=" is the session number you want. Committee minutes can also be accessed in hard copy by contacting the chief clerk of the House (switchboard number 515-281-3221) or Secretary of the Senate (switchboard number 515-281-3371).[22]

8. Reports

Reports associated with legislation or with a governmental body might also be available. *Interim Study Committees* meet between sessions to study issues on which legislation may be enacted. Each committee releases final reports with its recommendations, which may provide valuable insights into the motivations for a piece of legislation. Reports are available through the Iowa Legislature Heritage Digital Collections, 1956–2004; the State Law Library, 1965–current; the State Archives,[23] 1955–current; and the G.A. web site, 1995–current.[24] These reports are not currently indexed, so to see if there is a relevant report to your legislation, you have to search by topic. A good general rule is to check the committees for the four years preceding the introduction of your legislation.

In addition, the Legislative Services Agency prepares Legislative Guides and Legal Background Briefings. Both provide information on a particular topic; the guides survey the relevant law and the briefings provide background information. These are available from the G.A. website back to 2000.[25] The Legislative Services Agency also

---

22. E-mail contact information is at the bottom of http://www.legis.iowa.gov/Agencies/HCC.aspx for the House and http://www.legis.iowa.gov/Agencies/SOS.aspx for the Senate.

23. The State Archives are open to anyone, and the materials can be used on site during reading room hours. *See* http://www.iowahistory.org/archives/public-reference-services/index.html.

24. *See* http://www.legis.state.ia.us/aspx/Archives/Committees/Interim/CommitteeInfo.aspx for reports through 2008. For newer reports, link to the committee from the list at http://www.legis.iowa.gov/Schedules/Interim.aspx, then click on additional information to search for a report.

25. *See* http://www.legis.state.ia.us/Central/Guides or http://www.legis.iowa.gov/LSAReports/legalTopicPubs.aspx.

maintains a list of documents that state agencies have filed with the General Assembly. These reports can provide a wealth of data that may have influenced future legislation. Entries date back to 2003.[26]

9. Bill Drafting Files

The Legislative Services Agency maintains confidential bill drafting files for the current General Assembly plus the prior General Assembly.[27] Older files are sent to the State Archives, where they become publicly accessible. A file sent to the archives must include the request form for the LSA to draft the bill and the version of the bill as introduced. At the drafter's discretion, additional materials may be included, such as earlier bill drafts, notes, written comments from legislators, or model legislation from other states. However, it is uncommon for these additional materials to be maintained in the files. It is possible that notes written on or accompanying the request form might provide additional information about legislative intent.

The archives extend back to 1967 and include files for all Iowa bills, both enacted and unenacted. At a minimum, you will need to know the House or Senate file number and the number of the General Assembly to request a file. If you know the sponsor or LSA/LSB number, that might also be useful. Ask a reference librarian at the archives to find and retrieve the relevant file for you.

10. Newspaper Articles

Although unlikely to be persuasive to a court, newspaper articles from the time when the legislation was introduced and debated may provide context about the legislation. Articles from the *Des Moines Register*, which is the largest newspaper in the state and located in the capital city, can be found through news databases on LexisNexis and Westlaw. Your institution or a local public library may also offer access to *Register* stories through other newspaper article indexes, such as ProQuest or Newspaper Source-EBSCO.

---

26. *See* http://www.legis.iowa.gov/LSAReports/reportsfiled.aspx.
27. Confidentiality can be waived with permission from the bill sponsor.

The Welch Matter

In the hypothetical grandparents' visitation rights scenario, you would not likely research legislative history beyond looking at the prior version of the current statute, as described in Chapter 6. Remember that the courts look to legislative intent only when the statute's meaning is unclear.

However, for purposes of illustration, we will look at the major steps of the process considering the original statute, Iowa Code § 598.35.

Because this statute was repealed in 2007, imagine you have returned to 2002, when the district court in the *Howard* case held this statute unconstitutional.

First, look at the then current (2002) *Iowa Code Annotated* to see the legislative credits and other references. Figure 7-A in the chapter appendix shows that information on Westlaw.

The information under CREDITS gives you the list of statutes creating and affecting the code section. The information under LAW REVIEW AND JOURNAL REFERENCES and LIBRARY REFERENCES leads to interpretative materials. You might look first at the referenced law review journal articles or cases. If you decided you wanted to see the statute as it was originally introduced, you would follow up on the first line of the credits, indicating it was added by Acts 1974 (65th G.A.) ch. 1253, § 1.

Next, you obtain the referenced volume of the *Acts and Joint Resolutions of the General Assembly*. It is only available in hard copy, so you would obtain it from a law library. See Figure 7-B in the chapter appendix. From the top of the act you find the bill number, SF 500.

With the bill number, you can go to the bill book to see the original bill with explanation and the bill's progress through the legislative process. The Iowa Heritage Digital Collection offers the bill book for 1974 (the 65th G.A.); search that G.A.'s legislation by bill number, as shown in Figure 7-C in the chapter appendix.

This search brings up the original bill, with explanation and its amendments, as shown in Figure 7-D in the chapter appendix. (Note: If your clients were grandparents but not blood relatives, the adopted Senate amendment striking the term "by consanguinity" could be relevant to your argument.)

IV. Iowa Bill Tracking

Proposed legislation may affect a client's situation and, therefore, the way you advise that client. The General Assembly website's "Legislation" page offers a variety of options for following legislative proposals during and after the session.[28]

A. Alert Services

The General Assembly site provides several no-fee services that will alert you to legislative actions without the need to visit the home page. You can subscribe to an RSS feed that lists newly filed legislation with the bill number and a brief description. Alternatively, you can sign up for e-mail notification of the release of a new issue of a legislative publication, including such choices as "Daily Legislation and Analysis" or "Interim Calendar and Briefing."[29] Another e-mail service will deliver committee notices, subcommittee assignments, and approved minutes.[30] You can even follow the LSA on Twitter to learn of the publication of a variety of reports.[31]

From the legislation tab on the General Assembly site, you can also register for a no-fee service called Bill/Code Watch. This service allows you to set up customized lists to track the legislation of a specific committee, selected bills, or any legislation that would affect a specific Iowa code chapter or section. For each list you create, you can choose from among several options to have legislative actions e-mailed to you or available upon your login.

B. Search Options

The General Assembly "Legislation" page provides several ways to search for information about proposed legislation. You can access the bill requests log to ascertain what legislation the LSA has been asked to draft for the current session. Bills may be searched by bill number, subject, legislator, committee, and status. Amendments may be

---

28. *See* http://www.legis.iowa.gov/Legislation/BillTracking/billTrackingTools.aspx.
29. *See* http://www.legis.iowa.gov/Subscribe/subscriptions.aspx.
30. *See* http://www.legis.iowa.gov/Subscribe/committeeSubscriptions.aspx.
31. Follow at http://twitter.com/IowaLSA. *See* http://www.legis.iowa.gov/Subscribe/twitter.aspx.

searched by amendment number, bill number, sponsor, or date filed. A list of all filed amendments can also be created, as can a list of all resolutions for the session. User-friendly search options offer a combination of simple search boxes and drop-down menus, enabling you to find what you want.

C. Post-Session Publications

Two LSA publications, both linked from the "Iowa Law & Rules" page, are particularly useful in reviewing the developments of a legislative session. "Enrolled Bills" provides the file number with linked text, the bill title, and the dates the legislation passed, was signed by the governor, and will take effect. A separate "Code Sections Amended" list is organized by code section and lists the action taken, the file number with linked text, the relevant part of the bill, and the date when the law becomes effective.

V. Federal Legislative Research

A. Federal Legislative Process

The federal legislative process is very similar to the Iowa process described above, with legislation arising in one chamber, going to committee before possibly being considered on the chamber floor, and, if passed, being sent to the other chamber for consideration.[32] At the federal level, however, a bill may be drafted by others besides the chamber's legislative counsel. A federal bill does not need to include an explanation.

As in Iowa, federal bills are consecutively numbered and preceded by an S. if they originate in the Senate or H.R. if they originate in the House of Representatives. Once a bill passes both houses, it is given

---

32. For a detailed consideration of the federal legislative process, see John V. Sullivan, *How Our Laws are Made* 2007, which is linked from http://thomas.loc.gov/home/lawsmade.toc.html.

a public law number indicating the Congressional session in which it passed and assigning it a chronological number. For instance, Pub. L. No. 111-148 was the 148th bill passed by the 111th Congress: the Patient Protection and Affordable Care Act.

B. Federal Legislative History

1. Federal Legislative Documents and Their Uses

The federal legislative process is much better documented than the Iowa process, which means there are more solid sources of legislative history information to consult. A brief description of some of the more important sources follows.

Bill versions. Many bills are amended multiple times before they pass. Comparing bill versions may help determine legislative intent.

Committee reports. If a committee recommends passage of a bill, it will often introduce the bill with an accompanying written committee report that includes a statement of the bill's purpose and the reasons why the committee supports it. Conference committee reports are presented as joint explanatory statements from the floor managers of both chambers as they iron out differences in bill versions passed by each chamber. This analysis of the bill makes reports one of the most important sources for determining legislative intent.

Committee hearings. Congressional committees hold public hearings on significant issues. Published transcripts, available for most hearings, record the views expressed by the people invited to testify. Transcripts may also include introductory remarks or commentary from the committee members.

Congressional debates. Since 1873, the *Congressional Record* has served as the official record of U.S. Congressional proceedings and debates. Although it documents the actions taken and speeches given in Congress, it does not provide an exact transcript. Business conducted in an abbreviated form will be reported in full, and members have the opportunity to edit their remarks. Note that the *Congressional Record* is published first as a daily version and later in a permanent, bound edition with new page numbers.

Other sources. Additional sources, such as *committee prints* and *signing statements*, may also be referenced in a legislative history. However, these are generally considered less important and will not be discussed in this chapter.

2. Compiled Legislative History

Before attempting to build your own list of a bill's legislative documents and then locate them all, it is wise to try to find a history that has already been compiled. There are several ways to search for a compiled history.

First, check a law library catalog for relevant books. See Chapter 2 for suggested catalogs and how to use them. Search under the broad subject heading "Legislative histories — United States — Bibliography" to locate finding aids like *Federal Legislative Histories: An Annotated Bibliography and Index to Officially Published Sources* by Bernard Reams or the looseleaf *Sources of Compiled Legislative Histories: A Bibliography of Government Documents, Periodical Articles, and Books, 1st Congress–94th Congress* by Nancy P. Johnson, which is also available electronically via HeinOnline.[33] Search for the name of the law to find books specifically about that act, such as *Congress and Sports Agents: A Legislative History of the Sports Agent Responsibility and Trust Act (SPARTA)* by Edmund P. Edmonds.

Second, search a major legal database. LexisNexis, Westlaw, and HeinOnline all offer collections of compiled legislative history materials. In addition, LexisNexis Congressional (now called ProQuest Congressional), a separate database which you might find in general academic libraries, as well as law school libraries, provides options for locating compiled histories as well as compiling your own.

Next, search for law review articles. Using the periodical sources described in Chapter 3, search for articles that provide an act's legislative history. Try searching for the name of the act and the term "legislative history."

---

33. *See* http://heinonline.org.

Fourth, check *United States Code Congressional and Administrative News* (USCCAN), which reprints the text of laws passed by Congress in each session as well as selected legislative history documents. USCCAN is available as a Westlaw database and in print. When using it in print, be aware that the set is divided into two main parts. Volumes labeled "Laws" reprint the acts, and volumes labeled "Legislative History" reprint select reports and statements. In addition, a separate section reprints Presidential signing statements. All of these sections are organized by public law number. USCCAN also includes a helpful legislative history table that lists the public law number, *Statutes at Large* reference, bill number, House and Senate report numbers and reporting committees, and dates of passage.

Finally, examine an annotated federal code, such as USCA or USCS, both described in Chapter 6. As with ICA, an annotated version of a federal code will provide you a rudimentary compilation of acts that have affected a code section and references to other materials of interest.

3. Finding Legislative Documents

Particularly on the web, many sources offer access to multiple types of legislative documents. Key sources include THOMAS, the Government Printing Office, the U.S. Congressional Serial Set, LexisNexis, Westlaw, and HeinOnline. Each is described briefly below.

- THOMAS. The Library of Congress maintains this federal legislative information site. It includes a wealth of documents, such as bill and resolution text, summary, and status information; roll call votes; *Congressional Record* text, and committee reports. The full text of most of the documents on THOMAS can be searched. Some coverage dates back to 1967, with the site becoming more robust for recent years. Most information is available from 1995 to the present.[34]

---

34. *See* http://thomas.loc.gov/home/abt_thom.html for links to and descriptions of the types of information THOMAS contains and the dates covered.

7 · Legislative History   185

- Government Printing Office (GPO). GPO disseminates federal information for all three branches of government. It has a wealth of legislative materials available through its Federal Digital System (FDsys).[35] Materials may also be issued in print and available through federal government document depository libraries throughout the U.S.[36]
- U.S. Congressional Serial Set. Since 1817 this government title has published Congressional reports and documents, assigning each a sequential number. Select materials from 1833–1917 are freely available online; others may be available through a subscription database or library collection.[37]
- LexisNexis. This legal research system provides access to many legislative materials, particularly from 1990 forward. In addition, LexisNexis offers a specialty product, LexisNexis Congressional (now called ProQuest Congressional), which provides indexing or full-text access to legislative materials dating back to 1789. The print counterpart, the *CIS Annual*, offers an index to Congressional publications dating back to 1970.
- Westlaw. Westlaw also offers broad access to legislative materials, beginning with the late 1980s and early 1990s. In addition, the West title *United States Code Congressional and Administrative News* (USCCAN) offers laws and selected reports starting with the 78th Congress, 2nd Session (1944). Coverage on the parallel Westlaw database, USCCAN, extends to 1948.
- HeinOnline. In addition to its U.S. Federal Legislative History Library that includes compiled legislative histories, HeinOnline offers the U.S. Congressional Document Library. For federal legislative history, this collection most notably provides access to the *Congressional Record* and its predecessors and the *Statutes at Large*.

---

35. FDsys is available at http://www.gpo.gov/fdsys/search/home.action.
36. *See* http://www.gpo.gov/libraries/ for more information about the depository program, including library locations.
37. *See* http://memory.loc.gov/ammem/amlaw/lwss.html for the documents freely available online.

See Table 7-3 for further information on where to access each of the main types of legislative documents needed to determine legislative intent. For additional guidance, consult a more detailed federal legislative history research guide, such as the Law Librarians' Society of Washington D.C. *Federal Legislative History Research: A Practitioner's Guide to Compiling the Documents and Sifting for Legislative Intent.*[38]

C. Federal Bill Tracking

The web provides an abundance of aids to track federal legislation. THOMAS, discussed in Section V.B.3., provides up-to-date information about Congressional activities. You can also get updates via RSS feed, e-mail, Facebook, and Twitter. GovTrack provides similar information but offers additional search capabilities and the ability to set up customized trackers.[39] Additional news and analysis can be found at sites like the OpenCongress blog,[40] the Congress.org news site,[41] and *Roll Call*, a nonpartisan Congressional newspaper.[42] Through a library you may be able to access other print and electronic current awareness sources, such as those created by Congressional Quarterly, Inc., a publisher specializing in coverage of the U.S. Congress.

---

38. This guide is available at http://www.llsdc.org/Fed-Leg-Hist.
39. GovTrack is available at http://www.govtrack.us.
40. *See* http://www.opencongress.com.
41. *See* http://www.congress.org.
42. *See* http://www.rollcall.com.

7 · Legislative History

Table 7-3. Selected Sources for Key Legislative History Materials

	Bills	Reports (Serial Set)	Hearings	*Congressional Record* Debate
THOMAS Main page: http://thomas.loc.gov	Summary and Status: 1973+ Full-text: 1989+	1995+	Follow THOMAS links directly to House and Senate pages and then check the committee site. Coverage varies.	Daily 1989+
GPO FDsys Main page: http://www.gpo.gov/fdsys/search/home.action	Full-text: 1993+	1995+		Daily 1994+ Perm. 1999–2001
LexisNexis Congressional (ProQuest Congressional) Subscription Database	Full-text: 1989+	1789+ through Serial Set 1990+ through House and Senate Reports	1995+	Daily: 1985+
LexisNexis Subscription Database (Legis = library; filename listed)	Full-text: Current Congress BLTEXT 1997–last session BLREC	1990+ CMTRPT	1988+	Daily: 1989+ RECORD
Westlaw Subscription Database (Filename listed)	Full-text: 1994+ CONG-BILTXT-ALL	1990+ LH Selected from 1948+ USCCAN	1993+ POLTRN	Daily: 1989+ CR
Other	GovTrack.Us www.govtrack.us 1993+	U.S. Serial Set at American Memory http://memory.loc.gov/ammem/amlaw/lwss.html 1833–1917	1993+ USTestimony	HeinOnline (subscription database) Full runs of both daily and permanent editions
			Rutgers Congressional Documents Online http://lawlibrary.rutgers.edu/gdoc/search.shtml 1970s–1998	
Year+ indicates from that year to the present.				

188   7 · Legislative History

Appendix: Iowa Legislative History Excerpts

The following exhibits illustrate the Iowa legislative history example provided in the sidebar.

Figure 7-A. Screenshot of Westlaw's 2002 Version of Iowa Code § 598.35

IA ST § 598.35
598.35. Grandparent—great-grandparent—visitation rights
(Approx. 6 pages)

CREDIT(S)

2001 Main Volume

Added by Acts 1974 (65 G.A.) ch. 1253, § 1. Amended by Acts 1987 (72 G.A.) ch. 159, § 9; Acts 1996 (76 G.A.) ch. 1041, § 1; Acts 1997 (77 G.A.) ch. 118, § 1; Acts 1998 (77 G.A.) ch. 1104, § 1.

HISTORICAL AND STATUTORY NOTES

2001 Main Volume

The 1987 amendment rewrote the section, which prior thereto read:

"The grandparents of a child may petition the district court for grandchild visitation rights when:

"1. The parents of the child are divorced, or

"2. A petition for dissolution of marriage has been filed by one of the parents of the child, or

"3. The parent of the child, who is the child of the grandparents, has died, or

"4. The child has been placed in a foster home.

"A petition for grandchild visitation rights shall be granted only upon a finding that the visitation is in the best interests of the child."

The 1996 amendment added subsec. 7 relating to a parent unreasonably refusing to allow visitation by a grandparent.

The 1997 amendment, in the section name line, inserted "great-grandparent"; in unnum. par. 1, inserted "or great-grandparent", and inserted "or great-grandchild"; in subsec. 3, inserted "or who is the grandchild of the great-grandparent,"; in subsec. 5, inserted "or who is not the grandchild of the great-grandparent"; in subsec. 6, inserted "or the great-grandparent of the child is the grandparent of the father of the child", and inserted "or the great-grandparent of the child is the grandparent of the mother of the child"; in subsec. 7, inserted "or great-grandparent", and added the second sentence relating to application of the subsection; and in unnum. par. 2, inserted "or great-grandchild" and inserted "or great-grandparent".

The 1998 amendment rewrote subsec. 6 which prior thereto read:

"6. The paternity of a child born out of wedlock is judicially established and the grandparent of the child is the parent of the father of the child or the great-grandparent of the child is the grandparent of the father of the child and the mother of the child has custody of the child, or the grandparent of a child born out of wedlock is the parent of the mother of the child or the great-grandparent of the child is the grandparent of the mother of the child and custody has been awarded to the father of the child."

LAW REVIEW AND JOURNAL COMMENTARIES

Constitutional questions regarding grandparent visitation and due process standards. 60 Mo.L.Rev. 195 (1995).

Grandparent visitation law grows up: The trend toward awarding visitation only when the child would otherwise suffer harm. Joan Catherine Bohl, 48 Drake L.Rev. 279 (2000).

LIBRARY REFERENCES

2001 Main Volume

Child Support 282.
WESTLAW Topic Nos. 76D.
Comments.

Dissolution of marriage: grandparent visitation, see Volz, 2 Iowa Practice § 31.34 (2d ed.).
Forms.

Petition for grandparent visitation, see Smith, 6 Iowa Rules Civil Procedure § 25.26 (3d ed.).

UNITED STATE SUPREME COURT

Grandparent visitation rights, substantive due process rights of parent to make decisions regarding child's best interests, see Troxel v. Granville, 2000, 120 S.Ct. 2054.

Source: Westlaw. Published with permission of West, a Thomson Reuters business.

Figure 7-B. Sample *Acts and Joint Resolutions of the General Assembly*

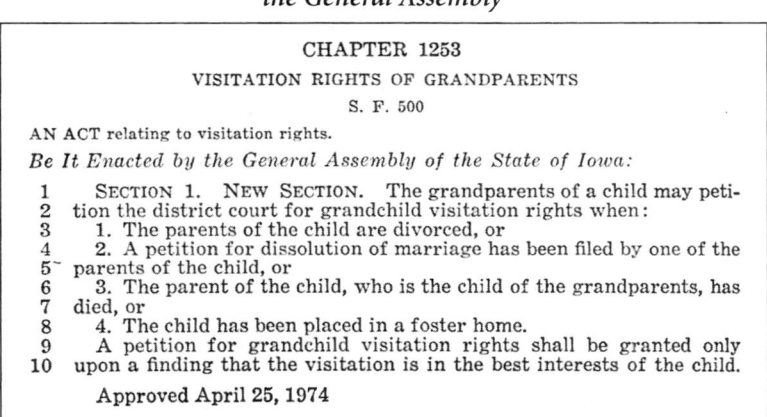

```
                         CHAPTER 1253
                 VISITATION RIGHTS OF GRANDPARENTS
                              S. F. 500
    AN ACT relating to visitation rights.
    Be It Enacted by the General Assembly of the State of Iowa:
     1     SECTION 1. NEW SECTION. The grandparents of a child may peti-
     2  tion the district court for grandchild visitation rights when:
     3     1. The parents of the child are divorced, or
     4     2. A petition for dissolution of marriage has been filed by one of the
     5  parents of the child, or
     6     3. The parent of the child, who is the child of the grandparents, has
     7  died, or
     8     4. The child has been placed in a foster home.
     9     A petition for grandchild visitation rights shall be granted only
    10  upon a finding that the visitation is in the best interests of the child.
       Approved April 25, 1974
```

Source: 1974 volume of *Acts of Joint Resolutions of the General Assembly*. Des Moines: General Assembly of Iowa.

Figure 7-C. Screenshot of Iowa Heritage Digital Collection Bill Book Search

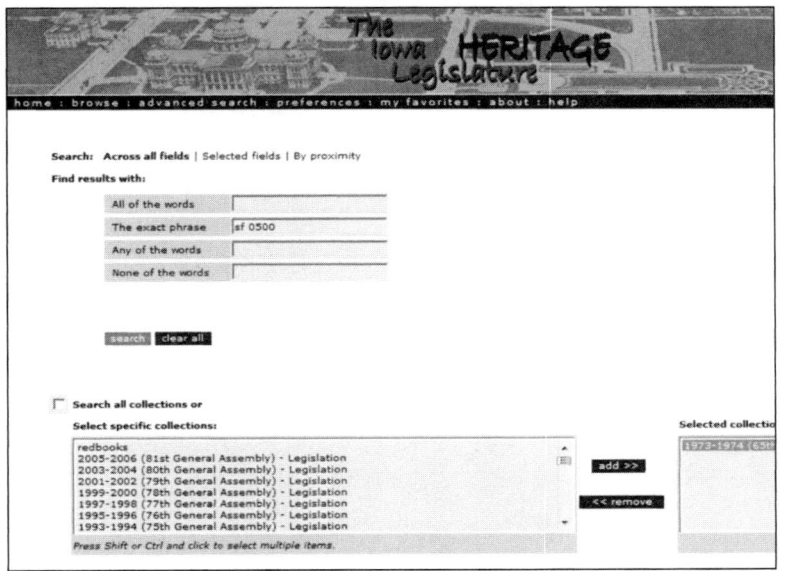

Source: Iowa Heritage Digital Collection, Iowa General Assembly. Available: http://contentdm.legis.state.ia.us/cdm4/search.php

190   7 · Legislative History

**Figure 7-D. Screenshots from the
Iowa Heritage Digital Collection**

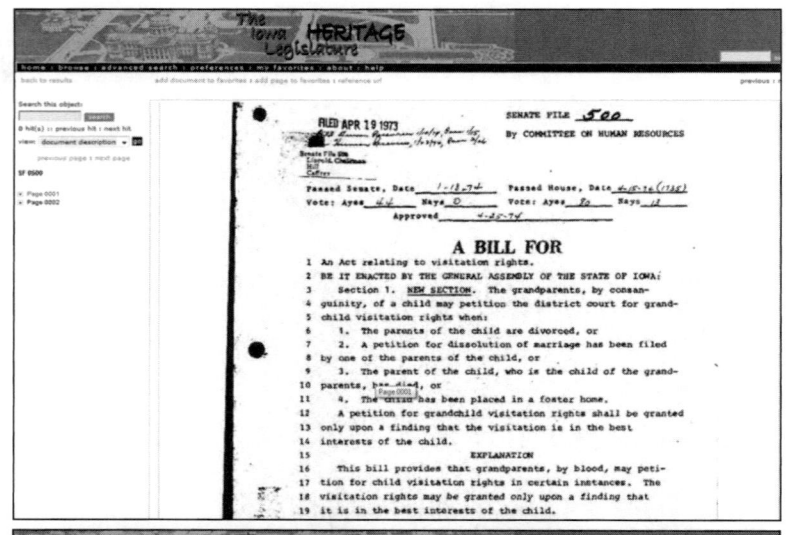

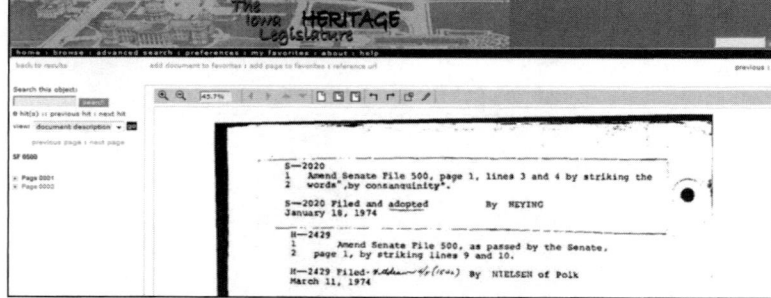

Source: Iowa Heritage Digital Collection, Iowa General Assembly. Available: http://contentdm.legis.state.ia.us/u?/65bills,4100.

Chapter 8

Administrative Law

I. Introduction

The area of administrative law consists of rules, regulations, orders, licenses, advisory opinions, and decisions that are promulgated by agencies. The Iowa General Assembly or United States Congress may delegate to an agency the authority to formulate rules or regulations through a statute. Alternatively, the Governor of Iowa or the President of the United States may delegate administrative rule-making authority through an executive order. Primarily, agencies have two types of actions: rule making and adjudication.

While statutes and many agency rules are relatively easy to access, some policies, regulations, guidelines, and decisions may be more difficult to locate. In fact, some information is never published.[1]

This chapter will cover general information about administrative agencies and rules, then move into specific information about Iowa rules followed by federal regulations. The chapter concludes with information about other documents from the executive branch, encompassing Iowa and federal agency decisions as well as executive orders and proclamations.

---

1. For example, federal agencies may have policy statements or manuals that do not require publication in the *Federal Register*. However, these documents can help the researcher determine how an agency perceives its mandate. Some agencies make this information available on their website (e.g., the Bureau of Prisons provides information at http://www.bop.gov/policy/index.jsp). Others may not make information accessible or, in some instances, even available.

II. Administrative Agencies

Although agencies are administered by the executive branch, they are generally established through enabling statutes enacted by the legislature. An *enabling statute*[2] is a law that confers powers on an executive agency to carry out delegated tasks. It dictates what the agency is permitted or forbidden to do. Agencies are created to administer and oversee government programs and to monitor and regulate certain industries. In order to perform their job, agencies promulgate *rules* or *regulations*,[3] which lay out how the laws are to be administered.

III. Administrative Rules

In operation, rules resemble statutes and are written in a format similar to statutes. Administrative agencies promulgate rules. Like statutes and judicial opinions, these rules and regulations are primary authority and have the force of law.

Administrative rules exist in part because, when a legislature passes a law, the statute may not specify all the details necessary to explain clearly how to comply with the law. The Iowa General Assembly and the U.S. Congress cannot legislate the detailed requirements of complex activities. Also, agencies have more subject-specific expertise to oversee the rules. For instance, when the U.S. Congress passed the Cigarette Labeling Act,[4] enforcement of the law was left to the Federal Trade Commission (FTC).[5] It was within the FTC's authority to

---

2. Sometimes enabling statutes are also referred to as enabling acts.

3. Both terms refer to rules originating from administrative agencies and are often used interchangeably. In Iowa, they are usually referred to as rules, while at the federal level they are normally called regulations.

4. Pub. L. No. 89-92, 79 Stat. 282 (1965).

5. 16 C.F.R. §0.4 lists 79 Stat. 282 as one of the laws that the FTC has the authority to administer. The original regulation on which the labeling act was based was reported in 29 Fed. Reg. 8325 (July 2, 1964).

determine when a cigarette manufacturer had failed to comply with the law by adding other information to the package that would negate the effectiveness of the warning label.[6]

Although both rules and statutes are primary authority, rules are subordinate to statutes. If there is any inconsistency between a rule and a statute, the statute is the prevailing authority. Also, if a statute is declared unconstitutional, a rule cannot be promulgated to remedy the deficiency in the statute.

IV. Iowa Administrative Rules

Iowa agencies are established through enabling statutes.[7] Except when otherwise expressly provided by statute, all agency rules are subject to the provisions of the Iowa Administrative Procedure Act (IAPA),[8] and the Uniform Rules on Agency Procedure.[9] The IAPA imposes a set of minimum requirements on each agency regarding access to its laws and policies. To have the force of law, agency rules must be published in the *Iowa Administrative Bulletin* and *Iowa Administrative Code*[10] unless they fall within a few specified exceptions.[11]

When beginning administrative research, it is helpful to have an idea of which agency is responsible for your area of research, because codified regulations are categorized by agency, as further discussed in Section IV.A.2. A complete list of Iowa agencies is available online[12] with links to official sites.

---

6. 30 Fed. Reg. 9485 (July 29, 1965).

7. Iowa Code §17A.23 (2009). The agency departments and their primary responsibilities are laid out in Iowa Code §7E.5 (2009).

8. Iowa Code §17A (2009).

9. The *Uniform Rules of Agency Procedure* can be found at the Iowa legislature site http://www.legis.iowa.gov/IowaLaw/AdminCode/adminLaw.aspx.

10. See Sections A. 1 and A. 2 below for locations and more detail on using these sources.

11. These exceptions are specified in Iowa Code §17A.2(11)(a–k).

12. State of Iowa Department Listing is available at http://phonebook.iowa.gov/agency.aspx.

A. Finding Iowa Rules

Iowa rules are published in two stages; they appear first in the *Iowa Administrative Bulletin* and are later organized by agency and published in the *Iowa Administrative Code*.

1. Iowa Administrative Bulletin

The *Iowa Administrative Bulletin* contains rules and proposed rules of administrative agencies and is published biweekly.[13] Issued chronologically, the *Administrative Bulletin* contains notices of intended actions, the text of rules adopted by state agencies, proclamations and executive orders of the governor, effective date delays and objections filed by the Administrative Rules Review Committee, and the agenda for monthly Administrative Rules Review Committee meetings.

Within the bulletin, underscored text indicates new material that has been added to existing rules while strike through designates deleted material. The *Iowa Administrative Bulletin* also contains other valuable information, such as a schedule for rulemaking and information about public hearings for proposed rules.

Libraries may have back issues of the bulletin, but it is no longer available in print. Issues of the bulletin from 1997 to the present are available through the Iowa legislature's website.[14] LexisNexis contains the bulletins from 1996 to the present. Westlaw has a database entitled "Iowa Regulation Tracking," which provides current information on proposed and recently adopted administrative rules.

2. Iowa Administrative Code

The *Iowa Administrative Code* (IAC) contains regulations arranged by agency. The table of contents for each agency section of the *Iowa*

---

13. The content of what is published as well as the publication schedule is set pursuant to Iowa Code chapters 2B and 17A.
14. The *Iowa Administrative Bulletin* can be found at http://www.legis.iowa.gov/IowaLaw/AdminCode/adminLaw.aspx.

Administrative Code provides references in parentheses after each rule number; see Table 8-1 for an example. These references indicate the statute that the rule implements.[15] The Iowa legislature's website also contains a Table of Rules Implementing Statutes,[16] as well as information about the fiscal impact of administrative rules.[17]

Iowa Administrative Code citations found in Iowa legal documents often follow the following structure: [agency number] IAC [chapter and rule]. For example, 11 IAC 4.3 tells you that 11 is the agency, in this case the Administrative Services Department, 4 is the chapter, Public Records and Fair Information Practices, and .3 is the rule, Requests for access to records. To reference a specific rule, the citation is 11 IAC 4.3; for a chapter reference, the citation is 11 IAC 4. However, note that the citation required by the *Bluebook* or *ALWD Manual* would be Iowa Admin. Code r. 11-4.3 (2010).

While libraries may have back issues of the code, it is no longer generally available in print.[18] The IAC is available from 1998 to the present via the Iowa legislature's website.[19] LexisNexis contains the code from 2004 to the present; a statement of how current the information is can be found at the top of the page. Westlaw contains the code from 2002 to the present; click on "Currentness" to determine when a particular rule was last updated on Westlaw.

---

15. These references are provided in accordance with Iowa Code § 7.17.

16. The Table of Rules Implementing Statutes is found at http://www.legis.iowa.gov/IowaLaw/AdminCode/adminLaw.aspx.

17. "House File 636 (Legislative Services Agency Consolidation Act), passed during the FY 2003 legislative session, requires the Legislative Services Agency (LSA) to analyze the fiscal impact of all administrative rules with an impact of $100,000 or more and provide a summary of the impact to the Administrative Rules Review Committee (ARRC)." http://www.legis.iowa.gov/IowaLaw/AdminCode/fiscalAnalysisProposedRules.aspx.

18. Only the Administrative Code Office now has an official print copy. Information about the office can be obtained at http://www.legis.iowa.gov/Agencies/nonPartisanStaff.aspx.

19. The *Iowa Administrative Code* is available at http://www.legis.iowa.gov/IowaLaw/AdminCode/adminLaw.aspx.

Table 8-1. Example from the Table of Contents of the *Iowa Administrative Code*

ADMINISTRATIVE SERVICES DEPARTMENT[11]
[Created by 2003 Iowa Acts, House File 534, section 2]
TITLE I
GENERAL DEPARTMENTAL PROCEDURES
CHAPTER 1
DEPARTMENT ORGANIZATION

1.1(8A) Creation and mission
1.2(8A) Location
1.3(8A) Director
1.4(8A) Administration of the department

CHAPTERS 2 and 3
Reserved
CHAPTER 4
PUBLIC RECORDS AND FAIR INFORMATION PRACTICES

4.1(8A,22) Definitions
4.2(8A,17A,22) Statement of policy, purpose and scope
4.3(8A,22) Requests for access to records
4.4(8A,17A,22) Access to confidential records
4.5(8A,17A,22) Requests for treatment of a record as a confidential record and its withholding from examination
4.6(8A,22) Procedure by which a person who is the subject of a record may have additions, dissents, or objections entered into a record
4.7(8A,17A,22) Consent to disclosure by the subject of a confidential record
4.8(8A,17A,22) Notice to suppliers of information
4.9(8A,22) Disclosures without the consent of the subject
4.10(8A,22) Routine use
4.11(8A,22) Consensual disclosure of confidential records
4.12(8A,22) Release to subject
4.13(8A,22) Availability of records
4.14(8A,22) Personally identifiable information
4.15(8A,22) Other groups of records
4.16(8A,22) Data processing systems
4.17(8A,22) Applicability
4.18(8A) Agency records

Source: Iowa Admin. Code Administrative Services Dept. Table of Contents p.1 (2010), http://www.legis.iowa.gov/DOCS/ACO/IAC/LINC/12-29-2010.Agency.11.pdf.

B. Researching Iowa Rules

Most researchers begin researching Iowa administrative rules in one of four ways: searching the administrative code index, starting with an annotated statutory code, searching the IAC by *Code of Iowa* section number, or conducting an advanced word search electronically. The first approach is similar to statutory research. Begin by generating a list of terms, using the TARPP or journalist techniques discussed in Chapter 1. Then, search for these keywords in the index[20] to the administrative code. Because the *Iowa Administrative Code* is organized by agency rather than subject, your topic may appear in more than one chapter. Using the index to find your research terms ensures you will find all relevant references. The sidebar on the Welch Matter and Figures 8-1 through 8-3 demonstrate this approach.

The Welch Matter

Regarding the grandparent visitation scenario, if you wanted to expand your research to include regulations, you could do so following the steps outlined in Section IV.B. Figures 8-1 through 8-3 illustrate this procedure.

Assume there is a question as to how financial support for the minor might be affected by a change in visitation. Even though the father is dead, you would likely want to investigate whether the granting of visitation rights might give rise to a financial obligation.

Try to locate your keywords in the index to the administrative code, Figure 8-1. For example, under "Children," there is a "Support" subheading that might be relevant. Next to the "Credits" entry, 441 is directing you to the agency number while 95.3 and 99.4(5) are the rules within that agency.

Locating the agency reference number in the *Iowa Administrative Code* (Figure 8-2), you see that 441 is the number for the Human Services Department, whose rules are accessible in PDF and RTF formats.

You would check both referenced rules to see if they apply to your case. 99.4(5) (Figure 8-3) addresses "extraordinary visitation adjustment" and may be relevant.

---

20. The index to the *Iowa Administrative Code* is located at http://www.legis.iowa.gov/IowaLaw/AdminCode/adminLaw.aspx.

Figure 8-1. Example from the Index of the
Iowa Administrative Code

```
CHIL                              Index                        IAC 4/21//10
CHILDREN (cont'd)


Placement agencies,   see Apartment Living, Supervised above; Guardianship Program above; ADOPTION; FOSTER
       CARE
Political contributions  351—4.29
Pornography, corrections facilities  201—20.6(5)
Pregnancy, adolescent,  see Adolescents above
Radiation exposure  641—40.21, 40.37, 41.2(14)f; 875—32.8(5)
Refugees  441—60.1(2), 60.7, 61.1, 61.14, 156.20(1)b(3)
Residential care  441—77.37(23), 78.41(10), 79.1(15), 83.61(1)a,k, 83.62(3)g, 83.70(3), chs 115, 116, 156.19;
       481—40.1, 57.13(1)j, 62.10"9," 63.13(1)j, see also RESIDENTIAL CARE FACILITIES
Respite care  441—77.30(5), 77.34(5), 77.37(15), 77.39(14), 156.8(7)
Runaways  441—85.25(2)c, ch 143, 156.10(1)c, 156.10(2)c; 661—ch 89
Shelter care/detention facilities  441—85.25(2)c, ch 105, 143.5, 150.3(5)a(8), 150.3(5)p, 151.22(1)b(5),
       156.10(3), 156.11(3), ch 167;  481—ch 40
Special needs,  see EDUCATION: Special Education; HUMAN SERVICES DEPARTMENT
Substance abuse,  see SUBSTANCE ABUSE
Support
   See also FAMILY INVESTMENT PROGRAM (FIP)
   Appeals/hearings  441—7.1"7," 95.13, 98.81(3), 98.97(3), 99.41(7,8), 99.61, 99.86(2), 100.7;  871—24.59(7)
   Collections
      See also Nonpayment; Overpayment this subheading below
      Accounts  441—95.24
      Contractors/attorneys, referral, costs  441—95.15, 98.121, 98.122
      Credits  441—95.3, 99.4(5)
      Lump sum settlements  441—95.5
      Services center, payments  441—ch 97
```

Source: Iowa Admin. Code Index page 12 (2010), http://www.legis.state.ia.us/ACO/Index/index.pdf.

A second research option is to look up a relevant statute in an annotated code to see if its notes reference applicable regulations. In the hypothetical grandparent visitation scenario, there are no rules referenced in the annotated code for the current relevant statute, § 600C.1. However, as noted in the Welch Matter text box, there are some regulations that may be relevant. The Welch Matter demonstrates why you cannot simply rely on references in the annotated code for all regulations applicable to a particular statute.

Because each administrative rule has to state the applicable code section,[21] if you know the section of the Iowa Code for which you are

---

21. Referenced in Section IV.A.2.

Figure 8-2. *Iowa Administrative Code*

Agency	Chapters	PDF	Analysis
Administrative Services Department [11]	View	View	View
Aging, Department on [17]	View	View	View
Agriculture and Land Stewardship Department [21]	View	View	View
Agricultural Development Authority [25]	View	View	View
General Services Department [401]	View	View	View
Human Investment Council [417]	View	View	View
Human Rights Department [421]	View	View	View
Community Action Agencies Division [427]	View	View	View
Criminal and Juvenile Justice Planning Division [428]	View	View	View
Deaf Services Division [429]	View	View	View
Persons With Disabilities Division [431]	View	View	View
Latino Affairs Division [433]	View	View	View
Status of African-Americans, Division on the [434]	View	View	View
Status of Women Division [435]	View	View	View
Status of Iowans of Asian and Pacific Islander Heritage [436]	View	View	View
Human Services Department [441]	View	View	View
Information Technology Department [471]	View	View	View
Inspections and Appeals Department [481]	View	View	View
Employment Appeal Board [486]	View	View	View
Foster Care Review Board [489]	View	View	View
Racing and Gaming Commission [491]	View	View	View

Source: Iowa Admin. Code Agency List, http://www.legis.iowa.gov/IowaLaw/AdminCode/agencyDocs.aspx.

trying to locate regulations, a third research option is to search the administrative code for the *Code of Iowa* chapter number. The only limitation to this method is that, because the rules are organized by agency, you would need to have a rough idea of what agency promulgates rules on the code section.[22]

If you are not finding your terms in the IAC index, a final research option is to do an advanced terms and connectors search on Iowa legislature's IAC page.[23] This option will allow you to bypass the

---

22. You do not need to know the agency number but can search the agency names via the agency list at http://www.legis.iowa.gov/IowaLaw/AdminCode/agencyDocs.aspx.

23. To access the Advanced Search option, from the Iowa Administrative Rules page (http://www.legis.iowa.gov/IowaLaw/AdminCode/adminLaw.aspx) click "Iowa Administrative Code Search."

Figure 8-3. Example from the *Iowa Administrative Code*

IAC 7/2/08	Human Services[441]	Ch 99, p.7

(2) The income of the parent whose location is unknown shall be determined by using the estimated median income for parents on the CSRU caseload and that parent shall be considered the custodial parent in calculating child support.

    c. When one parent is deceased or has had parental rights terminated, the method used to calculate support when one parent's location is not known shall be used. The parent who is deceased or has had parental rights terminated shall be considered the custodial parent with zero income.

    99.4(5) *Extraordinary visitation adjustment.* The extraordinary visitation adjustment is a credit to the guideline amount of child support as specified in the supreme court guidelines. The credit shall not reduce the child support amount below the minimum support amount required by the supreme court guidelines.

    The extraordinary visitation adjustment credit shall be given if all of the following apply:

    a. There is an existing order for the noncustodial parent that meets the criteria for extraordinary visitation in excess of 127 overnights per year on an annual basis for the child for whom support is sought. The order granting visitation can be a different order than the child support order. If a controlling order is determined pursuant to Iowa Code chapter 252K and that controlling support order does not meet the criteria for extraordinary visitation, there is another order that meets the criteria.

    b. The noncustodial parent has provided CSRU with a file-stamped or certified copy of the order.

    c. The court has not ordered equally shared physical care.

Source: Iowa Admin. Code r. 441-99.4(5) (2010), http://www.legis.state.ia.us/IAC.html.

index and search for your terms in the full text of the administrative code and bulletins. On the Advanced Search page, you can choose your search type in the upper right corner. Click "Boolean Search" from the "Choose Search Form" box. Then search for your terms. The only problem with this strategy is that it searches numerous Iowa publications such as the Iowa Code, Election Laws, and Iowa Court Rules. When you are perusing your list of results, be aware that many may not be from the *Iowa Administrative Code*. Use the expanders in the left column to go directly to results in the Administrative Code or Bulletin. You can also search the full text of the IAC databases in LexisNexis and Westlaw.

C. Currentness of Iowa Rules

Once you have found a relevant regulation, you need to (1) make sure the relevant regulation is still backed by current legislation; and (2) be sure the language hasn't been changed. This is a fairly straightforward procedure. First, check the *Code of Iowa* for the enabling statute.[24] Remember that the applicable Iowa Code section is noted next to the number of each rule. This step ensures that the regulation is still backed by current legislation.

On the *Iowa Administrative Code* agency list page,[25] there are a string of years at the top of the screen. Click on the link for the most recent year to see a list of the last update. Then, check the *Iowa Administrative Bulletin* issues that have been published since the last update. If both the code and the bulletin have the same date, check the most recent bulletin anyway as it lists notices on proposed rules so you can determine if your rule may be likely to change in the near future.

V. Federal Regulations

Federal administrative agencies are formed in much the same way as those in Iowa. As with Iowa, they are established and delegated authority by enabling acts. The scope of the authority of the agency, its internal organizations and procedures, and its rights of judicial review are all governed by enabling acts. The fundamental piece of legislation which dictates the actions of federal agencies is the Administrative Procedure Act (APA).[26]

One difference between Iowa and federal rules is that the latter are more readily available. In addition to the *Federal Register* (FR) and *Code of Federal Regulations* (CFR), which are discussed in Section V.A., there are many websites that contain federal regulations. The federal government provides GPO FDsys[27] as well as Regulations.gov,[28] which is the U.S. government portal for proposed and final regulations of ex-

---

24. See Chapter 6 for information on where to locate the Iowa Code.
25. The agencies are listed at http://www.legis.iowa.gov/IowaLaw/AdminCode/agencyDocs.aspx.
26. 5 U.S.C. § 551.
27. The government is phasing in GPO FDsys (http://www.gpo.gov/fdsys) and phasing out GPO Access (http://www.gpoaccess.gov).
28. Regulations.gov is located at http://www.regulations.gov.

ecutive branch agencies. Agency websites are also excellent resources for finding regulations. Many agencies' sites provide the text of the enabling statutes under which that agency operates as well as current regulations and information on proposed rules. The *United States Government Manual*,[29] the official handbook for the federal government, contains comprehensive information on the agencies of the legislative, judicial, and executive branches.

Some unofficial sites also provide access to proposed and final federal regulations. OpenRegs.com[30] contains the same information that can be found in the *Federal Register*, only in a more user-friendly format. It is an unofficial site intended to provide access to proposed and final federal regulations. One very useful feature is that it indicates when comment periods for regulations will close. The University of Virginia Library has an excellent site that links to administrative actions that are outside the scope of the CFR and FR. It can be searched by agency[31] or subject.[32]

A. Finding Federal Regulations

Federal regulations are published in two stages, first daily as the *Federal Register* (FR) and then by subject as the *Code of Federal Regulations* (CFR).

1. Federal Register

The *Federal Register*[33] is published five days a week and includes regulations, proposed rules, notices, and presidential proclamations

---

29. The *United States Government Manual* is available in print or online at http://www.gpoaccess.gov/gmanual/index.html.

30. OpenRegs.com is the brainchild of two men, Jerry Brito and Peter Snyder and is located at http://openregs.com.

31. The University of Virginia Library administrative agency list is at http://www2.lib.virginia.edu/govtinfo/fed_decisions_agency.html.

32. The University of Virginia Library administrative subject list is at http://www2.lib.virginia.edu/govtinfo/fed_decisions_subject.html.

33. The *Iowa Administrative Bulletin* is comparable to the *Federal Register*.

Figure 8-4. Example from the *Federal Register*

Dated: March 21, 2008. **Bernadette Dunham,** *Director, Center for Veterinary Medicine.* [FR Doc. E8–6601 Filed 3-28-08; 8:45 am] **BILLING CODE 4160-01-S** **DEPARTMENT OF THE TREASURY** **Alcohol and Tobacco Tax and Trade Bureau** **27 CFR Part 41** [T.D. TTB–68; Re: T.D. ATF–444 and Notice No. 912] **RIN 1513–AB38** **Puerto Rican Tobacco Products and Cigarette Papers and Tubes Shipped From Puerto Rico to the United States (2007R–368P)** **AGENCY:** Alcohol and Tobacco Tax and Trade Bureau, Treasury. **ACTION:** Final rule (Treasury decision). **SUMMARY:** The Alcohol and Tobacco Tax and Trade Bureau is adopting as a final rule, with some clarifying changes and editorial corrections, the temporary regulations set forth in T.D. ATF–444. These temporary regulations eliminated the onsite preshipment inspection of, and the requirement to complete several ATF forms for, shipments to the United States of tobacco products and cigarette papers and tubes manufactured in Puerto Rico. **DATES:** *Effective Date:* March 31, 2008. **FOR FURTHER INFORMATION CONTACT:** Amy R. Greenberg, Regulations and Rulings Division, Alcohol and Tobacco	Tax and Trade Bureau, 1310 G Street, NW., Suite 200E, Washington, DC 20220; telephone 202-927-8210; or e-mail *Amy.Greenberg@ttb.gov*. **SUPPLEMENTARY INFORMATION:** **Background** Chapter 52 of the Internal Revenue Code of 1986 (IRC) pertains to the Federal excise tax on tobacco products and cigarette papers and tubes. Section 5701 of the IRC (26 U.S.C. 5701) imposes a tax on such products manufactured in, or imported into, the United States. Section 7652(a) of the IRC (26 U.S.C. 7652(a)) imposes the same tax, with certain exceptions not pertinent here, on articles of merchandise of Puerto Rican manufacture coming into the United States and withdrawn for consumption or sale. The Alcohol and Tobacco and Trade Bureau (TTB) is responsible for administering the provisions of chapter 52 and section 7652(a) of the IRC as they pertain to the tax on tobacco products and cigarette papers and tubes, including promulgating regulations concerning payment and collection of the tax and other requirements that protect the revenue. Prior to January 24, 2003, our predecessor agency, the Bureau of Alcohol, Tobacco and Firearms (ATF) administered these regulations. On March 8, 2001, ATF published in the Federal Register (66 FR 13849) a temporary rule, T.D. ATF–444, amending the regulations in 27 CFR part 275 to eliminate certain regulatory requirements related to the shipment of tobacco products and cigarette papers and tubes of Puerto Rican manufacture	from Puerto Rico to the United States. Specifically, ATF amended §§ 275.105, 275.106, 275.110, and 275.111 to eliminate the requirement that persons who ship tobacco products and cigarette papers and tubes of Puerto Rican manufacture from Puerto Rico to the United States notify ATF prior to the shipment, and to eliminate the requirements that an ATF officer: (1) Inspect each shipment of such articles; (2) certify that the amount of tax on the articles has been calculated correctly; and (3) release each shipment. The amended regulations set forth recordkeeping requirements in place of the former processes of notification, physical inspection, certification, and release. Under the temporary rule, persons who ship Puerto Rican tobacco products and cigarette papers and tubes to the United States must keep and maintain records to show that the amount of tax is correctly calculated, paid (where applicable), and recorded for audit and examination purposes. The temporary rule amendments to §§ 275.106, 275.110, and 275.111 also eliminated the requirements for the completion of four specific forms. Two forms, ATF forms 2987 (5210.8) and 3075 (5200.9), were required to be submitted to ATF by the company shipping the products to the United States, and contained information readily available from common commercial records. The elimination of these forms was intended to relieve the taxpayer of a duplicative recordkeeping requirement. The other two forms, ATF forms 2989 and 3074 (5200.6), were certificates which were prepared by ATF officers and affixed to the outside

Source: Puerto Rican Tobacco Products and Cigarette Papers and Tubes Shipped from Puerto Rico to the United States, 73 Fed. Reg. 16755 (Mar. 31, 2008) (to be codified at 27 C.F.R. pt. 41).

and executive orders. It has a continuous page count for the entire year, and regulations are printed as they are promulgated. It contains extensive background information about regulation changes that is not available in the CFR, making the *Federal Register* an invaluable resource in understanding regulations and the policies behind them. (See Figure 8-4 for an example.)

The *Federal Register* includes two finding aids. One is the *Federal Register Index*, a separately issued, monthly publication that arranges entries by agency. The issues cumulate throughout the year. Also, a "CFR Parts Affected" section in each daily edition of the *Federal Register* indicates when an entry affects a part of the CFR. This section cumulates daily throughout the month.

The *Federal Register* is available in print and online. In print, check the catalog of your local library to determine its holdings. The FR is available not only at law libraries; any library that is a federal depository[34] should have print holdings. Online, the Government Printing Office (GPO) provides free access to the FR from 1994 to the present.[35] LexisNexis and Westlaw both provide access to the *Federal Register* although their coverage dates vary.[36] HeinOnline provides full-text access from 1936 to the present. Due to delays in the receipt of the paper edition, you can normally find more recent issues of the *Federal Register* on the Internet rather than in print.

2. Code of Federal Regulations

The *Code of Federal Regulations* (CFR)[37] is the codified form of all final regulations that have already been published in the *Federal Register* and that are currently in effect. The regulations are contained in fifty subject-specific titles, numbered one through fifty. Most agencies will have all of their rules in the same title. An example of a citation to the CFR is: 7 CFR § 319.76 (1999), where 7 refers to the CFR title number[38] and 319.76 is the section number.

The CFR is updated annually, but the updating process occurs throughout the year and not always on schedule. Technically, Titles 1–16 are updated January 1; titles 17–27 are updated April 1; titles 28–41 are updated July 1; and titles 42–50 are updated October 1. In print, the color on the paperback binding changes each year, providing a quick way to tell if a particular volume has been updated yet.

---

34. To find the federal depository nearest you, visit http://www.gpo.gov/libraries.

35. The *Federal Register* is located at http://www.gpoaccess.gov/fr (which is being phased out) and http://www.gpo.gov/fdsys (which is being phased in).

36. LexisNexis contains the *Federal Register* from 1980 to the present; Westlaw contains 1936 to the present.

37. While the *Iowa Administrative Bulletin* is comparable to the *Federal Register*, the *Iowa Administrative Code* is not analogous to the *Code of Federal Regulations* because the latter is arranged by topic or subject, not agency.

38. Note that not all of the fifty subject-specific titles of the CFR are identical to the fifty titles in the USC.

There are several finding aids for the CFR. Like the rest of the set, the volume entitled "Index and Finding Aids" is revised annually (see Figure 8-5 for an example). This volume contains a subject index as

Figure 8-5. Example of the *Code of Federal Regulations* Index and Finding Aids

---

Child support
Army Department; family support, child custody, and paternity, 32 CFR 584
Coast Guard personnel, allotments from active duty pay for certain support obligations, 33 CFR 54
Commerce Department, legal proceedings, 15 CFR 15
Enforcement programs
  Annual State self-assessment review and report, 45 CFR 308
  Comprehensive Tribal child support enforcement programs, 45 CFR 309, 45 CFR 310
  Computerized support enforcement systems, 45 CFR 307
  Operations standards, 45 CFR 303
  Program performance measures, standards, financial incentives, and penalties, 45 CFR 305
  State grants, Federal financial participation, 45 CFR 304
  State plan approval and grant procedures, 45 CFR 301
  State plan requirements, 45 CFR 302
Federal Retirement Thrift Investment Board, thrift savings plan, court orders and legal processes affecting accounts, 5 CFR 1653

Source: C.F.R. Index and Finding Aids Volume, page 107 (2009).

well as parallel tables of authorities including citations to the USC, the *Statutes at Large*, Public Laws, and Presidential documents. Another useful aid is the *List of CFR Sections Affected* (LSA), which is issued monthly and cumulates throughout the year. The LSA must be checked to make sure your section has not changed since being published.

The CFR is available in print or online. (See Figure 8-6 for an example of CFR in print.) In print, the same availability information as the *Federal Register* applies: check the catalog of your local library to determine its holdings. Online, the Government Printing Office provides free access to the full text from 1996 to the present.[39] While the online text is only updated as frequently as the print version, it is an official version. Another government option is the e-CFR,[40] which is updated daily and, although not an official version, is the most current of all the resources mentioned here. On the open web, FindLaw provides access to the CFR but it may not be as current as the GPO site.[41] Databases LexisNexis and Westlaw, contain the full text of the CFR, although their coverage dates vary.[42] HeinOnline contains the full text from 1938 to the present. Although commercial publishers update the text of the CFR more frequently than the federal government, they are not official versions.

B. Researching Federal Regulations

As with Iowa regulatory research, federal regulation research operates somewhat like statutory research. Before you begin your re-

---

39. The CFR is located at http://www.gpoaccess.gov/cfr (which is the process of being phased out) and http://www.gpo.gov/fdsys (which is being phased in).
40. E-CFR is located at http://www.gpoaccess.gov/ecfr.
41. FindLaw's CFR is at http://www.findlaw.com/casecode/cfr.html.
42. LexisNexis contains the CFR from 1981 to the present, while Westlaw contains 1984 to the present.

Figure 8-6. Example from the *Code of Federal Regulations*

Pt. 640

Blacktip shark, *Carcharhinus limbatus*
Blueline tilefish, *Caulolatilus microps*
Bonnethead shark, *Sphyrna tiburo*
Bull shark, *Carcharhinus leucas*
Cubera snapper, *Lutjanus cyanopterus*
Dog snapper, *Lutjanus jocu*
Finetooth shark, *Carcharhinus isodon*
Gag grouper, *Mycteroperca microlepis*
Lane snapper, *Lutjanus synagris*
Lemon shark, *Negaprion brevirostris*
Mangrove snapper, *Lutjanus griseus*
Marbled grouper, *Dermatolepis inermis*
Misty grouper, *Epinephelus mystacinus*
Mutton snapper, *Lutjanus analis*
Nurse shark, *Ginglymostoma cirratum*
Queen snapper, *Etelis oculatus*
Red grouper, *Epinephelus morio*
Red hind, *Epinephelus guttatus*
Red snapper, *Lutjanus campechanus*
Rock hind, *Epinephelus adscensionis*
Sand tilefish, *Malacanthus plumieri*
Sandbar shark, *Carcharhinus plumbeus*
Schoolmaster snapper, *Lutjanus apodus*
Silk snapper, *Lutjanus vivanus*
Snowy grouper, *Epinephelus niveatus*
Speckled hind, *Epinephelus drummondhayi*
Spinner shark, *Carcharhinus brevipinna*
Tiger shark, *Galeocerdo cuvieri*
Tilefish, *Lopholatilus chamaeleonticeps*
Vermilion snapper, *Rhomboplites aurorubens*
Warsaw grouper, *Epinephelus nigritus*
Yellowedge grouper, *Epinephelus flavolimbatus*
Yellowfin grouper, *Mycteroperca venenosa*
Yellowtail snapper, *Ocyurus chrysurus*

[64 FR 29135, May 28, 1999 as amended at 71 FR 58174, Oct. 2, 2006]

PART 640—SPINY LOBSTER FISHERY OF THE GULF OF MEXICO AND SOUTH ATLANTIC

Subpart A—General Provisions

Sec.
640.1 Purpose and scope.
640.2 Definitions.
640.3 Relation to other laws.
640.4 Permits and fees.
640.5 Recordkeeping and reporting. [Reserved]
640.6 Vessel and gear identification.
640.7 Prohibitions.
640.8 Facilitation of enforcement.
640.9 Penalties.

Subpart B—Management Measures

640.20 Seasons.
640.21 Harvest limitations.
640.22 Gear and diving restrictions.
640.23 Bag/possession limits.
640.24 Authorized activities.
640.25 Adjustment of management measures.
640.26 Tortugas marine reserves.

50 CFR Ch. VI (10-1-09 Edition)

640.27 Spiny lobster import prohibitions.
FIGURE 1 TO PART 640
AUTHORITY: 16 U.S.C. 1801 *et seq.*

EDITORIAL NOTE: Nomenclature changes to part 640 appear at 74 FR 1152, Jan. 12, 2009.

Subpart A—General Provisions

§ 640.1 Purpose and scope.

(a) The purpose of this part is to implement the Fishery Management Plan for the Spiny Lobster Fishery of the Gulf of Mexico and South Atlantic prepared by the South Atlantic and Gulf of Mexico Fishery Management Councils under the Magnuson-Stevens Act.

(b) This part governs conservation and management of spiny lobster and slipper (Spanish) lobster in the EEZ in the Atlantic Ocean and Gulf of Mexico off the Atlantic and Gulf of Mexico states from the Virginia/North Carolina border south and through the Gulf of Mexico. This part also governs importation of spiny lobster into any place subject to the jurisdiction of the United States.

(c) An owner or operator of a vessel that has legally harvested spiny lobsters in the waters of a foreign nation and possesses spiny lobster, or separated tails, in the EEZ incidental to such foreign harvesting is exempt from the requirements of this part 640, except for § 640.27 with which such an owner or operator must comply, provided proof of lawful harvest in the waters of a foreign nation accompanies such lobsters or tails.

[74 FR 1151, Jan. 12, 2009]

§ 640.2 Definitions.

In addition to the definitions in the Magnuson-Stevens Act and in § 620.2 of this chapter, the terms used in this part have the following meanings:

Bully net means a circular frame attached at right angles to the end of a pole and supporting a conical bag of webbing. The webbing is usually held up by means of a cord which is released when the net is dropped over a lobster.

Carapace length means the measurement of the carapace (head, body, or front section) of a spiny lobster from the anteriormost edge (front) of the groove between the horns directly above the eyes, along the middorsal

Source: 50 C.F.R. 640 (2009).

Table 8-2. Researching Federal Regulations

1.	Search the CFR to locate keywords on your topic.
2.	Search an annotated code for statutes related to your regulation.
3.	Search for cases that have examined the regulation.
4.	If you feel you need more information, look for law review articles and treatises that have addressed the regulation.

search, it is helpful to have an idea of what agency would have jurisdiction over your issue as well as the structure of the agency, both of which can be found in the *United States Government Manual*.[43] This information can aid in interpreting the regulation.

The first step is to search the CFR to locate keywords on your topic. In print, you can look up your terms in the Index and Finding Aids volume. Online, you can search for your keywords via full-text or the index[44] in any source (see Section V.A.2.) that contains the CFR.

After you have checked the CFR, you should search in an annotated code. Because regulations are used to implement statutes, annotated codes frequently include references to applicable regulations. *United States Code Annotated* (USCA) is available in print or via Westlaw. *United States Code Service* (USCS) is available in print or via LexisNexis and contains more extensive regulatory annotations than USCA. The USCS also has a table volume which provides citations for related statutes and regulations. References to the relevant sections of the CFR follow the text of the section in both the USCA and USCA.[45] See Table 8-2 for a streamlined explanation of researching federal regulations.

---

43. The *United States Government Manual* is available in print or online at http://www.gpoaccess.gov/gmanual/index.html.

44. Note that LexisNexis and FindLaw do not have an index search but GPO, Westlaw, and HeinOnline do.

45. See Chapter 6 for more detailed information on statutes.

The next step in administrative research is to search for cases, law review articles, or other texts that have examined a regulation. One of the most convenient ways to find court decisions is to use Westlaw's version of the CFR. It is annotated, like the USCA, and includes notes, decisions, references to relevant agency decisions, and statutes and secondary sources. You can also use KeyCite to get the most up-to-date reference to your regulation. LexisNexis does not annotate its version of the CFR but does have Shepard's *Code of Federal Regulations Citations* if you want to find citations to decisions, law reviews, and treatises that have examined your regulation.[46]

In addition to law review articles, other secondary sources might provide more information on the regulation you are researching. Treatises, such as Pierce's *Administrative Law Treatise*,[47] are excellent research options. *American Law Report*'s volume "Table of Laws, Rules and Regulations" provides a table listing parallel citations between the CFR and ALR annotations. Looseleaf services[48] collect and reprint agency regulations in a particular subject area. These topical looseleaf services focus on the work of one of the major agencies and provide up-to-date, annotated texts of federal regulations in their subject areas. However, no looseleaf services exist for certain areas of law. To locate a looseleaf in a particular subject area, check the catalog of your local law library or ask a librarian.

C. Updating Federal Regulations

Agencies can act at any time during the year, so updating your CFR research is essential. Although it is more common to update online, the process for print is also discussed in-depth.

---

46. See Chapter 9 for more detailed information on using citators.

47. Richard J. Pierce, *Administrative Law Treatise* (5th ed., Aspen Publishers 2010).

48. Refer to Chapter 3 for more detailed information about looseleaf services.

1. Online

The fastest and easiest way to update regulations is to use the GPO access site.[49] The quarterly publication schedule for the printed volumes is followed on the GPO access site where you can update your research for free. To update regulations via the GPO site,[50] follow these steps outlined in Table 8-3.[51]

You can also update your research in LexisNexis or Westlaw, although they are not as current as the GPO site. In LexisNexis, input

Table 8-3. Updating a CFR Citation Using GPO Access

1.	Search for your regulation by citation and note the date the section was last revised.
2.	At the main page, click "List of CFR Sections Affected" and click the most recent available month to see if your section is listed. If there has been a change, the LSA will refer you to the page in the *Federal Register* where the change was published.
3.	Go back to the "List of CFR Sections Affected" page and check the link "Last Month's List of CFR Parts Affected" for your citation. (Note this step may not be necessary if the most recent month listed in step 2 is very current.)
4.	Finally, check the links "Current List of CFR Parts Affected," and "List of CFR Parts Affected Today" for your citation. These are updated daily and allow you to update your citation to the current day.

---

49. The GPO access site for the CFR is http://www.gpoaccess.gov/cfr.

50. Although GPO Access is scheduled to be phased out and replaced with GPO FDsys (http://www.gpo.gov/fdsys) currently the updating process is slightly easier via GPO access. Regardless of which site you use, the updating process is similar. The notable exception is the absence on the GPO FDsys site of "Current List of CFR Parts Affected" and "List of CFR Parts Affected Today," which are available on the GPO Access site.

51. This updating process is covered in detail in: Patrick Charles, *How Do You Update the Code of Federal Regulations Using GPO Access?*, 17 Perspectives 119 (2009).

your citation in the "Citation" box at the top of the screen; information at the top of the text will indicate when the text was last updated. In Westlaw, input your citation through the "Find & Print" link at the top of the screen; information at the bottom of the entry will tell you how current the text is. If a section has been amended since that date, a note at the top of the screen will indicate there is an update to the section. Click the "update" link to get to the full text of the amended section in the *Federal Register*.

2. In Print

Begin by locating the desired regulation in the most recently revised edition of the CFR. Then consult the most recent monthly edition of the *List of CFR Sections Affected* (LSA). Because the LSA is cumulative, you only need to check the most recent issue to determine whether any changes to a regulation have taken place since the last CFR was published.

Then go to the most recent issue of the *Federal Register* for each month not covered by the LSA. At the back of each issue is a cumulative list called "CFR Parts Affected During [month]." This listing updates the most recent edition of the LSA. You can also update your research using the LSA online at the GPO site.[52]

If the CFR section is not listed in any of these places, there are several steps you can follow to ensure you have the most up-to-date information:

- Look in the LSA to see if it has been redesignated, i.e., given a new number.
- Look in the back of the appropriate CFR volume for a Redesignation Table.
- Look in the back of the appropriate CFR volume for an LSA table by year. This will reflect any changes that have occurred since 1986.

---

52. List of Sections Affected is located at http://www.gpoaccess.gov/lsa/index.html.

VI. Other Documents from the Executive Branch

A. Decisions of Agencies

1. Iowa

As stated at the beginning of the chapter, one of the primary actions of agencies is adjudication. Some Iowa agencies hold hearings to resolve disputes arising from their regulations. Some of these decisions are available online, as listed in Table 8-4.

Table 8-4. Partial List of Iowa Agency Decisions Available on the Web

Agency	Address	Available Dates
Iowa Civil Rights Commission	http://www.iowa.gov/government/crc/statutes/contested_cases.html	1987–present
Iowa Department of Education	https://www.edinfo.state.ia.us/web/appeals.asp	1975–present
Iowa Public Employment Relations Board	http://iowaperb.iowa.gov/agency_decisions/index.html	1991–present
Iowa Workers' Compensation Decisions	http://decisions.iowaworkforce.org/workerscomp/Pages/default.aspx	2000–present

2. Federal

As in Iowa, federal agencies hold hearings to resolve disputes. While some decisions are published in agency-specific reporters, others are available via agency websites. In print, Appendix 8 of the *ALWD Citation Manual* contains a list of major official agency publications.[53] In addition, Washburn University School of Law main-

---

53. This list is also available online at http://www.alwd.org/publications/pdf/CM1_Appendix8.pdf.

tains a list of agency sites with links to their opinions.[54] LexisNexis and Westlaw both contain databases that include the decisions of some agencies. HeinOnline also has a federal agency library, which includes opinions from select administrative bodies, such as the Atomic Energy Commission, the Comptroller General of the United States, the Federal Communications Commission, the Federal Trade Commission, and the Securities and Exchange Commission.[55]

B. Executive Orders and Proclamations

1. Iowa

Executive orders and proclamations from the governor have the force of law. *Executive orders* address issues such as creating task forces and committees, budgetary matters, and state resources. These executive documents are numbered in the order in which they are issued, beginning with number one. The numbering restarts for each governor.

Executive orders of Iowa governors are available on the State Law Library of Iowa's website.[56] The online holdings currently go back to 1921, and the library is in the process of adding orders from 1846 to 1921. More general information is available at the governor's official site.[57]

Executive proclamations include things such as the proclamation of a state of emergency after a severe weather event, for example, the floods of 2008, or the proclamation that a special event will be held. Current proclamations are available via the news archive on the governor's site.[58]

---

54. The Washburn site is available at http://www.washlaw.edu/doclaw/executive5m.html.
55. HeinOnline is available at http://heinonline.org.
56. The State Law Library of Iowa list of executive orders of Iowa governors is at http://www.statelibraryofiowa.org/services/collections/law-library/govexecorders.
57. The Governor of Iowa's site is http://governor.iowa.gov.
58. Press releases are located at https://governor.iowa.gov/category/press_releases.

2. Federal

At the federal level, executive orders and proclamations have basically the same legal effect as similar documents in Iowa, but are usually used for different purposes. Executive orders are issued for routine determinations under statutory authority, and proclamations communicate ceremonial or broad policy statements. Both are numbered, in separate series, in order of issuance. Numbering does not restart with each new president.

Presidential documents are published in the *Federal Register* and codified in Title 3 of the *Code of Federal Regulations*. However, a better source is the *Daily Compilation of Presidential Documents*,[59] as it includes press releases and signing statements as well as executive orders and proclamations. It is available in Westlaw from 2000 to the present. LexisNexis has a database entitled "Executive Orders," which contains all executive orders as printed in the *Federal Register* from 1980 to the present.

---

59. The *Daily Compilation of Presidential Documents* is available at http://www.gpoaccess.gov/wcomp/index.html. As of January 29, 2009, it replaced its predecessor the *Weekly Compilation of Presidential Documents*. An archive of the weekly compilation (from 1993 to January 2009) is available at http://www.gpoaccess.gov/wcomp/index.html. Both are available via GPO FDsys (http://www.gpo.gov/fdsys), which will replace GPO Access at some time in the future. Click the "Compilation of Presidential Documents" tab for documents from 1993 to the present.

Chapter 9

Updating with Citators

I. Introduction

The law is not static. Legal authorities change as they are interpreted by courts and modified by the legislature. As courts continue to decide cases in a particular area of law, determining which case to rely upon becomes increasingly difficult. Thus, a legal researcher must be able to locate all authorities applicable to an issue in order to evaluate cases and statutes in the context of developing law. As cases are questioned, reversed, or overruled and statutes are modified, the researcher must also be able to determine the status of a legal authority and whether it remains "good law."

The process of examining how a legal authority has been interpreted or changed subsequent to its issuance is known as *updating*. Updating is often referred to as "Shepardizing" because the first major updating tool, or citator, was *Shepard's Citations*. Shepard's is now available in print and online through LexisNexis. Westlaw also has an online citator known as KeyCite. This chapter focuses on online updating because of its relative ease and efficiency. Updating in print Shepard's is discussed in the chapter appendix.

II. Purposes of Updating

As a legal researcher, you must update all authorities you intend to rely upon for two major reasons. The first reason is to fulfill *ethical* and *professional* obligations to cite the most current and applicable sources. In this case, updating is done for validity purposes. The second reason is more strategic and practical; locating all applicable sources of law helps provide the most effective representation. In this situation, updating is done for research purposes. Using a citator to verify that you are relying on good law is a *requirement* of law practice. Using a citator as a research finding tool is an *optional* approach; there are many other ways to locate relevant authority.

A. Ethical and Professional Considerations

The *Iowa Rules of Professional Conduct* require that a lawyer provide competent representation, which "requires the legal knowledge, skill, thoroughness, and preparation reasonably necessary for the representation."[1] Moreover, lawyers are prohibited from "fail[ing] to disclose to the tribunal legal authority in the controlling jurisdiction known to the lawyer to be directly adverse to the position of the client and not disclosed by opposing counsel."[2] Comments to the rules explain that a "lawyer is not required to make a disinterested exposition of the law, but must recognize the existence of pertinent legal authorities.... The underlying concept is that legal argument is a discussion seeking to determine the legal premises properly applicable to the case."[3] Updating for both validity and research helps the lawyer ensure that she is presenting the court with the most relevant legal authority.

In addition to honoring clear ethical obligations to find and cite relevant authority, highlighting applicable authority for the court helps protect a lawyer's professional reputation. Courts are not hesitant to publicly criticize a lawyer's failure to locate and identify applicable authority.[4]

---

1. Iowa R. Prof. Conduct 32:1.1.
2. Iowa R. Prof. Conduct 32:3.3.
3. Iowa R. Prof. Conduct 32:3.3 (cmt. 4).
4. *U.S. v. Barnes*, 912 F. Supp. 1187 (N.D. Iowa 1996). In *Barnes*, the court noted:
> The government's brief was most unsatisfactory, indeed misleading, in that it failed to cite the decision of the Sixth Circuit Court of Appeals in *United States v. Brown*, 988 F.2d 658 (6th Cir.1993), which is not so recent as to excuse the government's failure to find

B. Practical Considerations

Updating is a sensible, as well as ethical, practice. Using citators is an efficient and effective way to conduct legal research. Once you have located a single applicable source for a client problem, you can use a citator to locate all of the other legal sources that have cited that source. As a result, the citator will lead you to a number of additional, potentially relevant and useful authorities.

III. Updating: An Overview

As noted, this chapter will focus on using online citators—Shepard's (available on LexisNexis) and KeyCite (available on Westlaw). For most research needs, online citators are the industry standard because they are far more current and easier to use than print citators. Refer to the chapter appendix for an overview of using print Shepard's.

Using a citator requires an understanding of some basic terminology. The source that you are updating is referred to as the *cited source*. The authorities listed in the citator that refer to your cited source are known as *citing sources* or *citing references*.[5] Your cited source may be a judicial opinion, constitutional provision, statute, rule, regulation,

---

and discuss it. The *Brown* decision is critical to disposition of any motion for a preliminary injunction under 18 U.S.C. § 1345, because of its discussion of the appropriate standards and burdens of proof for issuance of such an injunction as well as such an injunction's proper scope. Thus, the government's brief is an example of the kind of gross oversight that can result from failure to update a "canned" brief, however repetitive a specialized practice may become. Merely "Shepardizing" the cases cited in the government's brief would have revealed the *Brown* decision. At worst, the government knew of the case, and intentionally failed to cite it; at best, the government was negligent in failing to find and discuss applicable case law.

Id. at 1189.

5. For ease of reading, citing sources/references will be referred to as citing references throughout.

or agency decision. As explained in Chapter 1, you might base your legal argument on any of these primary sources. Because they may have been overturned or otherwise modified by a later primary source, you need to determine whether they are still current. You can also use a citator to update certain secondary authorities, such as a law review article or ALR annotation. In this instance, your objective would likely be to identify additional authorities, rather than to verify that the source is good law, because you rarely rely upon a secondary authority in a legal argument.

The general process for using online citators is the same for both Shepard's and KeyCite. You first need to access the online citator and enter the citation of the cited source. You must then select the type of citation list you prefer. Generally, your options are a short list showing the *direct history* (e.g., how a case proceeded through the court system to its present appellate level) and *negative treatment* of the cited source (e.g., a later case that overruled or questioned your case), or a longer list that shows all citing references. You will often select the more limited list when your objective is merely to check the validity of the cited source. When using a citator for research purposes to locate additional authorities, you want to select the more extensive list. Once you have selected the display option, you can then use the features of the online citator to limit the results and determine the potential effect of the citing references on the validity and currency of the cited source. These steps are discussed more fully below.

A. Using Shepard's on LexisNexis

1. Accessing the Citator

The first step in using Shepard's on LexisNexis is to access the citator. If you are already logged on to LexisNexis, select the "Shepard's" tab at the top left of the screen. If you are currently viewing a source that you want to update, simply click on the "Shepard's" link at the top of the screen. As you first logon to LexisNexis, there is also a shortcut to enter a citation and click on the "Shepardize" radio button.

On LexisNexis you can Shepardize case law, statutes, rules and regulations, a variety of federal and state agency decisions, patents, law reviews, restatements, and more. A searchable list of materials Shepardizable online is available by clicking on the "Citation Formats" link on the Shepard's tab.

2. Selecting the Type of Citing List

If you access the Shepard's tab, your next step is to select the type of citing list you would like to display. You can either select Shepard's for Validation, which is an abbreviated list intended only to show whether the case is still good law, or Shepard's for Research, which includes a complete list of citing references. Shepard's for Research also includes all prior history of the cited source and subsequent appellate history. If you access Shepard's from the case view or the shortcut, you will default to a Shepard's for Research search.

Figure 9-1 illustrates the Shepard's for Validation results for *Santi v. Santi*, 633 N.W.2d 312 (Iowa 2001), an Iowa case in which a portion of the grandparent's visitation statute, Iowa Code § 598.35(7) (1999), was declared unconstitutional. Figure 9-2 illustrates a portion of the results for a Shepard's for Research search for *Santi*. Figure 9-3 illustrates the results for a Shepard's for Validation result for Iowa Code § 598.35(7) (1999). Note that the Iowa statute was deemed unconstitutional in its entirety in *In re Howard*, 661 N.W.2d 183 (Iowa 2003), a case that naturally appears in the results list for Shepard's for Validation and Shepard's for Research, although not in the excerpts that are shown in Figures 9-1 and 9-2.

3. Analyzing the Citing Symbols and Limiting the Search Results

Review the list of citing references for your cited source to determine the effect that subsequent authorities have had on your cited source. Several features make this review an effective, efficient process. The first is the Shepard's Signal Indicator, which provides a symbol to show whether the cited source is still respected authority. At the top of the screen, a symbol to the left of the title of the cited

220   9 · Updating with Citators

Figure 9-1. Shepard's for Validation: *Santi v. Santi*, 633 N.W.2d 312 (Iowa 2001)

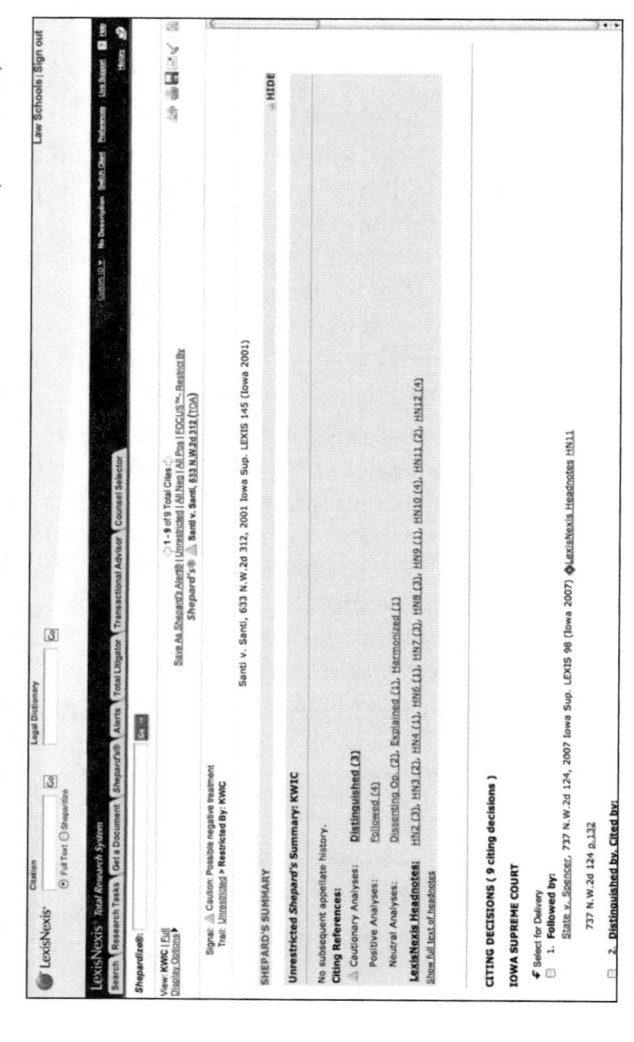

Source: Copyright 2009 LexisNexis, a division of Reed Elsevier Inc. All Rights Reserved. LexisNexis and the Knowledge Burst logo are registered trademarks of Reed Elsevier Properties Inc. and are used with the permission of LexisNexis.

9 · Updating with Citators 221

Figure 9-2. Shepard's for Research: *Santi v. Santi*, 633 N.W.2d 312 (Iowa 2001)

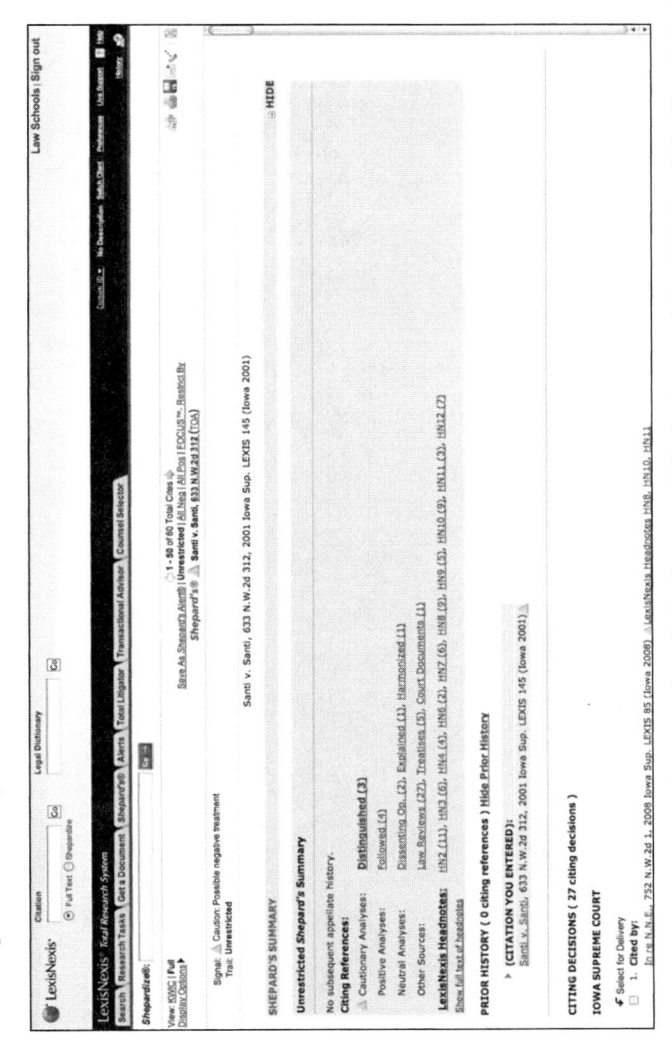

Source: Copyright 2009 LexisNexis, a division of Reed Elsevier Inc. All Rights Reserved. LexisNexis and the Knowledge Burst logo are registered trademarks of Reed Elsevier Properties Inc. and are used with the permission of LexisNexis.

222 9 · Updating with Citators

Figure 9-3. Shepard's for Validation: Iowa Code § 598.35(7) (1999)

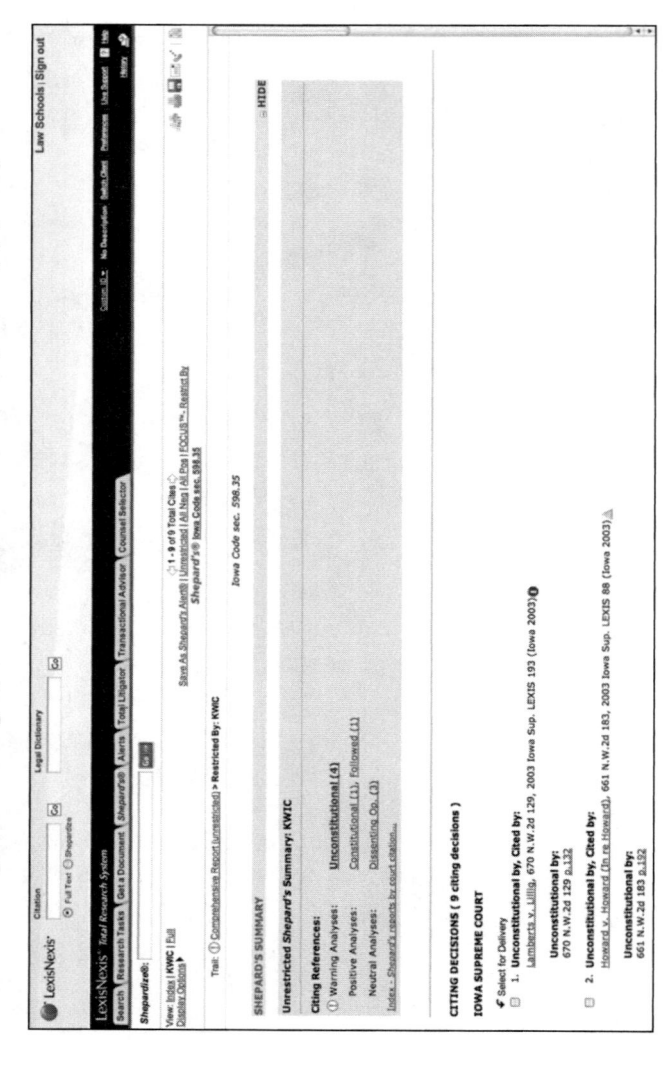

Source: Copyright 2009 LexisNexis, a division of Reed Elsevier Inc. All Rights Reserved. LexisNexis and the Knowledge Burst logo are registered trademarks of Reed Elsevier Properties Inc. and are used with the permission of LexisNexis.

Table 9-1. Shepard's Signal Indicators

Red stop sign
   Warning: Negative treatment is indicated

Red circle with exclamation mark
   Warning: Negative case treatment is indicated for a statute

Yellow square with black, capital Q
   Questioned: Validity is questioned by citing references

Yellow triangle
   Caution: Possible negative treatment

Teal diamond with + sign
   Positive treatment is indicated

Blue circle with white, capital A
   Cited and neutral analysis is indicated

Blue circle with white, capital I
   Citation information available

---

authority indicates how it has been treated by citing references. To determine what a particular symbol means, simply rest your cursor over the symbol. To access a full list of symbols and their meanings, scroll to the bottom of any Shepard's screen for a legend. A list of symbols and their meanings is provided in Table 9-1. As an example, Figure 9-3 shows the *Lamberts* case overturned the cited statute as unconstitutional.

Second, within the list of citing references, the Shepard's Signal Indicator provides a symbol to designate the status of each case. This symbol appears to the right of the citation of the citing reference.[6] Reviewing these symbols can reveal hidden weaknesses in a line of cases. Assume that you were Shepardizing a case that had received only positive treatment from its citing references, but each of those

---

6. In the event you Shepardize an authority and the symbol indicators do not appear, go to the top left of the screen and click on "Display Options." One of the options is "Citing Ref. Signals." When you select this, a check mark should appear. When you refresh your screen, the symbols for the citing references should appear.

citing cases had received negative treatment. If the negative treatment was based on analysis in those cases that is similar to the analysis in your cited case, you might want to reconsider relying on that analysis.

Recognize that you cannot rely entirely on the symbol indicator for your cited source to determine whether your case is valid for the point of law in which you are interested. Most cases contain more than one legal issue, and a symbol indicator on a source may be related to an issue that has nothing to do with your interest in the source. Therefore, your case may have a red stop sign signal indicating strong negative treatment, but for an issue unrelated to your research. Your cited source may still be good law for the issue related to your research, notwithstanding the red stop sign signal. It is your responsibility, therefore, to read the citing references and to determine for yourself how they affect the validity of your cited source.

Another helpful feature for online Shepard's is "Focus-Restrict By." This can be accessed through a link at the top of any Shepard's page. This feature allows you to limit the citing references by their analysis of your cited source, their jurisdiction, or headnote. Additionally, you can use the Focus feature to find issues or facts that are located in the text of the citing references. The Focus feature in Shepard's works in the same manner as Focus in other research using LexisNexis—you simply type your search terms in the Focus text box to locate a subset of documents from your original Shepard's citing references list that contain the search terms you entered. You will receive a list of citing references that include your search terms. You can click on any of these sources to move directly to the text that contains the Focus search terms. The Focus feature is illustrated in Figure 9-4.

Finally, note the option "Save as Shepard's Alert." This feature provides several choices for monitoring the status of your cited source and automatically receiving updates at the frequency you specify.

4. Reading and Analyzing the Citing References

Note that simply processing a request for a cited source on a citator is not sufficient to validate a source. As noted, you must analyze

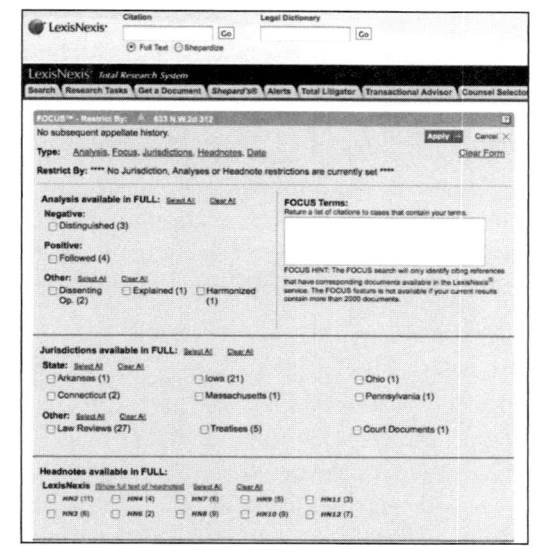

Figure 9-4. Focus Feature on Shepard's

Source: Copyright 2009 LexisNexis, a division of Reed Elsevier Inc. All Rights Reserved. LexisNexis and the Knowledge Burst logo are registered trademarks of Reed Elsevier Properties Inc. and are used with the permission of Lexis-Nexis.

the results that the citator retrieves. The symbols are a good, preliminary indication of how a citing reference may affect the validity of your cited source, but remember that the citing reference may challenge the validity of a point of law in your cited source that is not relevant to your research. In this respect, limiting the results by headnote can focus your evaluation of search results to cases likely to be on point. Even with a more limited list, however, you must actually review citing references to determine for yourself the impact the citing reference may have on the cited source. You should typically focus first on citing references that include negative treatment, determining whether the cited source has been overruled, reversed, or modified in some manner. It is also generally good practice to focus on cases from your jurisdiction, and to read the results in chronological order to determine how the law has developed.

B. Using KeyCite on Westlaw

KeyCite is similar in many respects to Shepard's, although there is no print version of KeyCite; it is only available online on Westlaw. Also, KeyCite's coverage is somewhat more limited than that of Shepard's. KeyCite is available for all cases and statutes on Westlaw, but its coverage is less complete for administrative decisions, state regulations, and secondary sources. Content is constantly being added, and you can check KeyCite coverage by accessing the "Scope" link toward the bottom of the main KeyCite web page.

1. Accessing the Citator

There are three ways to access KeyCite once you are logged on to Westlaw. First, you can click the KeyCite link at the top of the main menu, regardless of what page of Westlaw you are viewing. Second, at the home page you can enter a citation into the "KeyCite this citation" text box on the left side of the screen. Third, when you are viewing a document, you can either click on the symbol indicating subsequent treatment located to the left of the cited source name, or you can use the KeyCite options located in a text box in the left-hand margin. The text box allows you to view the Full History, Direct History, or Citing References. You can also select "Monitor with KeyCite Alert," which monitors the status of your case or statute and automatically sends you updates at the frequency you specify.

2. Selecting the Type of Citing List

As with Shepard's on LexisNexis, you can display your KeyCite results in a number of ways. The default option when you enter a citation in KeyCite and select "Go" is the Full History, which includes the prior and subsequent history of the cited source. The first sources in this list are the prior history of the cited source,[7] followed by Negative Citing References, Related References, and Court Documents. Figure 9-5 illustrates the Full History option for the *Santi* case.

---

7. You can select "Direct History (Graphical View)" to view this information in the form of a flowchart.

9 · Updating with Citators 227

Figure 9-5. KeyCite Full History: *Santi v. Santi*, 633 N.W.2d 312 (Iowa 2001)

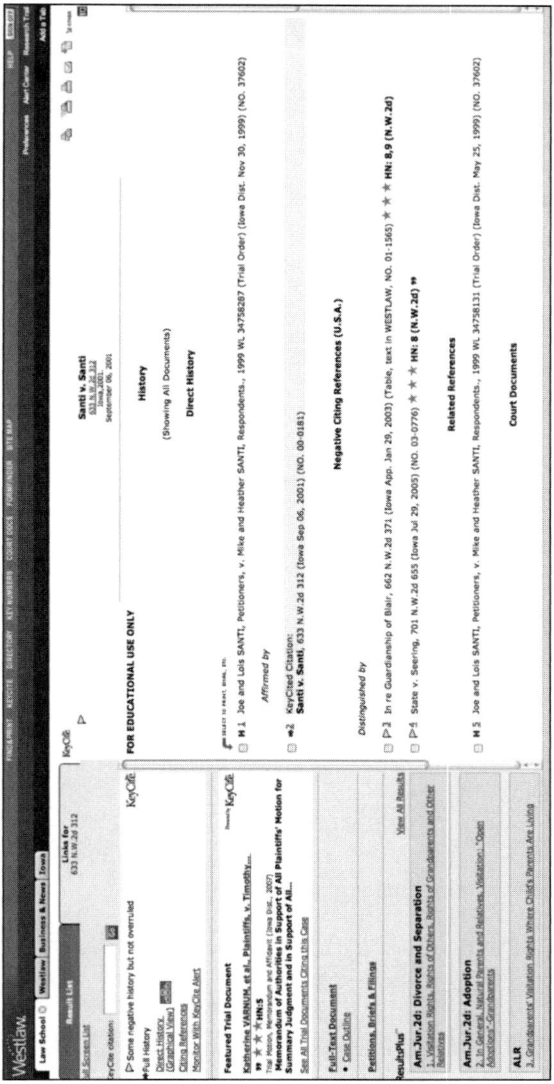

Source: Published with permission of West, a Thomson Reuters business.

You can view a more extensive list of citing references by selecting the Citing References link on the left hand side of the screen. Figure 9-6 illustrates this option for *Santi*. As you can see, this option first displays the citing references that have treated your cited source negatively, followed by non-negative citing references. The non-negative citing references are organized by Depth of Treatment stars. These indicate how extensively the citing reference addresses the cited source, ranging from four stars (examined), indicating an extended discussion of the cited source, to one star (mentioned), indicating that the cited source was briefly referenced.

You can also use KeyCite for statutes. Figure 9-7 illustrates the citing references for Iowa Code § 598.35(7) (1999). Note that the Iowa statute was deemed unconstitutional in its entirety in *In re Howard*, 661 N.W.2d 183 (Iowa 2003), the first case that appears in the citing references list.

3. Analyzing the Citing Symbols and Limiting the Search Results

As with Shepard's, KeyCite uses symbols to designate the status of sources that can be updated. The symbol appears in the left frame as well as to the left of the title of the source and can be used as a quick reference to help you determine whether the source is good law. Symbols also precede citing references in KeyCite. These symbols speak to the validity of the citing references themselves. Again, if your cited case is supported by cases that themselves have received negative treatment because of similar analysis, then you might not want to base your argument on that analysis. Figure 9-8 illustrates KeyCite's signal indicators and their meaning.

As with Shepard's, you can limit KeyCite search results to focus on the authorities that are most relevant to your research by accessing the "Limit KeyCite Display" box in the bottom-left of the right KeyCite frame. There, you can limit your citing references by document type, headnote, jurisdiction, date, or depth of treatment. You can also use the "Locate" feature on the left-hand screen to restrict your results to only those citing references that contain specific text.

9 · Updating with Citators 229

Figure 9-6. KeyCite Citing References: *Santi v. Santi*, 633 N.W.2d 312 (Iowa 2001)

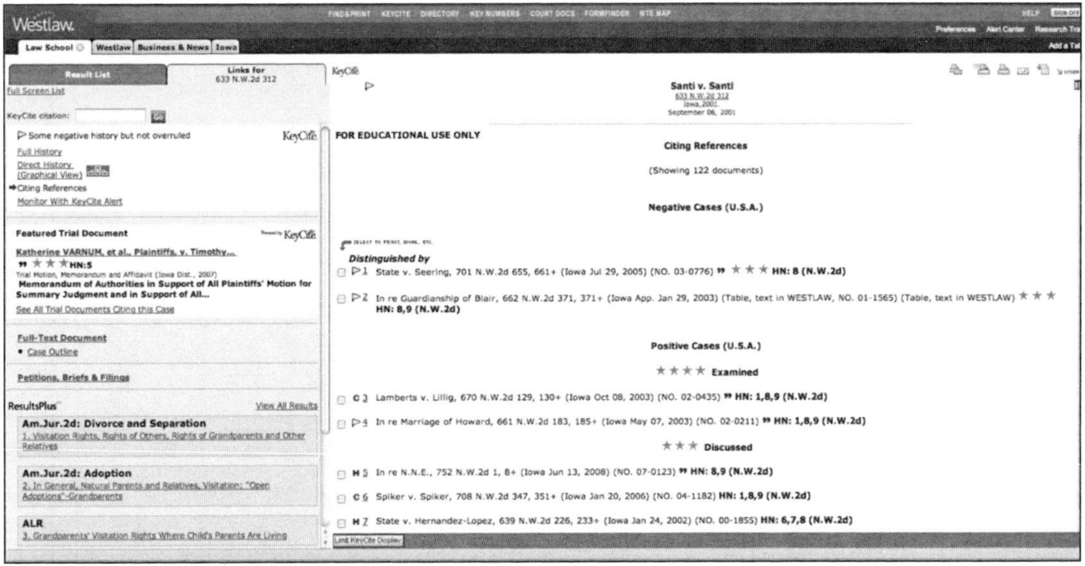

Source: Published with permission of West, a Thomson Reuters business.

230   9 · Updating with Citators

Figure 9-7. KeyCite Citing References: Iowa Code § 598.35(7) (1999)

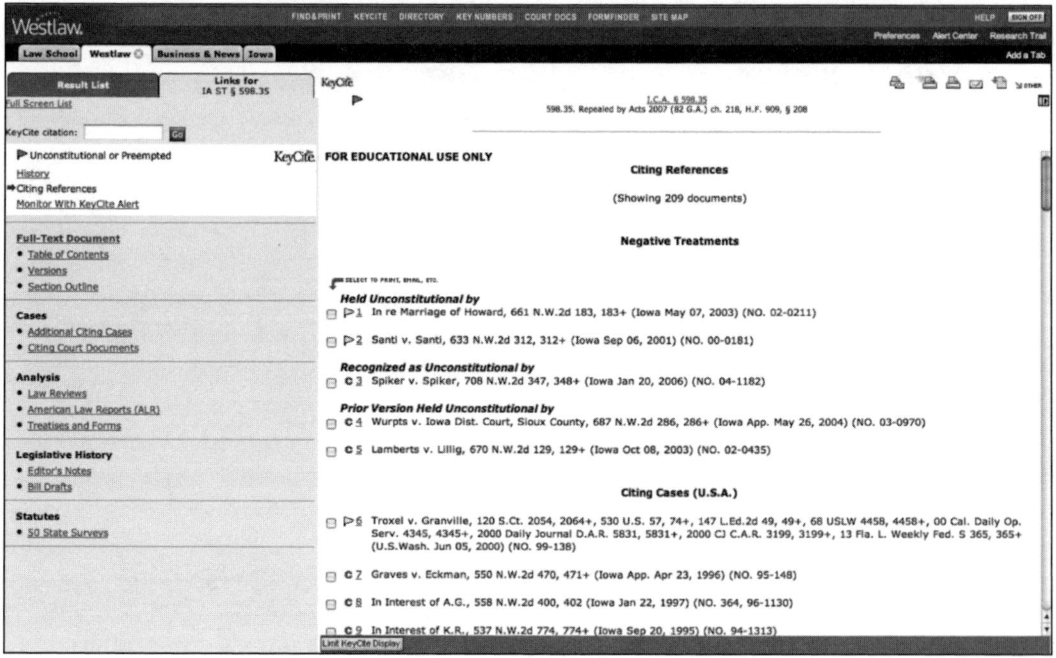

Source: Published with permission of West, a Thomson Reuters business.

9 · Updating with Citators   231

Figure 9-8. KeyCite Signal Indicators

▲
- In cases and administrative decisions, a **red flag** warns that the case or administrative decision is no longer good law for at least one of the points of law it contains.
- In patents, a **red flag** in Direct History warns that the court holds that all or part of the cited patent is invalid; that the court holds a patent to be unenforceable due the patentee's inequitable conduct before the patent board. A red flag in Negative Citing References warns that that court recognizes that a court in another case has held that the cited patent is invalid.
- In statutes and regulations, a **red flag** warns that the statute or regulation has been amended by a recent session law or rule, repealed, superseded, or held unconstitutional or preempted in whole or in part.

△
- In cases and administrative decisions, a **yellow flag** warns that the case or administrative decision has some negative treatment, but has not been reversed or overruled.
- In patents, a **yellow flag** in Direct History warns that court rules that the technology at issue does not infringe the cited patent, but does not otherwise rule on the patent's validity; or that the court upholds the validity of all or part of the cited patent, but rules that it is not infringed by the technology at issue. A yellow flag in Negative Citing References warns that the court recognizes that a court in another case has held that the cited patent has not been infringed.
- In statutes and regulations, a **yellow flag** warns that a statute has been renumbered or transferred by a recent session law; that an uncodified session law or proposed legislation affecting the statute is available (statutes merely referenced, i.e., mentioned, are marked with a green C); that the regulation has been reinstated, corrected or confirmed; or that the statute or regulation wa limited on constitutional or preemption grounds or its validity was otherwise called into doubt, or that a prior version of the statute or regulation received negative treatment from a court.

H
In cases and administrative decisions, a **blue H** indicates that there is direct history but it is not known to be negative.

In patents, a **blue H** indicates that the patent is:
- **Construed:** The court determines the meaning of words or phrases in a cited patent.
- **Infringed:** The court rules that the cited patent is infringed by the technology at issue.
- **Valid:** The court upholds the validity of all or part of the cited patent.
- **Valid and Infringed:** The court upholds the validity of all or part of the cited patent, and rules that it is infringed by the technology at issue.

C
A **green C** indicates that the case/administrative decision has citing references but no direct history or negative citing references. It also indicates that a statute/regulation has citing references, but no updating documents.

★★★★ **Depth of treatment stars** indicate how extensively a cited case or administrative decision has been discussed by the citing case.

" **Quotation marks** indicate that the citing case or administrative decision directly quotes the cited case.

Source: Published with permission of West, a Thomson Reuters business.

Figure 9-9. Limit KeyCite Display Options: *Santi v. Santi*, 633 N.W.2d 312 (Iowa 2001)

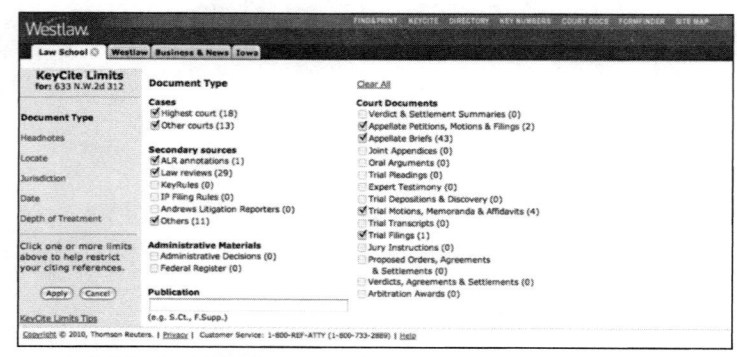

Source: Published with permission of West, a Thomson Reuters business.

Figure 9-10. "Locate" Feature within "Limit KeyCite Display"

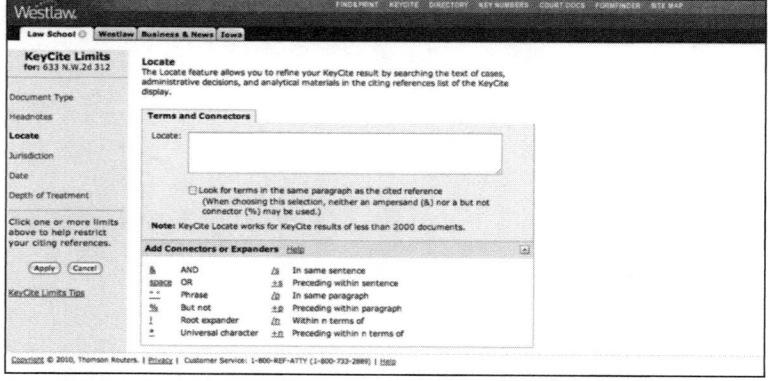

Source: Published with permission of West, a Thomson Reuters business.

Figure 9-9 illustrates the full "Limit KeyCite Display" option and Figure 9-10 illustrates the "Locate" feature within Limit KeyCite Display.

4. Reading and Analyzing the Citing References

As noted, you cannot effectively validate a source by simply running a search on KeyCite. You must also read and evaluate the citing references. Using the citator features, focus your review on cases involving your issue of law, preferably by headnote. Evaluate authorities with negative treatment first, focusing on the most recent cases from your jurisdiction.

C. Caution: Additional Limitations on the Use of Citators to Update

While updating with a citator is an essential step in legal research, citators do have limitations in terms of ensuring that you are relying upon good law. Citators only identify sources that actually cite to the cited source. A court opinion could change the rule of law relevant to your issue without citing the prior case, statute, or rule you are examining. In this instance, the newer case would not appear in your citator results. However, if you use citators in conjunction with the other legal research sources noted in this book, you should find proper authority for your issue.

Appendix: Shepardizing in Print

Shepardizing in print is far more time-consuming and cumbersome than using an online citator. If you must update with print Shepard's, you can consult the instructions, which are available online[8] and in the front of a Shepard's book.[9] This brief overview should give you an idea of how to Shepardize properly in print.

The first step in using print Shepard's is to locate the appropriate books. Shepard's are published for updating a variety of legal resources, including state and federal cases, statutes, rules, and sec-

---

8. The instructions are available at www.lexisnexis.com/shepards-citations/printsupport/shepardize_print.pdf.
9. Note that the online Shepard's usage guide begins by explaining the many advantages of the online version of the citator and later indicates there are a few specialized sources, such as U.S. trademarks, that can only be updated using the print.

ondary sources such as law reviews, restatements and ALRs. The sample case, *Santi v. Santi*, 633 N.W.2d 312 (Iowa 2001), is an Iowa state case and can be located in *Shepard's Iowa Citations* and *Shepard's Northwestern Reporter Citations*. Recognize that state citators and regional reporter citators may contain different citing references for a particular source. Check the table at the front of each Shepard's volume to determine what courts, codes, or other sources of law are searched to generate the citing references list.

You must also collect all necessary volumes of the applicable Shepard's to ensure that you are looking at the most complete and current information. Shepard's hard-cover maroon volumes are updated by a cycle of color-coded paper-bound supplements. To ensure you have all needed volumes, review all the dates on the covers of all the paper supplements and look more closely at the most recent. The cover should have a box titled "What Your Library Should Contain." This box notes the relevant bound volumes and any supplements you should consult. Supplements may include the annual cumulative supplement, which is gold-covered, the cumulative supplement, which is red-covered, or an advance sheet or express supplement, which is blue-covered or on newsprint.

Once you have located all the appropriate volumes and supplements for your cited source, you must go through each of them to locate citing references. Figure 9-A is an illustration of the result for *Santi v. Santi*, 633 N.W.2d 312 (Iowa 2001) in *Shepard's Iowa Citations*.

Note that the result may look like hieroglyphics to the novice. Pay meticulous attention to detail, as it can be very easy to miss a critical piece of information, such as reporter series designation. Also, familiarize yourself with the Shepard's history and treatment code abbreviations. A guide at the front of each Shepard's volume explains these codes. Parallel citations, if applicable, will appear underneath your cited source in parentheses. The first citing references will be history cases, which illustrate how your cited case proceeded through the judicial system.

History sources are citing references that refer directly to a different point in the proceeding of the cited source. They are followed by treatment sources, or citing references that refer to the cited source.

9 · Updating with Citators

Figure 9-A. Shepard's Results in Print

State v Campbell 2001 2003IowaApp [LX570	687NW 289 j 691NW412 701NW^{1}661 701NW^{2}661 701NW^{3}661 d 701NW664 702NW^{5}97 708NW351
—305— City of Des Moines v City Dev. Bd. 2001 2004IowaApp [LX975 2004IowaApp [LX1285 2006IowaApp [LX44 2006IowaApp [LX425 f 2007IowaApp [LX1052 2008IowaApp [LX233 637NW^{11}494 748NW512	f 737NW132 741NW806 752NW8 50DR267 88ILR865 116HLR2052 94VaL385 —322— IBP, Inc. v Harker 2001 f 2008IowaSup [LX112 2002IowaApp [LX764 2003IowaApp [LX957
—312— Santi v Santi 2001 2002IowaApp [LX1026 2002IowaApp [LX1065 2002IowaApp [LX1363 d 2003IowaApp [LX102 2004IowaApp [LX^{2}886 2004IowaApp [LX^{3}886 2005IowaApp [LX66 639NW^{2}233 639NW^{3}233 639NW^{5}237 639NW^{6}238 639NW^{7}238 641NW^{3}797 652NW209 661NW185 e 661NW187 f 661NW187 670NW130	f 2008IowaApp [LX556 641NW^{3}748 641NW^{4}748 641NW^{5}748 641NW^{6}748 641NW^{13}749 641NW^{11}750 648NW^{7}82 649NW^{2}750 649NW^{12}750 657NW^{12}489 662NW^{9}692 662NW^{10}692 663NW^{4}416 f 663NW^{3}864 f 663NW^{12}865 f 680NW^{3}374 706NW717 709NW541 ~ 729NW831 ~f 729NW832 737NW129 744NW361 747NW215 Cir. 8 437FS2d926

Source: Copyright 2009 LexisNexis, a division of Reed Elsevier Inc. All Rights Reserved. LexisNexis and the Knowledge Burst logo are registered trademarks of Reed Elsevier Properties Inc. and are used with permission of LexisNexis.

Once you have obtained a list of citing references, you will need to review those authorities to determine how they affect the validity of your cited source. This step is addressed more fully in Section III.A of this chapter.

Chapter 10

Practice Aids

I. Practice Aids: Types and Use

Lawyers have created a variety of materials, broadly referred to as practice aids, to help prepare litigation and drafting documents and provide additional practical, working guidance within various areas of law. Practice materials are a particularly useful secondary resource. Many contain both background analysis and commentary on specific legal issues and also forms or templates for specific legal documents commonly used in that area of law. In this respect, practice materials enhance efficiency, providing a starting point for drafting a document for a client.

Iowa legal researchers often turn to bar association manuals, form books, continuing legal education (CLE) materials, and other practice aids specifically devoted to Iowa law. Consulting practice aids may enable the researcher to find a relevant answer fairly quickly. However, practice aids have limitations. These materials are crafted for general use, but every client situation is unique. Therefore, the careful lawyer reviews forms and manuals in light of the specific circumstances at hand and adapts these materials accordingly. This chapter will describe techniques to identify relevant practice aids and highlight some resources frequently used in Iowa.

II. Finding Practice Aids

You find relevant practice aids much like you find other secondary sources, as described in Chapter 3. Library catalogs can be searched to identify practice aids, particularly those published as books.[1] Librarians can be consulted to recommend resources. Research guides are another excellent source for locating relevant practice aids in all formats. For instance, the Drake Law Library offers separate research guides on practice aids, law-related forms, and legal writing and drafting.[2] These kinds of web guides are often updated regularly, so they will point to the most recent versions of both print and electronic resources. They may also provide brief descriptions of available resources and tips on locating additional resources.

III. Bar Manuals and Practice Guides

A. Introduction to Bar Manuals and Practice Guides

Experts in different areas of law have written books that provide practical guidance to lawyers working in that field. These books typically include narrative descriptions of legal procedures; analysis of issues; references to primary law; and sample forms, letters, or other related documents. Titles addressing the same area of law may differ significantly in terms of depth of treatment, publication format, and frequency of updating.

B. Iowa Manuals and Practice Guides

The Iowa State Bar Association (ISBA) produces manuals in many key areas. Current titles are listed in Table 10-1.

These manuals provide practical information on common issues occurring in each area covered. Most manuals are divided into smaller topics and offer a succinct narrative analysis of each subtopic, with ci-

---

1. See Chapter 2 for a description of Iowa law libraries and brief instructions on searching a library catalog.
2. *See e.g.* http://drakelaw.libguides.com/PracticeAids, http://drakelaw.libguides.com/Forms, http://drakelaw.libguides.com/LegalWriting.

Table 10-1. Iowa State Bar Association Manuals

Appellate Practice Manual
Business Law Manual
Civil Jury Instructions Manual
Criminal Jury Instructions Manual
Family Law Manual
Federal Practice Manual
Fiduciary Tax Manual
Guide to Electronic Filing in the Iowa Courts
Labor and Employment Law Manual
Probate Law Manual
Real Estate Manual
Tax Manual
Title Standards
Workers' Compensation Manual*

* Most manual tables of contents may be viewed at http://iabar.net/store index.cfm?findprimarycategory=1425&findsecondarycategory=643.

tations to and brief descriptions of relevant cases, statutes, and regulations. All manuals also include sample materials, such as checklists, forms, and letters, which may be incorporated into narrative chapters or included in separate appendixes. Manuals are not indexed, so consult the table of contents to find a relevant section.

Manuals are typically issued in a looseleaf format. Most are updated periodically, but often infrequently. Therefore, you should always determine the date of the last revision and recognize that, while the manual is a good starting place for research, you will likely need to update the information using other sources. You can access the manuals at either the Drake or University of Iowa law libraries; members of the Iowa State Bar Association may purchase the manuals directly from the association at a reduced price.

West's Iowa Practice Series is another well-known practice guide which covers many areas of law, listed in Table 10-2. Available in print

Table 10-2. Topics in West's Iowa Practice Series

Methods of Practice (v. 1–3)
Criminal Law (v. 4)
Criminal Procedure (v. 4A)
Business Organizations (v. 5–6)
Evidence (v. 7)
Civil Litigation Handbook (v. 8)
Civil Procedure Forms (v. 9–10)
Civil and Appellate Procedure (v. 11–12)
Iowa Probate (v. 13–14)
Iowa Workers' Compensation Law and Practice (v. 15)
Lawyer and Judicial Ethics (v. 16)
Iowa Real Estate Law and Practice (v. 17)*

* Information on new editions is available at http://west.thomson.com.

and via Westlaw, this title provides expert commentary and analysis to help answer questions in specific areas of Iowa law. The series also includes references to primary law and forms. Volumes are revised and reissued annually in paperback. To find on-point information, you can consult either the General Index volume, which covers the whole series and is found at the end of the set, or the relevant article index, which covers only one particular topic and is included at the back of the last volume of that topic.[3]

In addition to these two series, a variety of other books offer valuable practice resources for the Iowa attorney. One of the best known is the looseleaf George A. LaMarca, *Iowa Pleading, Causes of Action and Defenses* (Iowa Tr. Lawyers Assn. 2000). Replete with forms, the LaMarca book is a great source to help determine the elements necessary for drafting pleadings in a variety of actions. Other books are subject-specific, such as Lawrence E. Blades & Charles A. Blades, *Iowa*

---

3. See Chapter 2 for more detail on using an index.

Tort Guide (5th ed., Iowa L. Sch. 2000) and Sheldon F. Kurtz, *Kurtz on Iowa Estates* (3d ed., Iowa L. Sch. 1995). These guides offer very detailed texts that summarize important issues in the area of law and include references to primary law. They may also include forms. These books tend not to be updated regularly, so you will want to pay particular attention to the copyright date and use additional sources to ensure the currency of your research.

C. Federal and General Practice Guides

An Iowa researcher will often have to research federal law as well as the law in other jurisdictions. Several well-known series cover federal practice, including James William Moore & Danile R. Coquillette, *Moore's Federal Practice* (3d ed., Matthew Bender 1997) and Charles Alan Wright, Arthur Raphael Miller & Mary Kay Kane, *Federal Practice and Procedure* (3d ed., West 1998).[4] These highly detailed, multi-volume works cover most issues likely to arise in a federal action.

Many law libraries also have materials devoted to general practice topics. These books can help you identify elements to draft pleadings, understand legal concepts, and prepare for trial. These books cover the entire country but may also include state-specific information. Some examples, updated regularly, include *American Jurisprudence Proof of Facts* (2d ed., West 1974), *American Jurisprudence Trials* (West 1964), and *Causes of Actions* (2d ed., West 1993).

IV. Legal Forms and Sample Documents

A. Introduction to Form Books

Because many transactions and court filings occur regularly, there is no need for practitioners to start anew creating related doc-

---

4. Now moving into its fourth edition, this title, first published in 1969, is still often called Wright and Miller, the names of two of its original authors. Several different authors now contribute to specific volumes.

Figure 10-1. Sample Forms

> **§ 4:14 Original notice—Proof of mailing**
> **Research References**
> West's Key Number Digest, Process ⇐135, 137
> C.J.S., Process §§ 79 to 82, 89
>
> STATE OF IOWA   )
>   ) ss.
> COUNTY OF _____)
>
> The undersigned, being first duly sworn, deposes and states:
> 1. On *[date]* I served the attached original notice and notification upon each of the Defendants named in the notification.
> 2. That such service was accomplished by mailing to such Defendant a copy of the notification, original notice, and petition, addressed to such Defendant at the Defendant's address specified in the notification, by restricted certified mail, such address being the Defendant's last known residence *[or place of abode]*.
> 3. That attached hereto is the receipt for restricted certified mailing as required by law.
>
> *[Signature]*
>
> *[Jurat]*
>
> **NOTES TO FORM**
> The mailing receipt, and this proof of mailing, must be attached to the original notification of filing and filed with the clerk "forthwith". I.C.A. § 321.505.

Source: Iowa Practice Series: Civil Practice Forms. Published with permission of West, a Thomson Reuters business.

uments each time. Sample forms and documents can be adapted to a particular issue, but care must be taken to ensure that forms adequately address the unique client situation. Consider how each draft provision might impact your particular client and modify as necessary.

Several multi-volume form series contain a broad array of procedural and transactional forms. Smaller series of forms may be limited to a particular jurisdiction or type of form. While form books sometimes contain forms with blank lines to fill in, more often they just suggest language and elements to address. Figure 10-1 shows two

Figure 10-1. Sample Forms, *continued*

---

§ 11:24   Statute—Unconstitutionality

Research References
West's Key Number Digest, Constitutional Law ⟜46(2); Statutes ⟜279
C.J.S., Constitutional Law §§ 86, 88; Statutes §§ 432 to 435

   I.C.A. § _____ is unconstitutional and affords Plaintiff no rights or protection against Defendant because . . . ..

[or]

   I.C.A. § _____ violates Article _____, § _____, of the Iowa Constitution because . . . ..

[or]

   § _____ violates Article _____, § _____, and the _____ Amendment to the Constitution of the United States because . . . ..

NOTES TO FORM
   All laws passed by the legislature are presumed to be constitutional. Therefore, any attack on the constitutionality of a statute must specifically set forth the grounds on which it is alleged the statute is constitutionally defective. Cole v. City of Osceola, 179 N.W.2d 524 (Iowa 1970).

Source: Iowa Practice Series: Civil Practice Forms. Published with permission of West, a Thomson Reuters business.

sample forms illustrating this range of complexity. Commentary accompanying a form may provide notes on the form's use and reference both primary authorities and other secondary sources that can help the researcher more fully understand the topic and use the source material effectively. As with all materials, references to primary sources need to be updated to ensure that they are still relevant.

Before using a form, do the necessary legal research to ensure you have selected the proper form and are using it correctly. If you do not understand an aspect of the form, you must research to clarify that point. When combining provisions from different forms, be sure to evaluate how those provisions impact your specific situation and whether the provisions you ultimately select are internally consistent in your final document.

B. Iowa-Specific Form Books and Electronic Resources

Relatively few form books are specific to Iowa. In most cases, you will need to adapt a generic form to fit your situation. To find print form books, search the law library catalog, as explained in Chapter 2. Searching for "forms" and "Iowa" should return relevant titles. Subject and/or title searches will return more refined results than keyword searches.

The *Iowa Code Annotated*, *Code of Iowa*, and the *Iowa Rules of Court* include standard forms prescribed by statute; where applicable, these forms should be used without modification. Other significant sources of Iowa forms include the Iowa State Bar Association (ISBA) manuals and the Iowa Practice Series, both described in Section III.B. Additionally, ISBA members can subscribe to IOWADOCS®, a collection of sample legal forms produced by the ISBA, including all forms in the ISBA manuals. This annually updated software allows you to open, modify, and save the form in a word processing program.[5] A print version of these forms can be accessed from the Drake and Iowa law libraries.

Electronically, Westlaw has copious Iowa forms databases, including the forms available in the Iowa Practice Series, described in Section III.B. Entering "Iowa Forms" in the "search for a database" box will return a range of form databases from Family Law (IA-FAMFORM) to Elder Law (IA-ELDFORM) to Estate Planning (IA-EPPFORM) to Real Estate (IAPRAC-REL). The database Iowa FormFinder (IA-FORMFINDER) contains Iowa-specific forms, clauses, and checklists. It can be searched through terms-and-connectors or natural language, and also provides a guided search screen to help you narrow your search. LexisNexis offers Iowa local bankruptcy forms.

On the web, you can find many law-related forms. However, remember to carefully assess the quality of these forms, as almost anyone can post almost anything on the web. Iowa governmental sites

---

5. *See* http://www.iowabar.org/iowadocs.nsf for more information about IOWADOCS®.

Table 10-3. Selected Internet Sources for Iowa Forms

Source	Web Address
Iowa Department of Human Services	http://www.dhs.state.ia.us/DHSForms.html
Iowa Judicial Branch	http://www.iowacourts.gov/Court_Rules_and_Forms
Iowa Secretary of State	http://www.sos.state.ia.us/business/form.html
Iowa State Bar Association	http://iabar.net. Click on Public.
LexisOne	http://www.lexisone.com/lx1/store/catalog?action=rootFreeCategory
USLegalForms.com	http://www.uslegalforms.com

are one good source for reputable forms. The Iowa judicial branch site contains court forms in nine categories, including family law, juvenile law, small claims, civil procedure, and probate.[6] Select forms are also available from other agencies, such as business incorporation forms from the Secretary of State's office. The ISBA offers a few free forms, such as a living will. Additional free or low-cost Internet sources for Iowa-specific legal forms are listed in Table 10-3.

C. Other Form Books and Electronic Resources

Many situations may not require Iowa-specific forms. General form books can provide helpful background information and draft provisions that can be adapted to the client's situation.

One of the major legal encyclopedias, *American Jurisprudence 2d*, publishes two helpful form series. *American Jurisprudence Legal Forms 2d* includes well over 20,000 forms arranged alphabetically by topic. *American Jurisprudence Pleading and Practice Forms* offers litigation

---

6. The web site of the judiciary is http://www.iowacourts.gov. Link to forms by clicking on the tab for Court Rules and Forms.

forms with procedural timetables and drafting checklists. Both have indexes that can help you locate the correct form. Another multi-volume series is *West's Legal Forms*, which is arranged by broad practice areas.

There are also several series that feature forms used in federal practice. These include *Bender's Federal Practice Forms* and *Federal Procedural Forms, Lawyers' Edition*, which are arranged by court rule. Another series, *West's Federal Forms*, is arranged by court, consisting of separate volumes covering forms needed in the Supreme Court, Courts of Appeals, District Courts, Bankruptcy Courts and other specialized national courts. Additional form books can be found through a search of the library catalog using search terms like "forms" and the specific legal area which you want the forms to cover.

LexisNexis and Westlaw contain extensive general forms. For Westlaw, the FORMFINDER database guides you through choices to help refine your search. LexisNexis contains two comprehensive forms databases: All Litigation LexisNexis Forms (LNFLTA) and All Transactions LexisNexis Forms (LNFABT).

Another electronic form database of note is Gale LegalForms. This database contains thousands of state-specific forms that have either been drafted by attorneys and approved for use at one or more law firms, or have been designated as official by the state. Many Gale forms are available in Word format, so they can easily be downloaded to your computer and edited. Gale LegalForms is accessible at some academic libraries. Moreover, Gale has actively pursued the public library market, so students and attorneys may also find this resource available to them through their community library.

In addition to these subscription databases, some other Internet resources provide free or low-cost forms. Many sites provide forms that can be used in multiple jurisdictions and might not work for your specific needs. As with all legal form use, be sure you have done your research and are using the correct form correctly. In addition, exercise extra caution in assessing forms you find on the open web. Remember that the web has no formal publishing or editing process; anyone with access to a connected computer and a little technical knowledge can put anything on the web. Some sources are excellent;

Table 10-4. Online Sources for Free or
Low Cost Legal Forms (General)

Source	Web Address
Forms.gov (through the U.S. government)	http://www.forms.gov/bgfPortal/main.do
LexisOne (through LexisNexis)	http://www.lexisone.com/lx1/store/catalog?action=rootFreeCategory
FindLaw	http://forms.lp.findlaw.com
Public Library of Law	http://partners.uslegalforms.com/partners/plol

some are suspect. Some more reputable online sites for free or low-cost legal forms are listed in Table 10-4.

D. Other Sample Materials

In addition to the sample materials included in form books, lawyers sometimes review actual documents and court filings for guidance.[7] Many law firms and legal departments have developed "brief banks" and other collections of sample documents to provide models for other attorneys' work. Institutional collections are only for members' use; however, sample documents can also be found online and in print. For instance, the Drake, Iowa Supreme Court, State of Iowa, and University of Iowa law libraries all maintain collections of briefs from Iowa appellate cases. In addition, Westlaw offers a database of these briefs. The University of Missouri-Columbia's Contracting and Organizations Research Institute (CORI) database provides another example of such a collection. CORI gathers and categorizes actual contracts, most drawn from filings with the U.S. Securities and Exchange Commission, and makes them available in a searchable database accessible without charge on the web.[8]

---

7. Form books may also include real-world examples.
8. The address is http://cori.missouri.edu/pages/ksearch.htm.

As with form books, sample documents provide only a starting point for the lawyer. Sample documents may suggest clear phrasing, persuasive arguments, important points of law to consider, and professional standards of presentation. However, the lawyer's knowledge of the particular client circumstances and requirements of applicable law must provide the basis for crafting any document.

V. Continuing Legal Education (CLE) Publications

A. Introduction to CLE Materials

Iowa court rules mandate that attorneys licensed to practice in the state must undertake a minimum of 15 hours of accredited continuing legal education (CLE) each calendar year.[9] Many of these CLE classes produce helpful written materials and resources. CLE materials cover a wide variety of topics. The accompanying print publications range from simple outlines that might not be very meaningful for those who did not attend the course to fully developed articles with sample forms or other useful exhibits.

B. Iowa-Specific CLE Resources

Iowa CLE materials can be located by searching a law library catalog. CLE or "continuing legal education" may not be very useful search terms. The materials are more likely to be found by searching using subject terms, possibly combined with the additional search term "practice of law." CLE materials can also be found by searching by both the legal subject and name of the CLE provider. Iowa's two law schools both provide CLEs, as do many Iowa legal associations. The Iowa State Bar Association's annual Bridge the Gap institutes are specifically designed to provide practical information for new attorneys. In addition, the National Business Institute and Lorman Edu-

---

9. Iowa Ct. R. 41.3(1).

cation Services both provide and publish CLE materials specific to Iowa, as well as to other states and federal practice. Sample titles include *Workers' Compensation Case Preparation Techniques*, *The Probate Process from Start to Finish*, and *Advanced Judgment Enforcement in Iowa*.

C. Other CLE Resources

On a national level, significant providers of CLE materials include the American Law Institute-American Bar Association (ALI-ABA), the National Institute of Trial Advocates (NITA), and the Practising Law Institute (PLI). Many of these materials are published as books and can be found by searching either a law library catalog or the publisher's catalog.[10] Many ALI-ABA materials are also available on Westlaw and LexisNexis, and many PLI materials are available on Westlaw.

VI. Jury Instructions

A. Introduction to Jury Instructions

Jury instructions provide plain-language explanations of the law intended to ensure members of the jury understand their duties and how to apply the law. The wording should be clear and unbiased, which can make drafting good jury instructions challenging. Consulting a collection of model or pattern instructions can save drafting time and ensure a proposed instruction has been carefully considered.

Jury instructions may summarize the elements of a crime or cause of action, showing what the attorney must prove. They may also provide references to cases, statutes, and secondary sources. In this respect, jury instructions can help an attorney focus on the most important aspects of a case and serve as a resource in crafting pleadings, analytical and persuasive documents, and opening and closing statements.

---

10. Check the website of the organization publishing the material for a catalog.

B. Iowa-Specific Instructions

The Iowa State Bar Association (ISBA) offers model Iowa jury instructions in a variety of categories. Drafted by the ISBA Committee on Iowa Jury Instructions and approved by the ISBA Board of Governors, instructions are then published in the *Iowa Criminal Jury Instructions* and the *Iowa Civil Jury Instructions*. Both titles are updated periodically and are available in print in law libraries and, for members, via the association's website.

C. Other Instructions

General practice and form book sets, such as *American Jurisprudence Pleading and Practice*, *American Jurisprudence Trials*, and *Causes of Action*, may provide jury instructions. Further, many courts provide jury instructions on their websites. For instance, the Eighth Circuit Court of Appeals offers model civil, criminal, and death penalty jury instructions. A variety of books offer instructions specific to a subject or jurisdiction. Search for these in a law library catalog under the subject heading "Instructions to Juries." The search can be limited with other relevant search terms.

The web journal LLRX.com offers a jury instructions research guide providing links to electronic versions of state jury instructions and other helpful resources.[11]

---

11. The web address is http://www.llrx.com/columns/reference53.htm.

Chapter 11

Legal Ethics

I. Introduction to Legal Ethics Research

Iowa attorneys are governed by rules of professional responsibility modeled after the American Bar Association's Model Rules of Professional Conduct (ABA Model Rules). The Iowa rules impose a number of ethical and professional obligations on attorneys, and an attorney's license to practice law in Iowa requires adherence to these rules. Therefore, you need to have a relatively sophisticated understanding of the rules that govern your professional conduct, and how those rules have been applied to other practicing attorneys.

Research involving issues of professional responsibility relies upon judicial decisions and statutes as well as the Iowa Rules of Professional Responsibility, the ABA Model Rules, and, at times, the ABA's earlier attempt to articulate rules regarding attorney conduct: the ABA Model Code of Professional Responsibility (ABA Model Code).[1] In addition to understanding the rules in Iowa, you may need to determine how courts in other jurisdictions have applied rules modeled after the ABA Model Rules or Model Code. Further, you will need to be familiar with a unique type of advisory opinion, the ethics opinion.[2] Finally, your research in judicial opinions involving lapses in attorney conduct may require inquiry into related substantive areas, such as attorney malpractice, rules of civil and appellate procedure, and criminal appeals.

---

1. The ABA Model Rules and the ABA Model Code, and their relationship to one another, are discussed in Section II.A.1. of this chapter.

2. Ethics opinions are discussed more fully in Section II.A.2. of this chapter.

II. Regulating the Conduct of Attorneys — An Overview

A. Sources of Regulation

1. ABA Model Code and Model Rules

Recognizing how the conduct of lawyers is governed and enforced is essential to understanding the ethical rules themselves. The legal profession is self-regulating; lawyers are subject to rules of ethics by virtue of their admission to the bar in a particular state. The American Law Institute's *Restatement of the Law Governing Lawyers* notes that, "upon admission to the bar of any jurisdiction, a person becomes a lawyer and is subject to applicable law governing such matters as professional discipline, procedure and evidence, civil remedies, and criminal sanctions."[3]

Therefore, you are subject to rules or standards of professional conduct that have been adopted by the state in which you are licensed to practice law. Most states have adopted some form of the various ethical rules promulgated by the ABA. The two main sources are the ABA Model Rules and the ABA Model Code. The term *model* is apt because the ABA is a private organization with no inherent authority to impose rules upon lawyers. The ABA suggests the rules, but only the adoption of the rules by the state bar associations or state court systems gives the rules legal effect.

The ABA's model rules have developed over time. In 1908, the ABA first published a set of ethical rules titled the Canons of Professional Ethics. This set remained in effect until the publication of the ABA Model Code in 1969. The ABA Code was designed to serve as a model for states to follow in adopting legal ethics rules. The ABA Code is comprised of nine *Canons*, which are described as "axiomatic norms, expressing in general terms the standards of professional conduct expected of lawyers in their relationships with the public, with the legal system, and with the legal profession."[4]

---

3. *Restatement (Third) of the Law Governing Lawyers* § 1 (1998).
4. Model Code of Prof. Conduct, Preliminary Statement.

The Canons are further explained by *Ethical Considerations* (ECs) and *Disciplinary Rules* (DRs). The ECs are aspirational and "represent the objectives toward which every member of the profession should strive."[5] DRs, unlike the ECs, are mandatory and "state the minimum level of conduct below which no lawyer can fall without being subject to disciplinary action."[6] The ABA Code was designed as a system under which lawyer conduct could be evaluated, and the ABA intended the enforcing agency at the state level to apply the DRs by using "the interpretive guidance in the basic principles embodied in the Canons and in the objectives reflected in the [ECs]."[7] The ABA Code was widely accepted at its inception and within a few years after its initial publication most states had adopted ethical rules modeled after the ABA Code.

Even though the ABA Model Code was extensively adopted, it was criticized for its arguably vague quality. So, the ABA next endeavored to draft a more straightforward set of rules. This attempt resulted in the publication of the Model Rules in 1983. The ABA intended for the Model Rules to replace the Model Code. Indeed, many jurisdictions, including Iowa, ultimately revised their ethics rules to be modeled after the Model Rules, rather than the Model Code. Distinct in approach from the Model Code, the "Scope" section of the ABA Rules describes the rules as "partly obligatory and disciplinary and partly constitutive and descriptive in that they define a lawyer's role."[8] Comments to the Rules are designed as guides to interpretation to explain and illustrate the meaning and purpose of the Rules.[9]

2. Legal Ethics Opinions

The ABA and states issue legal ethics opinions. At the state level, the opinions are often issued by the state bar association. The ABA

---

5. Model Code of Prof. Resp., Preamble.
6. *Id.*
7. *Id.*
8. Model Rules of Prof. Conduct, Scope § 14.
9. *Id.* at Scope § 21.

opinions are authored by the Standing Committee on Ethics and Professional Responsibility. Legal ethics opinions are typically drafted in response to questions posed by attorneys who want to know whether contemplated or past conduct comports with the ethical rules. Some opinions are designated as "formal," which means that the issuing body (e.g., the ABA or state bar association) deems them widely applicable to the practicing bar. These opinions generally provide an in-depth discussion of the issue. In contrast, an "informal" opinion is designed to provide a specific response to the requesting attorney. Even though the ABA has no independent enforcement authority, ABA ethics opinions that interpret the Rules are often cited by courts as they consider the propriety of lawyers' conduct.

3. *Other Sources of Law Relating to Attorney Ethics*

In addition to rules relating specifically to attorney ethics, some substantive and procedural rules impose ethical obligations on attorneys. For example, Federal Rule of Civil Procedure 11 prohibits attorneys from filing frivolous claims. This prohibition therefore implicitly obligates an attorney to conduct effective research, to investigate the matter carefully to ensure that there is a good faith basis in law and fact to support the claim, and to act truthfully. These are also the types of behavior required under ethical rules relating to competence and candor. Additionally, in some jurisdictions, certain claims of attorney malpractice related to ethical failures are addressed by statute or in the context of the common law.[10] In this way, ethics research involves investigation of the application of the ethics rules and can also extend beyond those rules to other substantive areas of law.[11]

---

10. In Iowa, for example, fraud is a common law matter, but allegations of fraud by an attorney will also likely implicate the duty of loyalty and the duty to avoid conflicts of interest. The latter duties arise in the context of rules of professional conduct. *See e.g. Iowa Sup. Ct. Bd. of Prof. Ethics and Conduct v. D.J.I.*, 545 N.W.2d 866 (Iowa 1996).

11. While an identification of these other, substantive sources of legal ethics are beyond the scope of this book, chapters relating to general research in statutes or cases cover the sources and research strategies associated with

B. State Regulation of Attorney Conduct

As noted above, most jurisdictions originally adopted some version of the Model Code. Following the release of the ABA Model Rules, almost all states incorporated material from the Model Rules into their rules of ethics.[12] Further, many states modify the Model Rules before adopting them. Consequently, it is important to be familiar with both the ABA Code and ABA Model Rules, as well as state rules and statutes regarding legal ethics.

In 1971, the Iowa Supreme Court adopted a form of the ABA Model Code. However, in keeping with the transition to the ABA's Model Rules, Iowa adopted the Iowa Rules of Professional Conduct in 2005. These have been amended over the past five years, but remain similar in many respects to the ABA Model Rules. They are codified in Chapter 32 of the Iowa Court Rules.[13]

In addition to the rules, you will likely want to examine cases that address how the rules apply. In this respect, you will consider judicial opinions that address attorney misconduct, as well as ethics advisory opinions and notices of disciplinary action, described more fully in Section III.C.

C. Regulation of Judicial Conduct

Similar to the rules regulating lawyers, the American Bar Association's Model Code of Judicial Conduct concerns the conduct of judges. This code has been widely adopted in some form by most

---

locating such authority. This chapter is designed to focus expressly on sources specific to legal ethics research, such as state ethics rules fashioned after the Model Rules and ethics opinions issued for the purpose of communicating advice regarding the propriety of lawyering conduct.

12. According to the Center for Professional Responsibility, California is now the only U.S. state that has not adopted some form of the ABA Model Rules. *See* http://www.abanet.org/cpr/mrpc/model_rules.html.

13. Iowa's rules are explained in Section III.B. of this chapter.

states. The Iowa Supreme Court adopted the Iowa Code of Judicial Conduct in 1973.[14]

III. The Process of Legal Ethics Research

A. Overview

The number of legal ethics research sources may seem somewhat overwhelming. Methodically consulting these sources can help ensure you find all relevant materials. Table 11-1 provides an overview of the basic research process for legal ethics research.

Table 11-1. Basic Process for Legal Ethics Research

1.	Identify relevant ethical or procedural rules within your jurisdiction.
2.	Identify cases related to each rule in your jurisdiction, including formal or informal ethics opinions.
3.	Examine the ABA Model Rule counterparts to your rules, any annotations to each rule, and any relevant cases or advisory opinions (formal or informal) issued by the ABA.
4.	Consider whether additional materials, including related ethics rules and opinions from other states or secondary materials, might be helpful and persuasive to your issue.

B. Iowa Rules of Professional Conduct

As noted, the Iowa Rules of Professional Conduct are codified in Chapter 32 of the Iowa Court Rules. Unannotated versions of the

---

14. Further discussion of judicial regulation is outside the scope of this book. Most law libraries have materials covering the topic, which often is listed in the online catalog under the subject of Judicial ethics. *See e.g.* James J. Alfini, *Judicial Conduct and Ethics* (4th ed., LexisNexis 2007).

rules are available both in print at law libraries and online.[15] You can access an annotated version of the Iowa Rules of Professional Conduct through an annotated version of the Iowa Code, as described in detail in Chapter 6.

One good starting point for research in the rules is to familiarize yourself with the topics addressed. The Table of Contents identifies the following subjects:

- Client-Lawyer Relationship
- Counselor
- Advocate
- Transactions with Persons other than Clients
- Law Firms and Associates
- Public Service
- Information about Legal Services
- Maintaining the Integrity of the Profession.

Every category includes a number of related rules. Each individual rule is followed by a series of comments that further explain how the rule should apply. For example, Rule 32:1.3 addresses diligence and provides "a lawyer shall act with reasonable diligence and promptness in representing a client."[16] The second comment to the rule explains "a lawyer's work load must be controlled so that each matter can be handled competently."[17]

The Welch Matter

Consider a question that might arise in the context of this book's hypothetical Welch matter if you are a new attorney, not entirely familiar with the law of domestic relations. To verify that you were competent to represent Mary Welch, you might consult the ethical rule that addresses the attorney's obligation of competent representation. The Iowa rule is logi-

---

15. Online, the rules are available from the website of the Iowa Judicial Branch at http://www.iowacourts.gov/Professional_Regulation/Rules_of_Professional_Conduct.
16. Iowa R. Prof. Conduct 32:1.3.
17. Iowa R. Prof. Conduct 32:1.3, cmt. 2.

cally located under the "Client-Lawyer Relationship" topic, and provides: "A lawyer shall provide competent representation to a client. Competent representation requires the legal knowledge, skill, thoroughness, and preparation reasonably necessary for the representation."[18] Comment 2 to this rule further explains the attorney's obligation:

> A lawyer need not necessarily have special training or prior experience to handle legal problems of a type with which the lawyer is unfamiliar. A newly admitted lawyer can be as competent as a practitioner with long experience. Some important legal skills, such as the analysis of precedent, the evaluation of evidence, and legal drafting, are required in all legal problems. Perhaps the most fundamental legal skill consists of determining what kind of legal problems a situation may involve, a skill that necessarily transcends any particular specialized knowledge. A lawyer can provide adequate representation in a wholly novel field through necessary study. Competent representation can also be provided through the association of a lawyer of established competence in the field in question.[19]

If you were to further review the annotated version of the rule, you would find two cases addressing this issue. In the first, the court concluded that an attorney had violated the rule by representing a client in an interstate adoption matter.[20] In the second, the court said that a normally competent attorney may have an obligation to become familiar with a new area of law contemplated by the representation.[21] With the case citations, you could easily obtain the full opinions to review in more detail to ensure that you take adequate steps to familiarize yourself with the area of law involved in the Welch matter.

C. Iowa Ethics Opinions

1. Iowa Ethics Opinions[22]

Prior to July 2005, the Board of Professional Ethics and Conduct (Ethics Board) issued Iowa formal ethics opinions. Beginning in July

---

18. Iowa R. Prof. Conduct 32:1.1.
19. Iowa R. Prof. Conduct 32:1.1, cmt. 2.
20. *Iowa Sup. Ct. Bd. of Prof. Ethics & Conduct v. Hill*, 576 N.W.2d 91 (Iowa 1998).
21. *State v. Schoelerman*, 315 N.W.2d 67 (Iowa 1982).
22. The discussion on the development and force of Iowa ethics opinions is based in large part on Gregory C. Sisk, *Iowa Practice: Lawyer and Judicial*

2005, the Iowa Supreme Court transferred responsibility for ethics opinions to the Iowa State Bar Association. This responsibility now lies with the Ethics and Practice Guidelines Committee. The Iowa Supreme Court issued an order explaining the transfer of responsibility from the Ethics Board to the Committee and the impact on the persuasive effect of the opinions:

> The Iowa State Bar Association has offered to undertake the issuance of advisory opinions and practice guidelines under the Iowa Rules of Professional Conduct in a manner similar to its activities regarding uniform jury instructions. The Iowa Supreme Court welcomes the assistance of the Bar Association to aid Iowa lawyers in their efforts to practice law in accordance with our new rules of professional conduct.
>
> Advisory opinions and practice guidelines issued by the Iowa State Bar Association do not have the force of law and are not binding on the court, as Iowa law places sole responsibility for the regulation of the practice of law in the supreme court.[23]

Committee opinions are typically reported in the bar association's journal, the *Iowa Lawyer*. Both committee opinions and the opinions

---

Ethics § 2:12 (West 2009) (citing Order of the Supreme Court of Iowa dated April 20, 2005).

23. *Id.* note 14. Sisk explains that the practical effect of relying on an ethics opinion is that of a safe harbor. He notes that the Supreme Court has the ultimate responsibility for regulating the conduct of attorneys in Iowa, and it therefore cannot transfer that responsibility and authority to the state bar association. Notwithstanding, Iowa attorneys should be encouraged to seek the opinion of the Ethics and Practice Guidelines Committee. Sisk explains:

> In cases where the court in the context of a disciplinary proceeding effectively rejects the analysis of a pertinent bar association advisory opinion, the respondent lawyer's reasonable reliance upon that opinion should be given considerable weight in evaluating the lawyer's culpability and the appropriate sanction if any.... [A] lawyer's careful compliance with the terms of an ethics opinion nonetheless should generally be a safe-harbor against disciplinary sanction.

Id.

previously issued by the Ethics Board are available on the website of the Iowa State Bar Association[24] and online on LexisNexis.[25] To search opinions on the bar association website, simply review the titles of the opinions. To search on LexisNexis, use terms and connectors to search by topic.[26]

2. Disciplinary Actions[27]

The Iowa Supreme Court has ultimate responsibility for regulating the conduct of attorneys in the state. In terms of disciplinary proceedings, the court has developed procedures for addressing complaints alleging ethical misconduct[28] of attorneys. Complaints against attorneys are initially investigated by the Attorney Disciplinary Board (Disciplinary Board). This is a confidential process. The Disciplinary Board may dismiss the complaint, admonish or reprimand the attorney, or file a complaint before another body, the Grievance Commission. If the Disciplinary Board files a reprimand with the clerk of the Iowa Supreme Court, the attorney has the option to file an exception to the reprimand. If he fails to do so, the reprimand becomes a public document and may be published in the *Iowa Lawyer*.

---

24. The Iowa Bar Association website address is http://iowabar.org. Use the Public tab to open the Attorney Discipline/Ethics link and click on Ethics Opinions or use http://www.iowabar.org/ethics.nsf/Ethics%20Opinions?OpenFrameset.

25. Use Area of Law — By Topic > Ethics > Search Legal Ethics Opinions > By State > Iowa. This link accesses materials compiled in the *National Reporter on Legal Ethics and Professional Responsibility*.

26. See Chapter 2 for information on conducting a terms and connectors search.

27. Much of the discussion on grievance procedures comes from the Iowa Judicial Branch website, which provides a more detailed explanation at http://www.iowacourts.gov/Professional_Regulation/Attorney_Discipline/Discipline_Procedures.

28. Note that these allegations can involve failings under the Iowa Rules of Professional Conduct or some other law that imposes an obligation on attorney conduct.

When the Disciplinary Board files a complaint at the Commission, a hearing is held. This is also a confidential process. At the conclusion of the hearing, the Commission may dismiss the complaint, issue a private admonition, or file a report recommending more serious sanction. Commission reports of recommendations regarding sanctions are filed with the clerk of the Iowa Supreme Court and are therefore public records. The attorney may file an appeal, which is then heard by the Iowa Supreme Court.

As public records, both reports of the Commission and final decisions on sanctions by the Iowa Supreme Court are available to view. Moreover, final determinations describing the conduct of the attorney and the type of sanction are published in the *Iowa Lawyer*. Archives of past issues of the *Iowa Lawyer* remain available on the website of the Iowa Bar Association.[29] Unfortunately from a research perspective, the disciplinary reports are published chronologically in the *Iowa Lawyer* and are not separately cataloged for topical searching. Thus, accessing the reports requires a general review of past issues of the bar journal. The wise attorney will therefore review monthly issues of the journal to stay apprised of conduct that results in sanctions.

D. American Bar Association Materials

1. *Model Rules of Professional Conduct*

The ABA Model Rules of Professional Conduct are available in annotated and unannotated versions, both in print and online. When conducting legal research, an annotated version is valuable because it contains citations to cases that have interpreted the rules. The annotated version is available in print, and online on LexisNexis[30] and

---

29. The Iowa Bar Association website is http://iowabar.org. Use the "Publications" link on the homepage to access the *Iowa Lawyer*.

30. To access the annotated Model Rules in LexisNexis, go to Area of Law — By Topic > Ethics > Find Statutes & Rules > ABA Model Rules of Professional Conduct and Code of Judicial Conduct.

Westlaw.[31] To search the rules, you can enter search terms or, in Westlaw, view the Table of Contents to find the rule(s) applicable to your situation.

The print version of the Annotated Model Rules of Professional Conduct is published by the ABA and includes a subject index, a Table of Amendments, and a Correlation Table between the Model Code and Model Rules. These are helpful resources if you are analyzing a topic that was previously considered in your jurisdiction under some version of the Model Code, rather than Model Rules (which were developed more recently).

2. *Model Code of Professional Responsibility*

Because most jurisdictions now have some form of the ABA Model Rules, it is unlikely that you will need to perform research in the ABA Model Code. However, because the same type of lawyering behavior is covered by both resources (e.g., candor, truthfulness, relationships with clients), you might consult a topic that had been previously addressed by the ABA Model Code to seek persuasive authority on an issue currently covered by the ABA Model Rules. To that end, the American Bar Foundation publishes an Annotated Code of Professional Responsibility. If your research is directed primarily to an issue involving the ABA Model Rules and you simply want to consult the issue as previously addressed under the ABA Model Code, it is most efficient to use an annotated version of the ABA Model Rules which should contain cross-references to the related ABA Model Code section.

3. *ABA Ethics Opinions*

ABA issues both formal and informal advisory ethics opinions in response to questions from attorneys about the propriety of certain conduct under the rules. Again, the formal opinions, issued in re-

---

31. In Westlaw, locate the annotated Model Rules by searching Topical Materials by Area of Practice > Legal Ethics and Professional Responsibility > American Bar Association Materials > ABA Annotated Model Rules of Professional Responsibility.

sponse to broadly applicable questions, are more likely to be relevant to you as you examine an ethical issue.

You can search the ABA opinions in the *ABA/BNA Lawyer's Manual on Professional Conduct*, which is available in print, as well as online through Westlaw,[32] LexisNexis,[33] and BNA.[34] The ABA Ethics Opinions section contains both ABA opinions and opinions from states. Search online using terms and connectors as described in Chapter 2. You can also review these opinions in print in a number of publications issued by the ABA.[35] In the print volumes, opinions appear in chronological order and can be best accessed by using the subject index at the end of the volume. Also, recent opinions are published in the *ABA Journal*.[36]

E. Materials from Other States

To locate materials from other states, including rules on professional conduct and state ethics opinions, a good place to start is the ABA website's Center for Professional Responsibility.[37] The site contains an alphabetical listing of all states with links to bar associations and rules of professional conduct. Another useful site is the American Legal Ethics Library from Cornell Law School's Legal Informa-

---

32. In Westlaw, you can also simply access the ABA-ETHOP database for formal and informal opinions.

33. In LexisNexis, you have the option of limiting your search to only formal opinions by accessing Area of Law—By Topic > Ethics > Search Legal Ethics Opinions > ABA Formal Ethics Opinions. Informal opinions are available in a separate file at Area of Law—By Topic > Ethics > Search Legal Ethics Opinions > ABA Informal Ethics Opinions.

34. For more information about the print title and online access through BNA, see http://www.bna.com/products/lit/mopc.htm.

35. The ABA publishes several compilations of ethics opinions. To access the most recent publications, go the ABA's Center for Professional Responsibility website at http://www.abanet.org/cpr/pubs/ethicopinions.html?gnav=global_publications_ethicsopinions.

36. ABAJ can be found at http://www.abajournal.com/magazine/archives.

37. This site is available at http://www.abanet.org/cpr/links.html.

tion Institute.[38] This digital library contains information on the codes and rules for professional responsibility by state. You can also access similar material on LexisNexis[39] and Westlaw.[40]

Locating individual state ethics opinions can be tricky because publication differs by state. Most state bar associations publish ethics opinions in their state bar journal or newsletter, but some do not. Two good resources are *ABA/BNA Lawyers' Manual on Professional Conduct,* available in print and online, which includes summaries of ethics opinions, and the *National Reporter on Legal Ethics and Professional Responsibility,*[41] available in print and on LexisNexis.[42] You can also use LexisNexis[43] or Westlaw[44] to search for selected state ethics opinions.

F. Secondary Sources for Legal Ethics Research

A variety of secondary resources assist in legal ethics research. The following are good starting points: *ABA/BNA Lawyer's Manual on Professional Conduct*; the *Restatement of the Law Governing Lawyers*;[45] the *National Reporter on Legal Ethics and Professional Responsibility*;[46]

---

38. This site is available at http://www.law.cornell.edu/ethics.
39. To find state codes in LexisNexis, use Area of Law—By Topic > Ethics > Find Statutes & Rules.
40. Westlaw has state databases for court rules that include codes of professional responsibility. Locate these by using the Materials by State link.
41. *National Reporter on Legal Ethics and Professional Responsibility* (Roy M. Mersky & Norman Quist eds., LexisNexis 1983–).
42. Use Area of Law—By Topic > Ethics > Search Legal Ethics Opinions > National Reporter on Legal Ethics and Professional Responsibility.
43. Use Area of Law—By Topic > Ethics > Search Legal Ethics Opinions > By State. Note that not all states are covered, and coverage for individual states varies.
44. Use the METH-EO database to determine which states are included, recognizing that coverage varies by state.
45. *Restatement (Third) of the Law Governing Lawyers* (2000).
46. *National Reporter on Legal Ethics and Professional Responsibility* (Roy M. Mersky & Norman Quist eds., LexisNexis 1983–).

Understanding Lawyers' Ethics;[47] *Legal Ethics in a Nutshell*;[48] *Legal Ethics: A Legal Research Guide*;[49] and *The Law of Lawyering*.[50]

There are also a number of law reviews and journals devoted to legal ethics and professional responsibility. These include the following: *Georgetown Journal of Legal Ethics*; *The Journal of Law, Medicine, and Ethics*; *Criminal Justice Ethics*; *Journal of the Institute for the Study of Legal Ethics*; *Journal of the Legal Profession* (University of Alabama School of Law); *Notre Dame Journal of Law, Ethics and Public Policy*; and the *Professional Lawyer*.

Finally, many resources are available on the Internet. The ABA's Center for Professional Responsibility website[51] contains a number of helpful links to material including state-specific resources, national organizations, law school websites, and general legal ethics material.

---

47. Monroe H. Freedman, *Understanding Lawyers' Ethics* (3d ed., Lexis-Nexis 2004).

48. Ronald Rotunda, *Legal Ethics in a Nutshell* (3d ed., West 2007).

49. Lee F. Peoples, *Legal Ethics: A Legal Research Guide* (2d ed., W.S. Hein & Co. 2006).

50. Geoffery C. Hazard & W. William Hodes, *The Law of Lawyering* (3d ed., Aspen 2001).

51. From the Center for Professional Responsibility webpage at http://www.americanbar.org/groups/professional_responsibility.html, select the "Resources" tab to find "Links of Interest."

Chapter 12

Research Strategies[1]

I. Introduction

When a client comes to a lawyer with a problem, the lawyer does not typically have an immediate answer. For most legal issues, the prudent course of action is more deliberate analysis. An effective lawyer listens well, hears the client's "story," and asks about the client's desired outcome. The lawyer will provide the client information and recommendations assessing the feasibility of the desired result and the best means of achieving it, whether through legal action or alternatives, such as mediation or counseling.

As you hear a story from a client, you will have to determine which facts are legally significant and identify the legal issues. This process may require that you ask questions to elicit facts the client might not have thought to mention. You might also need to review related documents, such as contracts, letters, bills, or public records. You may even need to interview others involved in the client's situation.

The legal issues are not always easily ascertained after the client meeting. If the facts involve an area of law in which you have limited experience, some preliminary research into potential legal issues could be required. When you complete the basic research to find the relevant law, you should be able to identify the legal issues that need to be addressed and begin to develop a research strategy. This chapter explains how to formulate that strategy and organize the materials you find.

---

1. Portions of this chapter are based on Suzanne E. Rowe, *Oregon Legal Research* (2d ed., Carolina Academic Press 2007).

II. Developing a Research Strategy

The research process in Chapter 1 outlines six basic steps: (1) identify the issues, jurisdiction, and scope of the project; (2) gather facts and identify preliminary search terms; (3) consult secondary sources and practice aids; (4) retrieve, read, and evaluate primary sources; (5) update authorities with a citator; and (6) determine when to stop. These steps provide a basic framework for research; as you become more experienced, you will begin to tailor your strategies to fit the specific project.

If you are researching an unfamiliar area of law, you probably want to begin with a secondary source. However, if you are already familiar with a topic, you could begin with primary sources. For example, in a matter governed by statutory law, such as the grandparents' visitation rights hypothetical used throughout this book, you could proceed directly to an annotated code. In another matter, perhaps you already have a citation to an applicable case. In that instance, you could begin by Shepardizing or KeyCiting the case to make sure it is still good law and find other cases that have cited it; you also could look at the relevant headnotes in the case and search the topics and key numbers corresponding to those headnotes in Westlaw or in a West digest. Using a citator and a digest should quickly retrieve additional cases of interest. As a final example, imagine you know that the issue is controlled by common law. Researching statutes or constitutions should be unnecessary or require minimal time, and you can focus on finding relevant case law as described in Chapter 5.

The research process itself is not always linear. Secondary sources often cite relevant cases or statutes. When you update your research with a citator you might find new cases or articles to review. As you search, you may find additional research terms to add to those you initially identified. Later in your research it may be helpful to review your initial work to see if you need to broaden your search in those sources. As you write your results, additional research could be needed if you discover new issues or if an argument needs further support.

III. Organizing the Research

A. Getting Started

One of the first steps in an organized research strategy is to make sure you understand the objective of the project you are undertaking. You need to know exactly what the supervising attorney (or client) expects. For example, does your supervisor want you to spend an hour or two finding a handful of applicable cases or does she expect you to compile a comprehensive review of the case law on the subject, involving many hours of research and writing? Many attorneys have had the misfortune of incorrectly assuming what the client wanted and wasting time needlessly. Beginning researchers in particular should ask enough questions to fully understand the research task.[2] Examples of the types of questions to ask a supervisor include: When is the assignment is due? What type of document is needed? Which jurisdiction's law is applicable?[3] Once you understand the scope of the project, you can begin the research process.

B. Structuring a Plan

With the goal clearly in mind, your first step is to develop your research *strategy*. This is just a list of the different types of legal resources you plan to search. By writing out a strategy you ensure that you check all the relevant sources of law. A written plan can also make a new project seem less daunting since you will have specific steps to follow. Referring to this document often can help keep your research on track and ensure you do not miss a step. As you develop your strategy, you want to stay cognizant of your goal and consider the structure of your research issue. Contemplate questions such as:

---

2. Drake's Research Reality Check webpage provides links to articles detailing what those questions should be at http://drakelaw.libguides.com/content.php?pid=101949&sid=766975.

3. For additional examples, see Mark E. Wojcik, *Quick Tip: Ten Questions for New Lawyers to Ask,* at http://www.lwionline.org/publications/seconddraft/dec06.pdf.

- How will the research be used? (For example, will I write a client advice letter or draft a motion?)
- What is the scope of the research? (For example, do I only need to provide a brief overview at this point or complete an extensive analysis of the issues?)
- What is the deadline to finish the project?
- Are there any cost constraints in the research and how much time is it expected to take?
- Is this issue controlled by state or federal law, or both?
- Are there statutes or constitutional provisions on point or is this something covered by the common law?
- Are administrative rules or decisions likely to be involved?
- Where in the research process will online sources be more effective and cost efficient than print sources?
- What period of time needs to be researched?

You should constantly assess your progress and feel free to revise your strategy as you learn more about the issues. For example, you might encounter a case or secondary resource that identifies a related cause of action that you had not previously considered. If that occurs, you will need to adjust your research.

Included in your strategy will be a list of research terms generated from the facts and issues in your problem. Develop an expansive list by brainstorming. As you work in each new resource, refer back to this list. On the list note which terms were helpful in which resource. As you discover new terms, add them to the list. If you are having difficulty identifying search terms, consider beginning with a secondary resource to give you some context for the project.

C. Implementing Your Plan

Once you begin consulting specific resources, you will keep a research trail. While the strategy document outlines what you intend to do in your research, the research trail notes what you really did. By comparing the two, you will keep on top of your research and minimize duplication. Some researchers keep detailed notes on their strategy document, so that becomes their process trail. With experience, you will be able to develop a system that works well for you.

Two hallmarks of effective research are good organization and documentation of what you find. Your research needs to be organized in the manner most effective to help you marshal the resources, understand the legal issues, and analyze the problem presented. Many people find a computer an efficient means of collecting their research, but a legal pad, note cards, or an organized folder can also be effective.[4] Software that provides fact and issue management, such as CaseMap, can help you organize information about the cases you find as well.[5]

In each step of your research, take careful notes. These notes need not be formal, but should be sufficient to indicate what you have done or found. Detailed notes help you avoid duplication, especially as you start and stop the process to do other work. In addition, keeping detailed notes that include the sources you searched and the ways you searched them will help you assess the effectiveness of your searches, which can save significant time when you review your initial research. For example, including both successful and unsuccessful index terms and searches will help you ensure that you don't repeat those same steps later. Your research notes can also help you relocate what you initially deemed an irrelevant or duplicative source that you later determine necessary.

When doing print research, note the volumes used, the indexes or tables checked, the terms searched, and the date of the search. For online research, the research trail should include the site, the database or link, the searches run, and the date of the search. Most electronic databases provide options for reviewing and often even saving

---

[4]. If you use a laptop, be sure to backup your work to a separate storage device. You don't want to be the subject in the oft-repeated horror story of the researcher whose computer crashed just before a deadline and had nothing backed up.

[5]. For information about CaseMap go to http://law.lexisnexis.com/casemap. Law students can find further details and download a free copy from http://www.lexisnexis.com/lawschool.

your research trail.[6] If you rely on these trails, make sure you know when they will expire and reference the trails in a single master research trail for your entire project. For example, you could keep a simple chart listing the following: (1) the date you searched, (2) the source consulted, (3) whether the research trail was captured by the database (and the date the trail expires) or if you kept your own notes on what you did, and (4) other notes briefly describing the research, such as "reviewed cases 2000–2010" or "good ALR annotation."

In addition to recording your research trail, take analytical notes about the information found. As you review the authorities, don't simply cut and paste the wording of the court or highlight or print it. Instead, summarize the issues in your own words (noting the pinpoint citations) and state what you learn from them. Such analytical notes should increase your understanding of the legal issues and prove invaluable as you organize and write your document. Strive to strike an appropriate balance. Taking notes that are too extensive or that include inappropriate detail may detract from more important tasks, such as the research itself or analyzing the results.

Whether you are working electronically, in print, or combining these approaches, you need a system for organizing your materials. For example, you may have a hard copy printout or copy of each of the most significant authorities. Those could be organized in a ring binder or set of files. Some possible headings or tabs include: strategy/process, secondary sources, primary authorities with statutes (plus any constitutional provision or rules) and cases, updating, and outline. Alternatively, you could set up similar computer folders to organize your materials electronically.

Be sure to keep focused on your objective and not become obsessed with creating a perfect research folder. Some researchers find that taking time to create a unique tab or file for each authority helps keep their work organized. However, if this process serves as a form of avoidance or procrastination, it can ultimately undermine the research process.

---

6. Westlaw provides a "Research Trail" and Lexis has a "History." Other services use different methods or terminology. Fastcase users, for example, see their last ten searches.

D. Secondary Authorities

Beginning your research with a secondary authority can help you gain a basic understanding of the relevant area of law and find references to primary authorities. When using a secondary authority, it can be helpful to prepare a short summary of what you have found and how it applies to your situation. Begin this process by summarizing the analysis the source provides, noting how it relates to your facts. If you discover issues that require more research, note those, and consider what the next source to consult might be. Secondary authorities include references to primary authorities, such as cases and statutes. As you find those cites, add them to your primary authority list. Resist the temptation to check that source immediately since it could break your train of thought.

Some inexperienced researchers underestimate the value of secondary authorities in the research process. Although you certainly want to emphasize relevant primary authorities in your legal documents, remember that secondary authorities can help you better understand the law and often enable you to do so more quickly than if you begin by perusing primary authorities. A few minutes with an on-point section of a legal encyclopedia may be more helpful in your initial research than wading through a number of case decisions trying to find the relevant law. After using a secondary authority you can more effectively turn to your primary authorities.

E. Primary Authorities

Once you are ready to review your list of primary authorities, eliminate the inevitable duplicates so you don't check the same source twice. While some novice researchers take the entire list of authorities and print or copy a voluminous stack of materials to review, taking the time to look at the authorities being retrieved is often more effective. That doesn't mean you need to read each word of each authority at this stage. You may just skim the authority to make sure it is relevant. Later you can be more deliberate and review it in more detail.

A few tips can help you skim to see if the authority is relevant. For statutes and rules, scan the sections that give definitions or explain the statute's purpose. Look for operative language that establishes duties or proscribes certain conduct. Browse the sections just before and after your code section to see if they are relevant. For cases, begin by reading the synopsis. The headnotes or core concepts follow and can help you zero in on the most relevant parts of the case. Jump from the relevant headnote(s) to the corresponding text of the case and make sure the language of the opinion addresses your issue. That jump enables you to skip unrelated points of law and other parts, such as the procedural history, that perhaps are not germane.

As you initially review sources, make a few notes on your list of authorities. For promising materials, briefly indicate their relevance. Strike through authorities that do not seem applicable. Do not delete them entirely, however, because they might ultimately become useful or relevant.

After you have selected a set of relevant authorities, develop an organizational schedule for reading them in groups. If there is a constitutional provision, statute, or rule on point, read it carefully, then read cases that interpret the provision. One approach is to read cases in chronological order, so that you see the development of the law over time. However, this may be time-consuming for causes of action that have continued for many years. Except for historical research, you should impose an artificial cut-off going back a set number of years so you can focus on more recent cases.[7] Another approach is to begin with the most recent cases. The benefit of reviewing recent cases is that you may be able to avoid reading law in old cases that has been revised or superseded.

After you have assembled this group of relevant authorities, read them with care, especially any areas you skipped initially. For statutory research, be sure to read the definitions section of the relevant

---

7. The cut-off may depend on the substantive issue involved. In an area with dramatic growth and change in law, such as patent infringement, the cutoff would be relatively short. A longer cut-off would be appropriate for an area that develops over time, such as an issue involving constitutional law.

statutory provision. In each court decision, make sure you understand the procedural history, including the standard each court applied. You want to have a good understanding of the facts of each case. A time line or chart of party relationships can be helpful. As you read the case, cross out parts that deal with issues not confronting your client so you won't reread those portions the next time you look at the case. If you find a case isn't relevant at all, clearly indicate that on the first page of the case so you don't read it more than once. If you are looking at several issues or related claims, consider them one at a time. Doing so will require separate lists of authorities for each claim being researched.

1. Taking Notes on Statutes

Notes on statutes should include both the actual language of the statute and your analysis or outline of it. Because the exact words of statutes are so critical, you should preserve that text in hard copy or electronic form. In order to effectively analyze a complex statute, you should outline it. Highlighting is sufficient only if a statute is very short and clear. A statute often includes the elements of the claim or indicates the time limitations for bringing the claim.

The definition sections of statutes are often the most important. If terms are not defined, you will need to make a note to look for judicial definitions. If a relevant statute includes cross-references to other statutes, be sure to read them as well.

2. Taking Notes on Cases

Once you determine that a case is relevant, you should brief it. Doing so does not require any formal style. The brief for each case should be a set of notes highlighting the key aspects of the case that are relevant to your research problem. Create a short summary of the pertinent facts, holding, and reasoning. Each case brief should include the following:

- *Citation.* Having the full citation will make writing your analysis easier because you won't have to refer back to the original case.

- *Facts.* Only facts relevant to your problem should be recorded.
- *Holding and reasoning.* Provide a summary of the court's analysis and include only those issues relevant to your problem. If the case includes a tort claim and a related contract claim, for example, but only the tort claim relates to your problem, then you only should take notes on the tort issues. Skim the contract information just to be sure nothing relevant is buried there and then move on.
- *Pinpoint pages.* Case citations require pinpoint references to the exact page where the cited information is found. When noting the page, be sure that you have the citation to the correct reporter if the case has parallel citations. Online versions of a case often have star pagination, which means you have to check to see which reporter page break corresponds to a single or double asterisk.[8]
- *Reflections.* Note your thoughts on the case: How do you expect to use the case in your analysis? Does it resolve certain issues in your problem? Does it raise new questions?
- *Updating information.* Provide a designate space on each brief for updating. Each case you use in your analysis must be updated with Shepard's or KeyCite.

F. Updating

Updating, described in detail in Chapter 9, will be helpful at several points in your research. Using Shepard's or KeyCite early on will lead you to other relevant authorities. Updating before you begin to rely on an authority is especially important; you must confirm that each authority you include in your analysis is still "good law." At the end of your research, before you submit the document, you will want to update again to make sure nothing has changed. Printing lists of

---

8. For more details on star pagination, see the discussion and illustrations in Chapter 2.

IV. Outlining Your Analysis

Because the most effective research often occurs in conjunction with the analysis of your particular project, try to develop an outline that addresses your client's problem as soon as possible. If outlining is not your forte, consider a chart that organizes all the primary authority into issues or elements, such as in Table 12-1.

Your initial analytical outline or chart could be based on information in a secondary source, the requirements of a statute, or the elements of a common law claim. As you conduct research, your outline will become more detailed. However, you cannot reread every case or statute in its entirety each time you include it in your outline.

Table 12-1. Sample Analysis Chart

Research Question: Is an automobile or truck an "occupied structure" within the meaning of the burglary statute so that breaking into a vehicle is a chargeable crime under that statute?

Controlling Statutes: Burglary is defined under Iowa Code §713.1 (2009): "Any person, having the intent to commit a felony, assault or theft therein, who, having no right, license or privilege to do so, enters an *occupied structure*, such occupied structure not being open to the public, or who remains therein after it is closed to the public or after the person's right, license or privilege to be there has expired, or any person having such intent who breaks an occupied structure, commits burglary."

Under Iowa Code §702.12 (2009), "An '*occupied structure*' is any building, structure, appurtenances to buildings and structures, land, water or air vehicle, or similar place adapted for overnight accommodation of persons, or occupied by persons for the purpose of carrying on business or other activity therein, or for the storage or safekeeping of anything of value. Such a structure is an 'occupied structure' whether or not a person is actually present."

Table 12-1. Sample Analysis Chart, *continued*

Case	General Rule	Facts of the Case	Holding/Reasoning
State v. Williams, 409 N.W.2d 187 (Iowa 1987).	An occupied structure as defined in the Iowa burglary statute includes land vehicles; a topper-enclosed pickup truck that is entered for the purpose of theft falls within that statutory language.	Defendant was observed opening the camper shell door on the back of a pickup, transferring two tires into his vehicle, and then driving away.	The illegal entry into an enclosed camper on a pickup truck is the entry of an occupied structure and may be the basis for a burglary charge under the Iowa statutes.
State v. Sylvester, 331 N.W.2d 130 (Iowa 1983).	Definition of occupied structure under the Iowa Code is very broad. An occupied structure not only includes buildings but extends to vehicles on land, water or air, without regard to whether a person is actually present.	While beer truck driver was making a delivery to a business establishment, the defendants were observed entering the beer truck and removing several cases of beer.	Definition of occupied structure includes any vehicle for the storage or safekeeping of anything of value. Plain meaning includes delivery trucks. Statute does not require the structure to be locked.
State v. Buss, 325 N.W.2d 384 (Iowa 1982).	Consistent with the rules of statutory construction, definition of occupied structure under the Iowa Code encompasses a dwelling and much more, including an automobile.	Defendant was charged with breaking into the cab of a Chevrolet pickup truck.	Although defendant contended that the truck was not an occupied structure because it was not *primarily* used for storage or safekeeping, the Court found that the statute lacked such qualifying language and that an automobile exclusion would eliminate car break-ins as aggravated theft. The Court held that the cab of the pickup was an "occupied structure" within the meaning of the burglary statute and reversed the district court.

A better approach would be to refer to your notes and briefs to find the key ideas supporting each step in your analysis.

With an outline or chart you should be able to synthesize the law, apply the law to your client's problem, and reach a conclusion on the desired outcome. As you apply the law to your client's facts, you may discover other research issues that were not apparent from an abstract review of the law.

V. When to Stop Researching

Deciding when to stop researching and start writing can be a difficult decision, especially for a novice researcher. If a client, supervisor, or court has set a deadline, that dictates the time that can be spent. Costs to the client will also be a factor.

The most significant misconception in legal research is that you will always find a clear answer in some resource if only you look long and hard enough. In reality, things are rarely this straight-forward. If you have that "Eureka moment," you can stop researching, but only if you are confident that you have actually located a straightforward answer to your problem. Be sure to carefully question whether a legal source can be distinguished or evaluated in a manner that is inconsistent with your position.

In most instances, there is no such Eureka moment or definitive resource, and you have to determine when to stop your research. Typically, you should feel comfortable stopping when you have come full circle, meaning that you are consistently coming back to the same authorities. When this occurs, you can be confident that you have been thorough. To double-check, you can go through each step of the basic research process to ensure you considered each one. Review your strategy and research trail.

If you work through the research process and find that you are not locating an on-point source, consider the possibility that nothing exists. More than one of the authors of this text was given a research assignment by a senior attorney and spent many fruitless hours without finding a single applicable authority. When those results were reported, the senior attorney responded, "I didn't think there were any. Thanks for confirming that."[9] Finding nothing on point is not unusual. In law practice, that often happens when the area of law is new, such as in the environmental law field, where there may be no appellate decisions or published trial decisions. However, before you throw in the towel, be sure to expand your research terms and look in a few more secondary sources. Also consider whether a persuasive authority from another jurisdiction could be used.

Keep in mind that your ultimate goal is to solve your client's problem and, if that is not possible because legal authority does not support a resolution, then your goal must be to advise your client accordingly. Sometimes the law will not seem to provide the answer your client wants. In that case you must think creatively. Although you must report to your supervisor what the law is and that your client's desired outcome is in question, be sure to consider if alternative options can be suggested. Finally, keep in mind your ethical obligation of candor, which requires you to deliver disappointing results if that is what your research reveals.

---

9. This was a great relief to the young researchers, who fully expected to be told otherwise. Now more experienced and wiser, both researchers realize this stress could have been avoided by asking more questions about the research task when it was assigned and checking back with the supervisor earlier.

Appendix

Legal Citations

I. Introduction

As explained in Chapter 2, legal citations indicate precisely where an authority can be found. Legal arguments normally include references to many authorities and accurate citations are essential so that a judge, opposing counsel, or anyone else viewing the document can find your supporting references. Each rule of law given must cite the authority on which it is based. Through citations the reader can be told not only where to find the authority but the level of support the authority provides.[1] (See Table A-1.)

Table A-1. Purposes of Legal Citations

- Show the reader where to find the cited material in the original case, statute, rule, article, or other authority.
- Indicate the weight and persuasiveness of each authority, for example, by specifying the court that decided the case, the author of a document, and the publication date of the authority.
- Convey the type and degree of support the authority offers, for example, by indicating whether the authority supports your point directly or only implicitly.
- Demonstrate that the analysis in your document is the result of careful research.

Source: *ALWD Manual*.

---

1. ALWD & Darby Dickerson, *ALWD Citation Manual* 3 (4th ed., Aspen Publishers 2010) ("*ALWD Manual*").

Citation rules are much more than technical requirements to which attorneys much adhere. Providing uniform citations ensures that anyone reviewing the document can find the cited sources. Correct citations help a lawyer or judge appreciate that the arguments were well researched and the conclusions supported by authority. Poor citation practices reflect adversely even if the balance of the document is well drafted. Judges can become very frustrated with citations that are inaccurate to the point of criticizing the author in an opinion that will be preserved forever.[2]

In a legal document an attorney normally provides citations for all relevant authorities within the text of the work. Law professors often support their academic writing with extensive footnotes. Although the value of including citations may not be apparent at first, experienced researchers appreciate the leads that these citations can provide. Great attention to detail is required in providing citations because a seemingly simple omission or error can misdirect the reader. For example, if a case is in the second series of the Federal Supplement and the citation is made to "F. Supp." rather than "F. Supp. 2d," the correct case will not be found.

Legal citation practice has developed over many decades to the point that a correctly formatted citation is something that most lawyers understand and recognize. Knowing how to prepare correct citations is an expectation many lawyers and judges have for those joining the practice of law. Most law students start learning those skills during the first year of law school. Two national citation manuals provide citation guidance: the *ALWD Citation Manual*[3] and *The Bluebook: A Uniform System of Citation*.[4]

---

2. *See e.g. Bradshaw v. Unity Marine Corp.*, 147 F. Supp. 2d 668 (S.D. Texas 2001)(the judge criticizes counsel for failing to give correct citations and for not giving pinpoint citations, among other problems).

3. ALWD & Darby Dickerson, *ALWD Citation Manual* (4th ed., Aspen Publishers 2010).

4. *The Bluebook: A Uniform System of Citation* (The Columbia Law Review et al. eds., 19th ed., The Harvard Law Review Assn. 2010)("*Bluebook*"). An online version also is available. See http://www.legalbluebook.com.

Most jurisdictions promulgate citation rules that attorneys filing documents in those jurisdictions must follow and those rules may or may not follow the style of one of the national manuals.[5] Whenever you are preparing a legal document be sure you know who your audience is and what citation rules must be followed.

II. The *Bluebook*

The Bluebook: A Uniform System of Citation was released in its nineteenth edition in 2010. The work is compiled by the editors of the Columbia Law Review, the Harvard Law Review, the University of Pennsylvania Law Review, and The Yale Law Journal. A new edition is released every five years and until the *ALWD Manual* was published in 2000, the *Bluebook* was the only national citation system that was widely recognized.[6] As a result, checking of citations became known as "Bluebooking."

The *Bluebook* provides citation examples aimed at two different groups: (a) those working with law review articles, and (b) practitioners. The bulk of the book, the "Whitepages," is devoted to the law review audience and the examples throughout the text show how to prepare citations for law review footnotes.[7] The footnote format requires a different typeface convention than what practitioners use, which sometimes is a bit confusing for first-time *Bluebook* users. For example, large and small caps are required in footnotes for periodical abbreviations, e.g., Iowa L. Rev., and book citations, e.g., James Adams, Pretrial Motions in Criminal Prosecutions. The inside front cover includes a Quick Reference for citing law review footnotes.

---

5. See Appendix 2 of the *ALWD Manual* for Local Court Citation Rules.

6. The University of Chicago attempted to do so with a *Maroonbook*, but that effort did not attract a following. It is available at http://lawreview.uchicago.edu/resources/style_sheet.html.

7. Bluepages cover the first 51 pages and Whitepages are from page 53 to 511.

The first section contains the "Bluepages" which provides citation guidance for practitioners for court documents and legal memoranda, which is what format that most lawyers and first-year law students use. The typeface convention is very simple and reminiscent of what can be produced on a typewriter: ordinary Roman type with underlining to show italics. The inside *back* cover gives a Quick Reference summary of the practitioner rules with examples. Tables in the back show which authority to cite and how to abbreviate properly.

III. *ALWD Manual*

The *ALWD Manual* was created by the Association of Legal Writing Directors "because lawyers, judges, law teachers, and law students need a citation manual that is easy to use, easy to teach from, and easy to learn from."[8] It codifies the most commonly followed rules for legal citation, serving much like a restatement. The *ALWD Manual* is consistent with the *Bluebook* on most practices and is increasingly so with the fourth edition changes released in 2010.[9] The primary difference is that the *ALWD Manual* uses a single, consistent system of citation using ordinary type for all materials, whether they be legal memoranda, court documents, law review articles, or some other authority.

IV. Legal Citation in Iowa

A. Introduction

Although some jurisdictions reference a particular citation manual in their rules, Iowa does not. Iowa follows generally accepted ci-

---

8. *ALWD Manual* Preface xiii.
9. *See e.g. ALWD Manual* Preface (contractions as abbreviations, such as Dep't and Ass'n, are acceptable now, which matches *Bluebook* rules). *See also* Peter W. Martin, *Introduction to Basic Legal Citation* § 1-100 (LII 2010), http://www.law.cornell.edu/citation.

tation practices and outlines its rules for citation at Iowa Rule of Appellate Procedure 6.904:[10]

Rule 6.904 References in briefs.

6.904(1) *To the parties.* In briefs counsel should minimize references to parties by such designations as "appellant" and "appellee" and should use the actual names of the parties or descriptive terms such as "the plaintiff," "the defendant," "the employee," "the injured person," "the taxpayer," or "the decedent."

6.904(2) *To legal authorities.*

a. Cases. In citing cases, the names of parties must be given. In citing Iowa cases, reference must be made to the volume and page where the case may be found in the North Western Reporter. If the case is not reported in the North Western Reporter, reference must be made to the volume and page where the case may be found in the Iowa Reports. In citing cases, reference must be made to the court that rendered the opinion and the volume and page where the opinion may be found in the National Reporter System, if reported therein. *E.g.,* _ N.W.2d _ (Iowa 20_); _ N.W.2d _ (Iowa Ct. App. 20_); _ S.W.2d _ (Mo. Ct. App. 20_); _ U.S._, _ S. Ct._, _ L. Ed. 2d _ (20_); _ F.3d _ (_Cir. 20_); _ F. Supp. 2d _ (S.D. Iowa 20_). When quoting from authorities or referring to a particular point within an authority, the specific page or pages quoted or relied upon shall be given in addition to the required page references.

b. Iowa Court Rules. When citing the Iowa Court Rules parties shall use the following references:

(1) "Iowa R. Civ. P."; "Iowa R. Crim. P."; "Iowa R. Evid."; "Iowa R. App. P."; "Iowa R. of Prof'l Conduct"; and "Iowa Code of Judicial Conduct" when citing those rules.

(2) "Iowa Ct. R." when citing all other rules.

---

10. Iowa Court Rules are available at http://www.iowacourts.gov/Court_Rules_and_Forms.

c. Unpublished opinions or decisions. An unpublished opinion or decision of a court or agency may be cited in a brief if the opinion or decision can be readily accessed electronically. Unpublished opinions or decisions shall not constitute controlling legal authority. When citing an unpublished opinion or decision a party shall include an electronic citation indicating where the opinion may be readily accessed online.

E.g., No. _____, _____ WL _____, at *__ (____ 20__).

d. Other authorities. When citing other authorities, references shall be made as follows:

(1) Citations to codes shall include the section number and date.

(2) Citations to treatises, textbooks, and encyclopedias shall include the edition, section, and page.

(3) Citations to all other authorities shall include the page or pages.

e. Internal cross-references. Use of "supra" and "infra" is not permitted.

As noted in Chapter 2, for most Iowa authorities the citation will look the same whether you are using the *Bluebook*, *ALWD Manual*, or following the Iowa court rules. Below are additional examples. The *Bluebook* examples follow the format for Court Documents and Legal Memoranda.

B. Cases

Iowa Supreme Court:

McCarty v. Jeffers, 154 N.W.2d 718 (Iowa 1967).

Beebe v. Funkhouser, 2 Iowa 314 (1855).[11]

---

11. The official Iowa Reports must be cited if the case is not reported in the North Western Reporter, which began publication in 1879. The North Western Reporter became the official reporter in 1968 when Iowa Reports ceased publication.

Iowa Court of Appeals (since 1977):

    Iowa Court Rules and *Bluebook*:

        Cooper v. Kirkwood Community College, 782 N.W.2d 160 (Iowa Ct. App. 2010).

    ALWD Manual:

        Cooper v. Kirkwood Community College, 782 N.W.2d 160 (Iowa App. 2010). [drop Ct.]

U.S. District Court for the Southern District of Iowa:

    Fields v. NCR Corp., 683 F. Supp. 2d 980 (S.D. Iowa 2010).

U.S. Court of Appeals for the Eighth Circuit:

    Kluesner v. Astrue, 607 F.3d 533 (8th Cir. 2010).

U.S. Supreme Court

    Iowa Court Rules (parallel citations):

        Iowa v. Tovar, 541 U.S. 77, 124 S. Ct. 1379, 158 L. Ed. 2d 209 (2004).

    ALWD Manual and *Bluebook* (no parallel citations):

        Iowa v. Tovar, 541 U.S. 77 (2004).

        Gross v. FBL Fin. Servs., Inc., 129 S. Ct. 2343 (2009). [use S. Ct. if U.S. not available]

C. Statutes

A citation to a statute includes the state code, section number, and year. Federal codes begin with title number.

    Iowa Code § 232.102 (2011). [official version]

    Iowa Code Ann. § 232.102 (West 2006 & Supp. 2010).

    19 U.S.C. § 2411 (2006). [official United States Code]

    19 U.S.C.A. § 2606 (West 2009). [United States Code Annotated]

    12 U.S.C.S. § 84(a)(2) (Lexis 2008). [United States Code Service]

D. Constitutions

Constitution citations include the abbreviated name followed by the pinpoint reference. Citations to current constitutions do not require a date.

> Iowa Const. art. XII, § 1.
>
> U.S. Const. amend I.

E. Administrative Regulations

Administrative codes typically are cited by title number, abbreviated name of code, pinpoint subdivision, and year. The *Code of Federal Regulations* begins with the title number but most state administrative codes do not.

> Iowa Admin. Code r. 17-13.3 (2010).
>
> 31 C.F.R. § 515.329 (2010). [Code of Federal Regulations]

F. Books and Periodicals

Books typically are cited by the book's author(s), title, page or section where the information is found, edition, publisher, and copyright date.[12]

> Jerry L. Anderson & Dennis D. Hirsch, *Environmental Law Practice: Problems and Exercises for Skills Development* 123 (3d ed., Carolina Academic Press 2010).

Periodical citations normally include the author(s), title, volume of the periodical, abbreviated periodical title, beginning page, page on which the information is found, date.

> Allan W. Vestal & J. William Callison, *Taming the Mandibles of Death: Secrecy, Disclosure, and Fiduciary Duties in the Re-*

---

12. For more examples, see *Bluebook* Rule 15 and *ALWD* Rule 22. *Bluebook* form omits the publisher.

vised Uniform Limited Liability Company Act, 59 Cath. U. L. Rev. 183, 185 (2009).

About the Authors

John D. Edwards is Associate Dean for Information Resources and Technology and Professor of Law at Drake University Law School. He has directed Drake's Legal Research program since 1985 and served as Executive Director of Legal Research and Writing for more than two decades. He received his J.D. from the University of Missouri-Kansas City School of Law, his M.A.L.S. from the University of Missouri-Columbia, and his B.A. from Southeast Missouri State University.

M. Sara Lowe served as Reference Librarian and Assistant Professor of Librarianship at Drake University Law School from 2009–2011. She has worked in academic, special, and public libraries over the past decade. She received her M.L.S. and M.A. from Indiana University-Bloomington and her B.A. from the University of Missouri-Columbia. She is currently Electronic Resources Librarian at Claremont University Consortium.

Karen L. Wallace is Circulation/Reference Librarian and Professor of Librarianship at Drake University Law School, where she has worked for over a decade. Prior to joining Drake, she worked in public libraries for over five years. She received both her M.A. and B.A. from the University of Iowa.

Melissa H. Weresh is a Professor of Law and the Director of Legal Writing at Drake University Law School. She received her B.A. from Wake Forest University and her J.D. from the University of Iowa College of Law. She is the President-Elect of the Legal Writing Institute and an active member of the Association of Legal Writing Directors and the Association of American Law School's Section on Legal Writing, Reasoning, and Research. She has been teaching at Drake University Law School since 1997.

Index

ABA Journal, 263
ABA Model Code of Judicial Conduct, 255–256
ABA Model Code of Professional Responsibility, 251, 252–253, 262
ABA Model Rules of Professional Conduct, 251, 252–253, 261–262
Abbreviations,
  ALWD citation, 9, 67, 282, 284
  Bluebook citation, 48, 67, 283–284
  Citations, generally, 35–37
  Federal reporters, 118
  In digests, 130, 132
  Regional reporters, 112
  Tables of, 32, 79–81, 132
Abstracts, 65
Acts and Joint Resolutions (Iowa Legislature), 141, 170, 179, 189
Administrative agencies,
  Agency publication list in *ALWD Citation Manual*, 212
  Federal, 107, 201
  Generally, 192
  Iowa, 194
  Regulations, 192
Administrative law, 53, 70, 191–214
  Enabling statutes,
    Federal, 202
    Generally, 192
    Iowa, 193
  Iowa, 193–201
  Research process,
    Federal, 206–211
    Iowa, 197–201
  Rules and regulations, 7, 270
    Federal, 201–206
    Iowa, 192–195
  Statutory law, relation to, 192
  Updating,
    Federal regulations, 209–211
    Iowa rules, 200–201
  See also Code of Federal Regulations (CFR); *Iowa Administrative Code* (IAC); *Iowa Administrative Bulletin* (IAB)
Administrative Law Treatise (Pierce), 209
Administrative Procedure Act (APA), 201
Administrative rules,

294 Index

See Rules and regulations, administrative agencies
Adoption by reference, 60
Advance sheets, 109, 110, 121, 130
Agency decisions, 191, 209, 219
 Federal, 212–213
 Iowa, 212
ALI,
 See American Law Institute (ALI)
ALR,
 See American Law Reports (ALR)
ALWD Citation Manual, 67, 212, 282
 Abbreviations, 67
 Association of Legal Writing Directors (ALWD), 284
 Generally, 9
American Bar Association (ABA), 59, 65
American digest system, West's, 122–128
American Jurisprudence, Second Edition (AmJur), 77–81
American Law Institute (ALI), 56, 57, 59, 62, 249
American Law Reports (ALR), 52, 53, 72–75
 In AmJur, 77
 In administrative law research, 209
Analysis of American Law, West's, 127
Annotations,
 Constitutional research, 95–96, 101

Court rules, 158
 In *Iowa Code Annotated*, 95–96, 98, 147
 LexisNexis, 208
 Regulatory research, 208
 Statutory research, 147, 154
 See also American Law Reports (ALR)
Appellate courts, 104, 108, 119, 127
 Federal, 9, 107, 119, 120
 Generally, 8–9, 104
 Iowa, 8, 104, 106–107
Association of Legal Writing Directors,
 See ALWD Citation Manual
Authority,
 Case law, 103, 109 n. 15, 116, 286
 Constitution, 87
 Dispositive, 16
 Ethical duty to provide, 11, 280
 Mandatory authority, 6, 8, 139
 Mandatory v. persuasive, 5–8, 280
 Persuasive authority, 6–7, 8, 262, 280
 Primary authority, 5–6, 273–275
 Primary v. secondary, 5–6, 51
 Regulations, 192–193
 Secondary authority, 6, 15–16, 218, 273
 Statutes, 139, 193
 See also Updating

Ballentine's Law Dictionary, 75–76
Bar journals, 63, 66, 68
  See also Iowa Lawyer
Bieber's Dictionary of Legal Abbreviations, 36 n. 23, 67
Bill tracking,
  Federal, 186
  Generally, 176
  Iowa, 179
Bills,
  Federal, 181–182, 187
  Iowa, 141–142, 150, 163–165, 167, 172, 174–176, 178, 180–182
  See also Bill tracking; Legislative history; Legislative process
Black letter law, 77
Black's Law Dictionary, 76
Bluebook (*The Bluebook: A Uniform System of Citation*), 10, 47–48, 67, 70, 195, 282, 283–284, 286–287
BNA,
  See Bureau of National Affairs (BNA)
Boolean connectors, 40–41
Brief banks, 247–248
Bureau of National Affairs (BNA), 55, 70

Canons of Professional Ethics, 252–253
Case analysis, 137–138, 275–276, 278
Case research, 36, 43, 46, 111, 129, 132, 134

Citation, 36, 46
  Headnotes, 43
  In secondary sources, 56–59, 70–71, 72–75, 84
  Online research, 37–45, 46
  Opinions, 108
    Unpublished, 109, 286
  Prior history, 219, 226
  Updating online, 136
  See also Digests; Reporters; Subsequent history
Catalog,
  See Library catalog
CCH,
  See Commerce Clearing House (CCH)
CFR,
  See Code of Federal Regulations (CFR)
Circuit courts, federal,
  See United States Courts of Appeals
Citation manuals, 9–10, 47, 108, 281
  See also ALWD Citation Manual; *Bluebook* (*The Bluebook: A Uniform System of Citation*)
Citation rules, generally, 35–37, 47–49, 281–289
Citators, generally, 99, 136, 215, 217–218, 233–234
  See also KeyCite; Shepard's citators
Civil procedure, 240, 245
CJS,
  See Corpus Juris Secundum (CJS)

CLE,
　See Continuing legal education (CLE)
Code of Federal Regulations (CFR), 201–202, 204–206, 214, 288
　List of CFR Sections Affected (LSA), 210, 211
　Updating, 209–211
Code of Iowa, 95–96, 142–144, 170, 180, 244, 256–257
　In statutory interpretation, 150–151
Codification, defined, 140
Codified statutes, 140
　Federal, 154–157
　Iowa, 142–144
　Other states, 151–152
Commerce Clearing House (CCH), 55, 70
Common law, 5–6, 53, 56, 167
　Defined, 103
　Researching, 6–7, 56, 268, 270, 277
　Statutory law, relation to, 103
Concurring or dissenting opinion, 108
Congressional Information Service (CIS), 185
　See also LexisNexis Congressional
Congressional Record, 182, 184–185, 187
Constitutional law research, 93–95
　See also Iowa Constitution
Continuing legal education (CLE), 237, 248–249

Contracting and Organizations Research Institute (CORI), 247
Controlled vocabulary, 63–64
Corpus Juris Secundum (CJS), 76, 77, 95
Cornell Legal Information Institute, 62, 152
Cost-effective searching, 28–29, 67
Court of last resort, 106
Court rules, 157, 160
　Federal, 158–159, 160
　Iowa, 105, 157–158, 160, 255–256
Court systems, 8–10, 104–108
　Federal, 9, 106–107
　Iowa, 8, 104–106
　Other states, 9, 107–108

Daily Compilation of Presidential Documents, 214
Databases,
　Cost-effective searching, 28–29, 67
　Using, 29, 30, 37–46, 55, 72, 244, 246
　See also Bureau of National Affairs (BNA); Commerce Clearing House (CCH); EBSCO; HeinOnline; LexisNexis; OCLC; Research Institute of America (RIA); Scopus; Westlaw
Descriptive-Word Index,
　See Digests, Descriptive-Word Index
Dictionaries,

See Legal dictionaries
Digests, 122–128
  Decennial Digest, West's, 123
  Descriptive-Word Index, 129–132
  Generally, 122
  Headnotes, 127
  Key numbers, 29–30, 126–127
  Online, 133–134
  Research process, 128–133
  Table of Cases, 128
  Topics, 126–27
  Updating, 136
  Words and Phrases, 127–128
  See also Iowa Digest; *North Western Digest*
Disciplinary action, 253, 255
Disciplinary rules (DRs), 253
Disposition tables, 143
Dissenting opinion, 108
District courts, 8–9
  Iowa, 104–105
  Reporters for, 118, 119
  United States, 8–10, 104, 106–107
Docket number, 109 n. 18, 115

EBSCO, 66
Eighth Circuit Court of Appeals, U.S., 9, 107
Enabling statutes,
  See Administrative law
Encyclopedias,
  See Legal encyclopedias
Engrossed bill, 166
Enrolled bill, 181
Environment Reporter, 71
Ethical considerations (ECs), 253

Ethics, 251–265
Examples and Explanations series, 54
Executive orders and proclamations, 213, 214

Fastcase, 28, 29, 37, 272 n. 6
Federal Appendix (Fed. Appx.), 118, 119
Federal Practice Digest, 123
Federal Register, 201–202, 202–204
Federal Reporter (F., F.2d, F.3d), 118, 119, 120, 123
Federal research,
  Administrative law, 206–209
  Cases, 128–135
  Digests, 122, 123, 127
  Reporters, 118–121
  Statutes, 152–157
  See also Bill tracking; Constitutional law research; Court rules; Legislative history
Federal Rules Decisions (F.R.D.), 118, 119
Federal Supplement (F. Supp., F. Supp. 2d), 118, 119, 123
Finding tools, 13, 24, 31–35, 52, 130, 154, 178, 195, 217, 246
  See also Citators, generally; Digests; Disposition tables; Indexes; Key numbers; LexisNexis; Parallel tables; Popular name tables; Tables of cases; Tables of contents
FindLaw, 27, 101, 120, 121, 151, 159, 206, 208, 247
Fiscal notes, 172–173

Forms and formbooks, 237, 241–247
Full-text sources, 63–65

Gale LegalForms, 246
General Assembly of Iowa, 191, 192
Google Books, 55
Google Scholar, 69
Government Printing Office (GPO), 152, 184–185, 204, 206
GPO Access, 101, 157, 210
GPO FDsys, 187, 201

Headnotes, 43, 126, 127
  Defined, 116
  Westlaw, 129
  Words and Phrases, 127–128
  See also Digests
Hearings, 182, 187, 194, 212
HeinOnline, 29 n. 11, 55, 65, 121, 152, 153, 154, 183–185, 187, 204, 206, 213
Hornbooks, 54
House Journal (Iowa), 169, 175–176

IAB,
  See Iowa Administrative Bulletin (IAB)
IAC,
  See Iowa Administrative Code (IAC)
ICC,
  See International Code Council (ICC)

ILL,
  See Interlibrary loan (ILL)
Index to Periodical Articles Related to Law, 65
Index to Legal Periodicals (ILP), 65
Indexes, 13–14, 31–33, 68, 75, 85, 130, 178, 246, 271
  Defined, 63–65
  In specific sources, 56–57, 60, 71, 73, 79–81
Interim committees, 177, 180
Interlibrary loan (ILL), 68
Internet,
  See Online legal research; Search engines
International Code Council (ICC), 59
Iowa administrative agencies, 193
  See also Agency decisions
Iowa Administrative Bulletin (IAB), 193, 194
Iowa Administrative Code (IAC), 60, 193, 194–195
Iowa Administrative Procedure Act (IAPA), 193
Iowa administrative rules, 193–194, 197–201
  See also Rules and regulations, administrative agencies
Iowa cases, 117–118, 122
Iowa Code,
  See Code of Iowa
Iowa Code Annotated, 61, 90, 95–96, 97, 98, 99, 100, 141, 143–144, 170, 244, 287

Iowa Code of Judicial Conduct, 256, 285
Iowa Constitution, 6, 8
 Amendments, 88, 90–91
 History, 87–89
 See also Constitutional law research
Iowa Court of Appeals, 8, 104–106
Iowa courts, 8, 104–106, 150, 172, 173
Iowa Digest, 122
Iowa Lawyer, 63
Iowa legislative history, 166, 168–169
 Research process, 169, 176, 188–190
 Sources, 168–179
 See also General Assembly of Iowa; *House Journal*; *Senate Journal*
Iowa legislative process, 163–166
Iowa legislature,
 See General Assembly of Iowa
Iowa Pleading, Causes of Action and Defenses (LaMarca), 240
Iowa Practice Series, 239–240
Iowa Reports, 117
Iowa Rules of Court: Federal, 158–159
Iowa Rules of Court: State, 158, 244
Iowa Rules of Professional Conduct, 10, 216, 255, 256–257, 259–260
Iowa State Bar Association (ISBA), 259–261
Iowa State Bar Association manuals, 238–239
Iowa Supreme Court, 8, 106, 111, 117, 157–158, 255–256, 259–261
Iowa trial courts,
 See Trial courts, Iowa
IOWADOCS, 244
ISBA,
 See Iowa State Bar Association (ISBA)

Journal finders, 67
Journal of the House (Iowa),
 See House Journal
Journal of the Senate (Iowa),
 See Senate Journal
Judicial opinions, 5–6, 108–111
 Researching, 6–8
 Updating, 136
Jury instructions, 28, 239, 249–250
 Model jury instructions, 250

Key numbers, 29–30, 126–127, 128–134
KeyCite, 99, 209, 217–218, 226–233
 Generally, 45
 Updating with, 136, 149, 215, 217–218, 226–233, 276–277
Keyword searching, 38–41, 64, 82
 Defined, 23 n. 1

Law Library of Congress, 68

Law reviews, 6, 39, 53, 61, 65, 67–69, 168, 183, 208, 209, 219, 265
  Annotations as finding tools, 168, 179
  Citing, 52, 209, 283–284
  Defined, 63
Lawyers' Edition,
  See United States Supreme Court Reports, Lawyers' Edition (L. Ed., L. Ed. 2d)
Legal citation,
  See ALWD Citation Manual; *Bluebook* (*The Bluebook: A Uniform System of Citation*)
Legal dictionaries, 8, 52, 53, 75–76
Legal encyclopedias, 6, 52, 53, 76–82, 95, 245, 273, 286
  See also American Jurisprudence, Second Edition (AmJur); *Corpus Juris Secundum* (CJS)
Legal ethics opinions, 253–254
Legal Looseleafs in Print, 70
Legal periodicals, 8, 39, 52, 53, 62–69, 85, 95, 168
  See also ABA Journal; Bar journals; *Iowa Lawyer*; Law reviews
LegalTrac, 65
Legislative history, 163, 179
  Federal, 182–187
  Iowa, 166–169, 172, 176, 188
Legislative process, 150, 163–165, 179, 181–182
LexisNexis, 28, 37
  Search techniques, 38–47, 82, 122, 132–135, 149, 210–211, 272
  Sources in, 39, 55, 59, 65, 67, 72, 76, 77, 85, 98–99, 100, 103 n. 4, 119, 121, 142, 144, 148, 151, 153, 154, 158, 170 n. 7, 176, 178, 183–185, 187, 194, 195, 200, 204, 206, 208, 209, 213, 214, 244, 246, 249, 260, 261, 263, 264
  Topic and headnote system, 134
  See also Shepard's citators
LexisNexis Congressional, 183, 185, 187
LexisONE, 29, 120, 121, 245, 247
Library catalog, 22–24, 25–26, 55–56, 63, 70, 84, 183, 244, 246, 248, 250
List of CFR Sections Affected (LSA),
  See Code of Federal Regulations (CFR)
Looseleaf services, 52, 53, 70–72, 209
  Table of titles in *Bluebook*, 70

Mandatory authority,
  See Authority, mandatory
Majority opinion, 108–109
Model codes, 52, 53, 59–62
Model jury instructions,
  See Jury instructions
Model Rules of Professional Conduct, ABA, 251, 261–262

National Association of Insurance Commissioners, 59
National Conference of Commissioners on Uniform State Laws (NCCUSL), *See* Uniform Law Commission (ULC)
National reporter system, 110–111, 112, 127
National Survey of State Laws, 152
Natural language searching, 41–42
Newspaper articles, 169, 178
North Western Digest, 122, 123
North Western Reporter (N.W., N.W.2d), 111, 112, 117, 122, 123
Notes of decisions, 96–97
Nutshells, 54

OCLC, 66
Online legal research, 24, 37–46, 135, 148–149
  Boolean search queries, 40–41
  Choosing online sources, 38–39
  Commercial databases, 28–29, 37–38
  Free online resources, 22, 98, 120, 121, 157, 160, 184–185, 247
  Generally, 4
  Internet, 135
  Search techniques, 37–46
  Specialized legal databases, 28–29
  See also Bureau of National Affairs (BNA); Commerce Clearing House (CCH); Databases; EBSCO; HeinOnline; KeyCite; LexisNexis; OCLC; Research Institute of America (RIA); Scopus; Search engines; Shepard's citators; Westlaw
Ordinances, local, 159–161
Organizing research, 17, 269–270
Outlining, 277–279

PACER, 109
Paragraph numbers, 71
Parallel citations, 43, 287
  Defined, 36
Parallel tables, 154, 206
Persuasive authority,
  See Authority, persuasive
Pinpoint page, 276
Pocket parts, 30, 55
Popular name tables, 143, 154
Portfolios, 8, 52, 53, 70–72
Practice aids, 237–250
  Defined, 237
  Federal, 241
  Finding, 237–238
  See also Brief banks; Continuing legal education (CLE); Forms and formbooks; Iowa Practice Series; Iowa State Bar Association manuals; Jury instructions
Primary authority,
  See Authority, primary

Prior history, 219, 226
ProQuest Congressional,
 See LexisNexis Congressional
Public law number, 152, 182

Query structure, 37–42, 99, 133–134

Regulations,
 See Administrative agencies, regulations; Rules and regulations
Regulations.gov, 201
Reporters, 110–117
 Agency decisions, 212
 Federal court opinions, 118–121
 Generally, 110–111
 Iowa court opinions, 117
 Nominative, 117
 Regional, 111, 112
Research guides, 27, 52, 53, 82–85, 186, 238, 250, 265
Research Institute of America (RIA), 70
Research process,
 Generally, 4, 12–17, 38, 93, 104, 168, 279–280
 Unfamiliar area of law, 268
Research strategy, 12–17, 140, 267–273
Research terms,
 See Search terms, generation of
Restatement (Third) of the Law Governing Lawyers, 252, 264
Restatements, 7, 8, 51, 52, 53, 56–59, 219, 234
RIA
 See Research Institute of America (RIA)
Rule-making, 191
 See also Court rules
Rules and regulations,
 Administrative agencies, 107, 192
 Federal regulations, 201–202
 Generally, 191–193, 192 n. 3
 In secondary sources, 70
 Iowa administrative rules, 193–195

Scope notes, databases, 38, 55, 65, 77, 81, 99
Scopus, 66
Search engines, 68, 84, 135
Search terms, generation of, 12–16, 40–42, 82, 84, 130, 246, 248, 250, 268, 270
 Journalistic approach, 14–15, 130
 TARPP approach, 14–15, 130
Searching, cost-effective,
 See Cost-effective searching
Searching online,
 See Online legal research
Secondary authority,
 See Authority, secondary
Secondary sources, 51–85, 137, 154, 209, 226, 243, 249
 Citing to, 52
 Defined, 6–7, 51–52
 Use in research, generally, 12, 14–15, 21, 51–53, 104, 129, 134, 249, 264–265, 268, 272
Senate Journal (Iowa), 169, 175–176

Session laws,
  Defined, 140
  Federal, 153
  Iowa, 141–142, 146, 170–171
  Other states, 151
Shepard's citators, 136, 209, 215, 217–225, 276
  Case-finding tool, 218
  Code of Federal Regulations Citations, 209
  Print, 136, 233–236
  Updating with, 136, 217–225, 276
Shepardizing, 215, 217–225, 233–236, 268
  See also Shepard's citators
Signals, in citations, 223, 231
Signing statements, 183, 184, 214
Singer,
  See Statutory construction; *Statutes and Statutory Construction* (Singer)
Skeleton and popular name index, 61
Slip opinions and laws,
  Federal, 152–153, 157
  Generally, 109, 139–140
  Iowa, 141, 146
SSRN, 69
Star pagination, 43
Stare decisis, 103–104
State Bar of Iowa,
  See Iowa State Bar Association (ISBA)
Statutes,
  Citation of, 49, 287
  Defined, 139
  Enabling statutes, 192
  Federal, 152–157
  Generally, 139
  In secondary sources, 51, 53, 59–62, 64, 70–71, 75, 83–84
  Iowa, 141–144, 146
  Popular name table, 154
  Reading of, 150–151, 275
  Research process, 144–149, 275, 277
  See also Bill tracking; Codification, defined; KeyCite; Legislative history; Shepard's citators; Statutory construction
Statutes at Large (Stat.), 153, 157
Statutes and Statutory Construction (Singer), 150
Statutory construction, 150–151
Study aids, 55
Subject Compilations of State Laws, 83, 152
Subject headings or descriptors, 63–64
Subsequent history, 226
Supreme Court,
  See Iowa Supreme Court; United States Supreme Court
Supreme Court Reporter (S. Ct.), 118, 121
Supreme Court Reports, Lawyers' Edition (L. Ed., L. Ed. 2d), 118, 121

Tables of cases, 128
Tables of contents, 33–35
  In specific sources, 57, 61, 72, 73, 81, 82, 96, 99, 148, 149, 194, 196, 239, 257, 262

Terms and connectors searching, 40–41, 244, 260, 263
THOMAS website, 157, 184, 186, 187
Topic and Key Number System, West's,
See Key numbers
Topical research, 13, 177, 209, 261
Treatises, 6, 8, 36, 39–40, 43, 51, 52, 53, 54–56, 61, 168, 208–209, 286
Updating, 54–55
Trial courts, 106–107
Federal, 8, 106–107
Generally, 104
Iowa, 8, 104–105
Other states, 9, 107–108

ULC,
See Uniform Law Commission (ULC)
Uniform Commercial Code (UCC), 59, 61
Uniform jury instructions,
See Jury instructions
Uniform Law Commission (ULC), 59, 62
Uniform laws, 51, 52, 53, 59–62
Uniform Laws Annotated (ULA), 60–61
Uniform Rules on Agency Procedure (Iowa), 193
United States Code (USC), 154–157
United States Code Annotated (USCA), 154

United States Code Congressional and Administrative News (USCCAN), 152–153
United States Code Service (USCS), 154–155
United States Constitution,
See Constitutional law research
United States Courts of Appeals, 9, 107
United States District Courts, 8–10, 104, 106–107
United States Reports (U.S.), 118, 120–121
United States Statutes at Large,
See Statutes at Large (Stat.)
United States Supreme Court, 9, 107
United States Supreme Court Reports, Lawyers' Edition (L. Ed., L. Ed. 2d), 118, 121
Unpublished opinions,
See Case research, opinions, unpublished
Updating, 16, 30–31, 161, 204, 209–211, 215–218, 233
Research process, 136, 149, 276–277
See also KeyCite; Pocket parts; Shepard's citators; Treatises, updating

Veto, 165–166

Westlaw, 28
Search techniques, 38–47, 61, 82, 95, 122, 126–127, 133–134, 149, 210–211, 268, 272 n. 6

Sources in, 39, 55, 59, 61, 65,
67, 69, 72, 73, 75, 76, 77,
98–99, 100, 103, 119, 121,
123, 128, 142, 144, 148,
151, 152, 153, 154, 158,
170, 176, 178, 183–185,
187, 188, 194, 195, 200,
204, 206, 208, 209, 213,
214, 240, 244, 246, 247,
249, 262, 263, 264
See also KeyCite; Key numbers
West's topic and key number system,
See Key numbers
Words and Phrases, 76, 127–128